THE UNIVERSITY OF WINCHESTER

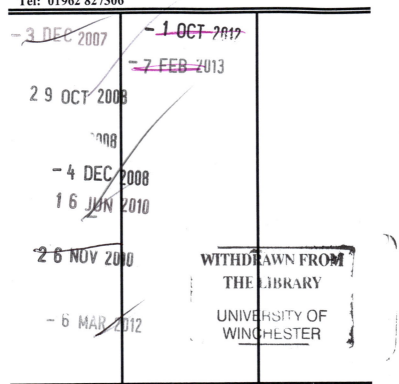

Early Modern Literature in History

General Editors: **Cedric C. Brown**, Professor of English and Dean of the Faculty of Arts and Humanities, University of Reading; **Andrew Hadfield**, Professor of English, University of Sussex, Brighton

Advisory Board: **Donna Hamilton**, University of Maryland; **Jean Howard**, University of Columbia; **John Kerrigan**, University of Cambridge; **Richard McCoy**, CUNY; **Sharon Achinstein**, University of Oxford

Within the period 1520–1740 this series discusses many kinds of writing, both within and outside the established canon. The volumes may employ different theoretical perspectives, but they share an historical awareness and an interest in seeing their texts in lively negotiation with their own and successive cultures.

Titles include:

Andrea Brady
ENGLISH FUNERARY ELEGY IN THE SEVENTEENTH CENTURY
Laws in Mourning

Martin Butler (*editor*)
RE-PRESENTING BEN JONSON
Text, History, Performance

Jocelyn Catty
WRITING RAPE, WRITING WOMEN IN EARLY MODERN ENGLAND
Unbridled Speech

Dermot Cavanagh
LANGUAGE AND POLITICS IN THE SIXTEENTH-CENTURY HISTORY PLAY

Danielle Clarke and Elizabeth Clarke (*editors*)
'THIS DOUBLE VOICE'
Gendered Writing in Early Modern England

James Daybell (*editor*)
EARLY MODERN WOMEN'S LETTER-WRITING, 1450–1700

Jerome De Groot
ROYALIST IDENTITIES

John Dolan
POETIC OCCASION FROM MILTON TO WORDSWORTH

Tobias Döring
PERFORMANCES OF MOURNING IN SHAKESPEAREAN THEATRE AND EARLY MODERN CULTURE

Sarah M. Dunnigan
EROS AND POETRY AT THE COURTS OF MARY QUEEN OF SCOTS AND JAMES VI

Andrew Hadfield
SHAKESPEARE, SPENSER AND THE MATTER OF BRITAIN

William M. Hamlin
TRAGEDY AND SCEPTICISM IN SHAKESPEARE'S ENGLAND

Elizabeth Heale
AUTOBIOGRAPHY AND AUTHORSHIP IN RENAISSANCE VERSE
Chronicles of the Self

Pauline Kiernan
STAGING SHAKESPEARE AT THE NEW GLOBE

Arthur F. Marotti (*editor*)
CATHOLICISM AND ANTI-CATHOLICISM IN EARLY MODERN ENGLISH TEXTS

Jean-Christophe Mayer
SHAKESPEARE'S HYBRID FAITH
History, Religion and the Stage

Jennifer Richards (*editor*)
EARLY MODERN CIVIL DISCOURSES

Sasha Roberts
READING SHAKESPEARE'S POEMS IN EARLY MODERN ENGLAND

Rosalind Smith
SONNETS AND THE ENGLISH WOMAN WRITER, 1560–1621
The Politics of Absence

Mark Thornton Burnett
CONSTRUCTING 'MONSTERS' IN SHAKESPEAREAN DRAMA AND EARLY
MODERN CULTURE

MASTERS AND SERVANTS IN ENGLISH RENAISSANCE DRAMA AND CULTURE
Authority and Obedience

The series Early Modern Literature in History is published in association with the Renaissance Texts Research Centre at the University of Reading.

Early Modern Literature in History
Series Standing Order ISBN 0–333–71472–5
(*outside North America only*)

You can receive future titles in this series as they are published by placing a standing order. Please contact your bookseller or, in case of difficulty, write to us at the address below with your name and address, the title of the series and the ISBN quoted above.

Customer Services Department, Macmillan Distribution Ltd, Houndmills, Basingstoke, Hampshire RG21 6XS, England

Shakespeare's Hybrid Faith

History, Religion and the Stage

Jean-Christophe Mayer

Senior Research Fellow
French National Centre for Scientific Research (CNRS)

First published 2006 by
PALGRAVE MACMILLAN
Houndmills, Basingstoke, Hampshire RG21 6XS and
175 Fifth Avenue, New York, N.Y. 10010
Companies and representatives throughout the world

PALGRAVE MACMILLAN is the global academic imprint of the Palgrave Macmillan division of St. Martin's Press, LLC and of Palgrave Macmillan Ltd. Macmillan® is a registered trademark in the United States, United Kingdom and other countries. Palgrave is a registered trademark in the European Union and other countries.

ISBN-13: 978–0–230–00525–9 hardback
ISBN-10: 0–230–00525–X hardback

This book is printed on paper suitable for recycling and made from fully managed and sustained forest sources.

A catalogue record for this book is available from the British Library.

Library of Congress Cataloging-in-Publication Data
Mayer, Jean-Christophe.
   Shakespeare's hybrid faith : history, religion, and the stage /
Jean-Christophe Mayer.
      p.   cm. — (Early modern literature in history)
   Includes bibliographical references and index.
   ISBN 0–230–00525–X (cloth)
   1. Shakespeare, William, 1564–1616—Religion.   2. Christianity
and literature—England—History—16th century.   3. Catholics—
England—History—16th century.   4. Christian drama, English—
History and criticism.   5. Historical drama, English—History and
criticism.   6. Religion in literature.   I. Title.   II. Series: Early
modern literature in history (Palgrave Macmillan (Firm))
   PR3011.M39 2006
   822.3′3—dc22   2006043227

10   9   8   7   6   5   4   3   2   1
15   14   13   12   11   10   09   08   07   06

Printed and bound in Great Britain by
Antony Rowe Ltd, Chippenham and Eastbourne

For Hélène,
Jacqueline and Paul,
Marie-France and Claude,

with love

Contents

List of Figures

Acknowledgements

Illustrations for the cover of the book and for Chapter 5 are reproduced by permission of the National Archives (UK). Some of the material used in Chapter 3 was previously published in *Bulletin de la Société d'Études Anglo-Américaines des XVIIe et XVIIIe siècles* 59 (2004), edited by A. Crunelle Vanrigh, while part of Chapter 6 appeared in *Reformation & Renaissance Review* 5.2 (2003), edited by P. Ayris and published by Equinox. I am grateful to the editors and publishers of both these journals for permission to adapt this material here.

This project would never have been completed without the warm and unfailing support of Charles Whitworth, Director of the Institute for Research on the Renaissance, the Neoclassical Age and the Enlightenment (IRCL) at the Université Paul Valéry, Montpellier, who encouraged me and kindly agreed to cover many of my research expenses. I am also greatly indebted to those among my colleagues, friends and family who read the manuscript, in part and for some, in whole, and came up with invaluable suggestions and useful corrections. These are: Jean-Marie Maguin, Nick Myers, Yves Peyré and Jacqueline Mayer, my mother. All remaining errors or misconceptions are of course my own.

I should also like to thank Professor Cedric Brown and Professor Andrew Hadfield for believing in the project and for agreeing to publish the book in their series. I am especially grateful to Andrew Hadfield for his kind support both during and after the evaluation process. Special thanks are also due to Palgrave's anonymous external reader for the very generous report and all the extremely judicious suggestions, which I have tried to follow to the letter.

My heartfelt thanks go to Jacqueline and Paul Mayer for their enthusiasm and constant support and to Marie-France and Claude Morzadec for looking after me so well during the writing of this book and for those wonderful Brittany vistas! Hélène Morzadec, my partner, was her usual self – comforting and good-humoured.

Introduction: Shakespeare's Hybrid Faith

The question of Shakespeare's religious affiliation has sparked much interest in recent years – no serious biography of the playwright is without its discussion of the subject and the issue regularly resurfaces not only in academic discussions, but also in the media. The subject in itself, however, is hardly new – nor is the view recently upheld again with renewed strength that the dramatist may have been a Catholic, a partisan of the Old Faith, that is, someone holding on firmly to what historian Eamon Duffy has called 'Traditional Religion'.[1]

The claim that Shakespeare was a Catholic was never a neutral statement to make. It was always in one way or another an act of appropriation, an ideological, even a political act, as this was the man who, from the second half of the seventeenth century onwards, rose to almost undisputed fame as England's National Poet – England which regarded itself primarily as a Protestant nation.[2]

Political or even sectarian agendas loomed in many of the statements made over the centuries about the poet's Catholic faith. Even the claim that 'he died a papist' made by a near-contemporary – Richard Davies, a Protestant clergyman who lived not far from Stratford-upon-Avon – may not have been devoid of partisan afterthought.[3] In 1801 the French romantic poet, François René de Chateaubriand, was adamant that 'if Shakespeare was anything at all, he was a Catholic', while the historian and critic Thomas Carlyle described Shakespeare in a lecture he delivered in 1840 as 'the noblest product of the Catholicism of the Middle Ages'.[4] Catholic Shakespeare came under different guises – the Romantic hero or the traditionalist poet imbued with the spirit of ages past.

Writing in a century marked in England by Catholic renewal, the Victorian essayist Richard Simpson was the first to put forward a sum of arguments propounding the theory of a Catholic Shakespeare.[5] In a series of elegant essays, published in the mid-1850s in a Catholic journal entitled *The Rambler*, Simpson buttressed his case with a number of documents he found in the public archives. Many of his arguments would serve as a basis for later Catholic readings of Shakespeare's life and works.[6] His method, however, was not entirely historical, nor was his approach solely literary. When he had finished with his demonstrations, it came down to a simple matter of faith. Simpson actually believed in Shakespeare's Catholicism and his creed placed the matter beyond scrutiny and beyond the necessity of having to prove anything conclusively. In other words, personal faith in the matter – or rather, in Simpson's case, an avowed mysticism – was deemed sufficient proof. Yet what Simpson was really asking for was a leap of faith on the part of his readers, as in this striking conclusion:

And there is a *spirit* in the workings of genius too subtle to be seized or analysed; like those finer properties of the air which escape all detection of chemistry, and yet communicate to it either an exquisite sweetness or an oppressive deadness. It is in this subtle spirit of Shakespeare's poesy, which we cannot *catch* (so to speak) and set down in citations, that we find the main force of our argument. It is pregnant with latent Catholicity. It breathes forth, in a hundred delicate touches and indescribable beauties of feeling, the influence of Catholicity upon his soul.[7]

Such statements, expressing the critic's intimate convictions, were to become an essential hallmark of the type of criticism that explored Shakespeare's religious credentials. This way of wanting to prove a point almost purely by the force of one's personal convictions remains to this day attached to the delicate task of pinning down the dramatist's religious beliefs.

Happily, however, Simpson steered clear of the social prejudices which surfaced in the work of some later proponents of the Catholic Shakespeare theory, especially in the first half of the twentieth century. Heinrich Mutschmann and K. Wentersdorf's *Shakespeare and Catholicism* (1952) sums up many of the themes which are now recognized as being the familiar hunting-ground of the supporters of a Catholic Shakespeare.[8] Unfortunately, the book is marred from the outset by a sketchy and somewhat slanted historical synopsis. Moreover, the authors later speak of Shakespeare's native Warwickshire as a county famous 'for the conservative and patriotic spirit of its sons' and of the poet's ancestors as 'gentlefolk' – the implication, of course, being that Shakespeare had a touch of nobility in him.[9] These are arguments commonly found in the writings of those who contest Shakespeare's authorship of the plays and attribute them not to the player from Stratford-upon-Avon, who had not been to university, but to some person of more noble stature: William Stanley, Edward de Vere (the 17th Earl of Oxford), Francis Bacon or indeed Elizabeth I herself. Such conservative agendas have thrived mainly on the fact that very little is known of Shakespeare's early years and that it has seemed convenient either to polish up the playwright's image by associating him with the so-called prestigious networks of the Elizabethan (Catholic) nobility, or to try to prove that he could not be the author of those plays and poems – which of course is a more radical solution to the problem posed by Shakespeare's social origins.

One of the most serious claims for the dramatist's affinities with the Catholic faith was made by E. A. J. Honigmann two decades ago in his tentative and carefully documented account of Shakespeare's so-called 'lost years' – twenty-eight years (between 1564 and 1592) – which were no doubt his crucial formative years, but which remain largely a mystery. It is Honigmann's view that Shakespeare was born and educated in a Catholic milieu, first in Stratford and then perhaps in the north of England, where he may have worked as a schoolmaster and player for a wealthy Catholic family at Hoghton Tower in Lancashire. Honigmann also sees Shakespeare changing his religion perhaps in the late 1580s and possibly returning to it in later life, or indeed on his deathbed.[10]

Even if some aspects of his theory have been disputed, Honigmann's account remains influential and has attracted much critical attention.[11] One important aspect of Honigmann's demonstration, in our view, is that it is not built on an either/or premise in the sense that it does not seek to pronounce itself definitively on Shakespeare's faith and it also takes into account the possibility that the dramatist may have had one or several sea changes – a fact not uncommon for many individuals in the course of their lives, especially in a century as spiritually troubled as the sixteenth century.

It is noteworthy, for that matter, that despite the many active scholarly debates on the vexed question of the dramatist's religious faith, the majority of the scenarios which have been put forward remain somewhat entrenched. Indeed, most of the answers proposed are either still expressed in partisan terms, or the perspectives adopted tend to be mutually excluding – in other words, the scholars who argue that

Shakespeare leaned towards Catholicism cannot conceive that he may have been influenced by Protestantism, the reverse also being true.

Many of the other more recent arguments in favour of a Catholic Shakespeare have indeed – despite the sophistication of the demonstrations – relied mostly on a straightforward scenario of a lasting faith in Catholicism.[12]

Demonstrations must of course be sustained by facts and arguments, but we may wonder whether even an accumulation of facts presented as evidence is enough to be convincing. 'Cumulatively', wrote Gary Taylor, 'the evidence for Shakespeare's Catholic sympathies is convincing enough that we should be arguing about it'.[13] But is 'cumulative' evidence enough?

When reading recent accounts of Shakespeare's career and alleged Catholicism, we are often caught in a whirl of names and associations and are under the impression that the links between Shakespeare and Catholicism were strong, if not tight.[14] Yet, on closer scrutiny, most of these associations remain hypothetical, as the authors of these accounts are in fact constructing a bridge over a biographical void.

Far from claiming that such endeavours are of no value, I am only saying that we as critics should acknowledge what is truly speculative in our work and that it may also be worthwhile to ask ourselves whether 'cumulative' evidence does actually demonstrate anything, whether associations and kinship are always relevant, whether it is not the degree of relevance that makes all the difference, as not all associations of facts or persons are systematically meaningful.[15]

Thus, the scenarios constructed by critics recently beg the question of whether one can – or indeed should – try to *prove* anything conclusively when it comes to the personal religious creed of a man who died more than four centuries ago and who has left no private testimony whatsoever of his beliefs, apart from his poems and plays. All too often, proving by not proving has been the sleight of hand that scholars have forced themselves to perform for the benefit of their readers for fear of not coming home with the demonstrative goods.[16] Many of those who argue the case for a Catholic Shakespeare have to admit that they cannot prove it and lack of proof thus becomes proof, as it were.[17]

Are we not also unconsciously reproducing the somewhat artificial polarities of Elizabethan polemical literature when we construct equally polarized scenarios about Shakespeare's religious beliefs?[18] Is proving one's point by not proving it the only answer that criticism can offer to the problem of religious allegiance? What if religious identity – in the labile world of late Elizabethan England – was not more of a quest than a secret certainty? What if our natural will as critics to prove our point categorically – or, failing that, intuitively – was in fact misguided?

These are some of the questions which this book sets out to pose.

Indeed, faith can be a matter of momentary allegiance, a quest for meaning, one that does not necessarily take the road of conformity or dissent, either open or secret.[19] The claim that this book tries to make is that religion for Shakespeare was not so much a matter of systematic allegiance as one of *constant* debating and questioning. After all, Shakespeare was a dramatist and this is how good drama functions – through asking questions, probing and giving voice. The problem is and has been that the terms of this questioning among scholars have often been incomplete, one-sided or partisan, whereas the cultural and religious universe around Shakespeare was fast-moving, ever-changing and largely hybrid.[20]

Shakespeare's hybrid faith

At present, we have to recognize that only Shakespeare's father's Catholicism can almost certainly be proved. The evidence, as even historians have pointed out, 'is very nearly conclusive'.[21] Much of it is now in the public domain and will not need to be rehearsed in great detail.[22] Suffice it to say that for a man of John Shakespeare's generation this does not come as much of a surprise. Moreover, until the 1580s early Elizabethan Stratford had been little affected by Protestantism and after that period, even when some more hard-line Catholics such as Shakespeare's probable schoolmaster, Simon Hunt, or his school friend, Robert Dibdale, had already fled to the Continent to become Catholic priests, the dramatist's father stayed and, like a not so negligible number of Englishmen, remained 'an unreconstructed Catholic of the old sort'.[23]

As for Shakespeare, his Catholicism still has to be inferred negatively, as we have suggested – for lack of definitive proof has to be taken for an assured sign of his Catholicism. Yet, however interesting the hypothesis, Shakespeare's apparent silence about his religious credentials may not only be attributable to the necessity of protecting his crypto-Catholic identity.

It is indeed an important premise of this book that one has not hitherto paid enough attention to what was no doubt Shakespeare's *mixed* upbringing in Stratford, both Catholic (at home and possibly with his schoolmasters) and Protestant, when he went to church, was forced to absorb the language of the Book of Homilies and read the Geneva Bible.[24] Shakespeare, furthermore, was born into a society which was spiritually in crisis, where Catholics, Protestants and others were engaged in a quest for meaning:

> The world into which William Shakespeare was born was fragmented, with, in John Donne's telling phrase, all coherence gone. Shakespeare and countless others of his generation did not know what to believe or, if they did, could not tell when they might be called on to believe contrary things.[25]

'Was anything "settled" by the so-called religious "settlement" of 1559? Not much, and not yet', wrote Patrick Collinson, neatly summing up the opinions of many other modern historians.[26] After all, even the Queen's own form of Protestantism was 'deeply idiosyncratic' – Elizabeth had a dislike for the Protestant institution of clerical marriage (she never appointed a married Archbishop of Canterbury after Matthew Grindal); she loved elaborate church music and employed Catholic composers such as William Byrd in her chapel royal. Furthermore, she did not really see preaching as a necessity, which of course went counter to the opinions of many Protestants who called for more evangelism.[27] The Queen's mixed signals in the religious domain were also part of a strategy of appeasement highlighted in an anonymous memorandum entitled the 'Device for the Alteration of Religion', which had circulated early in Elizabeth's reign. The author of the document acknowledged revealingly that some would call the settlement 'a cloaked papistry or a mingle-mangle'. Yet, in the words of this anonymous senior official, 'better it were that they did suffer than her highness and commonwealth should shake or be in danger'.[28]

Most specialists also agree that 'the Reformation' was something which did not happen until the second or third decade of Elizabeth's reign.[29] The form which it then took, and certainly the degree of change which it brought to the minds of individuals, are questions which are still open to debate, but there is a growing consensus around the idea of reformation as something which was more akin to an open and ongoing process than a movement which had almost reached its objectives and was in its final stages.[30]

As J. J. Scarisbrick famously wrote, 'on the whole, English men and women did not want the Reformation and most of them were slow to accept it when it came'.[31] What was also to become another revisionist motto was Christopher Haigh's assertion that in the last years of the sixteenth century England had become 'a Protestant nation, but not a nation of Protestants'.[32] More importantly, Haigh's work brought to the fore the fact that the Reformation as such never really existed, that there was a series of reformations, that these movements were discontinuous and parallel, and that they were far from straightforward – religious reform even in late Elizabethan England was still a story of reaction, reversals and alternatives, a fundamental quest for solutions and compromises and a constant cultural negotiation.

One of the vital points made by Haigh and others was that religious change happened as a result of *interaction* between religious groups: 'Reformations were made by Catholics as well as by Protestants, because the Reformations came out of the clashes between them'.[33]

In a world where 'one person's superstition may be another's spirituality, and one person's freedom another's guideless anarchy' – the society in which Shakespeare grew up and later wrote his plays – it is easy to understand why there was a constant obsession with labelling, ascribing religious identities, setting down differences or, as Debora Shuger has usefully noted, with 'the placement of boundaries'.[34] When the sense of flux created by the religious rifts of the reformation(s) became too much to bear, the urge was to look for meaning at all costs. But meaning itself is not solely the product of ideology. Indeed, it is important to understand that the construction of religious meaning and belief remained a task largely performed by individuals. The 'mediating role of the psyche in all cultural production' has to be acknowledged, as 'ideology is not simply a function or an entity but the creation of people feeling, thinking, interpreting, persuading, and struggling for meaning'.[35]

It is thus indispensable to take this into account when one discusses the question of Shakespeare's religious beliefs and when one looks at how they may have transpired through his work. Indeed, religious beliefs are not just a question of acculturation, which would suppose that individuals receive some kind of religious imprint which will never leave them, or that the state has the power to erase such imprints and replace them by others – faith is also a question of personal debate and conviction.

Debate is perhaps the word that best describes these spiritually troubled times, as deep differences of opinion existed even among those who were members of the national Protestant Church. In fact, there was no truly united Protestant front which opposed those whom propaganda literature named the dissenters – the Puritans and the 'papists'. The situation was far more complex, as Puritanism, for instance, was a set of attitudes which was part and parcel of the Protestant movement rather than 'the symmetrical counterpart of Catholic recusancy'.[36] The Protestant movement itself was in crisis in the sense that it 'could not agree on what it was supposed to be'.[37] As for English Catholicism, it is essential to note that it was 'not in this period clearly and totally separated from the established Church' and this fact largely explains why 'it remained a focus of intense anxiety'.[38] As the work of Alexandra Walsham has shown, there were a considerable number of Catholics who attended Protestant church services, who conformed outwardly only, or remained 'in between'. They were branded by both Protestant *and* Catholic polemicists, who labelled them 'church papists'.[39] In other words, Catholicism was not detached from mainstream Protestant culture; it was itself deeply integrated within the debates of that culture and of the whole of society itself. Catholicism was thus not just a residue of the past in Elizabethan England, it formed an important and inextricable part of what must be called a hybrid culture, a society so fluid in its religious affiliations that – in Patrick Collinson's words – its faith was placed in a 'mongrel religion'.[40]

It is time to ask where this leaves us as far as the debate around Shakespeare's religious affiliations is concerned.

It is one of the main arguments of this book that, far from being silent on religious issues, Shakespeare in fact came back to the religious question again and again throughout his career as a poet and dramatist, and that he did so primarily to find answers to the religious questions which haunted him and his fellow Elizabethans. What we know about his life and works indicates, as we shall see, that he may at times have been indecisive, that he may have wavered in his faith, and that true to his mixed confessional identity, he had an eye for the contradictions and complexities of his society. The extent of his conversion to a form of Protestantism is difficult to determine – we shall none the less venture a few informed guesses in the course of this study – but what remains important to bear in mind is the fundamentally unstable character of religious faith in Elizabethan England:

All in all, a study of conversion tells us that instability was as much a defining characteristic of English religion in this unsettled period as the placid acquiescent conformity for which some historians have argued, or, as others have it, a stubborn conservative adherence to the values and practice of the past in opposition to Protestant novelty . . . . During this time, within the apparently rigid constraints of doctrinal formulation and political loyalism, flux in religion was the norm rather than the exception in religious experience, actually expected rather than regarded with astonishment. Confessional polemical conflict itself undermined certainty and questioned uniformity.[41]

Why should Shakespeare, despite his personal history, respond differently to his social environment from his contemporaries? His work indicates that he had an ear finely tuned to many of the debates of his time and there is thus good reason to believe that he too may have been affected by the contemporary widespread 'flux in religion'. Not only was there flux, but also the amount of religious material which remained as the debris of successive attempts at reformation since the beginning of the sixteenth century had created a confessional wasteland where one was left to pick up the pieces and reassemble them creatively in an attempt to find a meaning. Indeed, as Peter Lake explains, 'the religious scene of Elizabeth's reign is best seen as a number of attempts, conducted at very different levels of theoretical self-consciousness and coherence, at creative bricolage, mixing and matching'.[42]

Shakespeare, history and the stage

It is a rarely mentioned fact that the plays that contain the most allusions to religion in the whole of the Shakespeare corpus are the dramatist's English history plays – the ten or so plays which encompass the reigns of six medieval English monarchs, with the exception of *All is True*, which partly covers that of Henry VIII.[43] Strangely enough, no extended study has been devoted to religion in the histories. Instead, most of the critics interested in religion have concentrated on the tragedies, notably *King Lear, Measure for Measure, Hamlet* and *Macbeth*,[44] or on Shakespeare's romances, *Cymbeline, The Winter's Tale* in particular[45] and his late plays, such as *The Tempest*.[46]

This might be explained by the fact that religion in the histories is often considered to be a byword for politics.[47] Indeed, much of the scholarship produced in the 1980s and early 1990s was influenced by secularist perspectives, partly produced by the New Historicist and Cultural Materialist movements, characterized by their will to throw light on the workings of power and by their broadening of the field of politics to adjacent fields, such as that of religion – a trend which has often resulted in the blurring or oversimplification of confessional issues.[48] Among the many influential essays of that period was Stephen Greenblatt's study of *King Lear* which set a pattern for a decade or so for the analysis of religious allusions and for early modern theatre's cultural positioning. Indeed, Greenblatt argued in 'Shakespeare and the Exorcists' (an essay published in his *Shakespearean Negotiations* (1988)) that 'performance kills belief; or rather acknowledging theatricality kills the credibility of the supernatural' represented on stage, and concluded that '*King Lear* is haunted by a sense of rituals and beliefs that are no longer efficacious, that have been *emptied out'*.[49] Implicit in Greenblatt's argument is a theory of containment of religious dissent: theatre is there to confirm for the state and for the representatives of its official religion that the rituals of the Catholic faith are illusory. Theatre, in other words, practises meta-drama to serve the state and rid it of Catholic magic, by reducing it to an empty and meaningless spectacle.[50] Such views considerably oversimplify the links between religion and the state (these links being far more complex and fluid), but also the relation between religion and theatre.

For one thing, it is not at all certain that religious ritual when performed in the theatre loses its initial dynamic – several chapters in this book will point to contrary examples.[51] It is doubtful that Greenblatt's 'emptying out' of religious magic actually functions on stage; it is more likely that the alleged secularising powers of theatre stem from an anachronistic perception of the nature of Elizabethan society.[52]

What is more, Greenblatt's implicitly secularist view of theatre is overstated. Several scholars have shown that theatre was closely tied to the evangelical movement, that it was used by Protestants as an instrument of propaganda.[53] Matters admittedly became more complex in the 1580s, which can be seen in many ways as a watershed. Whereas the theatre had been a shared culture between Catholics and Protestants, both sides making use of it for their own didactic purposes, the second generation of Protestants became more circumspect about using theatre for the preaching of religious doctrine.[54] Many Protestants had nothing against theatre itself – Protestant publicists, however, began to disregard theatre for the teaching and the spreading of faith. This corresponded roughly to the period when Puritanism was on the rise and when many Protestants felt that the reformation they had expected had still not happened and when reasons had to be found to explain why this was not the case.[55] By turning their backs on theatre they added grist to the mill of the anti-theatricalists who denounced theatre as an art-form which was 'popishly affected' and which used the same illusionist magic as the Catholic Church, thus implicitly (or explicitly at times) branding theatre people as Catholics, or even worse, as 'papists'.[56]

Catholics had indeed used the theatre for both didactic and propagandist purposes – but some Catholics had also denounced the inappropriateness of such media when it came to questions of faith.[57] Be that as it may, theatre people found themselves at the heart of the confessional debates of the time – and this, as Jeffrey Knapp has recently argued, put both dramatists and actors in a delicate situation.[58] Indeed, Knapp's point is that: 'Shakespeare's reluctance to preach Christian doctrine seems a mark not of his secularism, as most scholars have claimed, but rather of his fears regarding the potential divisiveness of his religious beliefs'.[59] I agree with Knapp's view that Shakespeare's theatre was certainly not fully secularized and that to embark on religious issues was risky for a dramatist in that he could increase the deep confessional rifts and uncertainties of his society. I do not, however, see Shakespeare as a playwright wanting to preach anything,[60] but as a theatre person who was engaged in the same quest as many of his contemporaries and who inevitably touched on some extremely sensitive religious issues, as will be shown in the course of this book.

Theatre at large – and this is an insufficiently acknowledged fact – was deeply involved in the debate around 'true faith', a controversy which raged during the whole of the sixteenth century. This meant that theatre could both serve as a polemical instrument and become a direct target of the anti-theatricalists, whose reactions we have already mentioned. Those who refused to become the mouthpieces of propaganda – dramatists like Shakespeare or Ben Jonson, for instance – none the less saw themselves as fulfilling a religious and social function to a certain extent.

Theatre and particularly the English history play which purported to tell the story of the English nation – however selective in their view of history these plays may have been – was particularly engaged in this debate around religion and faith, in the same way as retelling the history of the nation brought Shakespeare to acknowledge the inextricable entanglement of state and religious issues. The playwright's anachronisms amply testify to the fact that retrospection was dramatists' favoured prospective mode, in that it was the safest way to explore the future of the nation without attracting too much attention.[61]

There are indeed times, as we shall see, when Shakespeare seems to be probing into the present and future of the nation and its confessional issues. What better instrument than the history play for a quest into the religious and political roots of the nation – a quest which had contemporary resonances. Indeed, the history play *per se* is not about closure, it is a fundamentally open form, which echoes the ongoing process of history and its multifaceted unfolding:

> The histories . . . reveal time to be intractable stuff. It cannot be recalled, and it cannot be rejected; at best it can be understood. The histories would help us to that understanding, as their open-ended structures make us confront our fragile existence as 'time subjects' . . . released in a world of contingency and flux.[62]

It is precisely this 'world of contingency and flux' which this book tries to recapture by studying how the complexities of faith, of religious conscience and identity, and of confessional polemics are reflected in Shakespeare's histories.

Indeed, the current project was born out of the idea that there was a need for a book that was neither a sectarian manifesto nor a work emanating solely from the so-called 'Christian criticism' school – a study that would combine the methodologies of theatre studies and history without the temptation of looking for ready-made or over-rounded truths.

The book offers selected readings of Shakespeare's history plays. It does not seek to cover all Shakespeare's histories; the aim is rather to concentrate on the histories which are central to the topic at hand and which have received comparatively less attention. This explains why the plays of the Second Henriad have not been included. The economy of the work and the fact that religious issues in these plays had been well covered by several recent and distinguished studies were deciding factors.[63]

As this book endeavours to demonstrate, claims that Shakespeare was a Catholic are somewhat of a shortcut – perhaps it would be better to suggest that despite the menace of censorship (which has been a trifle overstated) and of potential polemical involvement, Shakespeare – whose religious identity was mixed – liked to explore the contradictions of his age, in a society where print, polemics, pulpit, politics and stage were sometimes so dangerously close. Even if Shakespeare was indeed brought up in a Catholic family, the dramatist's multifarious living and working environments explain why, as many scholars have recognized, his plays send conflicting signals. Far from being a mere expression of his so-called scepticism, or of the fact that he had no faith at all,[64] these mixed signals were, I should like to argue, the traces of a spiritual quest conducted by the dramatist's own creative mind.

This book also tries to take Shakespeare's Catholic audience into account, as there is a key question which needs to be investigated – how his histories were received by that fraction of his audience which leaned more towards Catholicism. There is reason to believe that the tensions at the heart of his history plays had a particular ring for that audience and that, as we shall see, he may have had that audience in mind *at times*.[65] While the links between Shakespeare's histories and his Protestant audiences have been well sketched by scholars,[66] it is high time to add to such studies – not to counter them, but to suggest how issues involving religion could speak to Elizabethans of different denominations. Maurice Hunt confirms this view with his observation that 'Shakespeare's syncretistic method for incorporating Protestant and Catholic elements into his plays is virtually singular among early modern English playwrights...'.[67] The chapters which follow explore some of the implications of this view.

This study begins with a chapter on *1 and 2 King Henry VI* in which the many allusions to witchcraft and magic are examined and set in context. Indeed, it soon becomes apparent that witchcraft was not simply used to validate political power or as a denunciation of the Catholic Other; witchcraft signalled the urgent need for answers in the religious domain. The world of *Richard III* is equally imbued with magic, but Chapter 2 concentrates more on the hybrid world which Shakespeare has created in this fascinating play, where the ghosts of the dead are present in ways which are unsettling and where Catholic elements interact in a pre-Reformation world which feels strangely Elizabethan. Chapter 3 suggests that debates about religious conscience may have been latent in *Richard II* and that the play's more than passing references to Parliament could have had dangerous overtones in the polemical and religious climate of the mid-1590s. Chapter 4 looks at how and why Shakespeare handled polemical and sectarian material in his account of the reign of *King John*. Chapter 5 also explores the workings of propaganda; it shows how easily a 'Popish Plot' could be constructed, and suggests that Shakespeare and his fellow players may have been required to play a dubious part in the 1601 Essex rebellion. The book closes with Shakespeare and Fletcher revisiting many of the political and confessional issues of the sixteenth century with their complex account of the Henrician reformation – *All Is True (Henry VIII)* – a play filled with humour, hope and religious contradiction.

1
Theatre, Witchcraft and the Crisis of Faith in *King Henry VI, Parts 1 and 2*

> So long (righte Gentle and Courteous Reader) as wee live heere in this wretched vale of miserie, and myserable estate of our Probationership, we are all even the best of us all, to account no better of our selves, then that we live in a perpetuall warrefare, and most dangerous and deadlie combat.

Thus wrote the author of *A most wicked worke of a wretched witch*, a pamphlet published in London in 1592.[1] The writer has harsh words for those he describes as God's enemies and the destroyers of all social unity: 'O rebels towards God: enemies to mankinde: catterpillers of a common wealth, the fire is too good to consume them'.[2] Witches, he argues, are the moral vermin of society, and life is a constant struggle against evil, which itself can appear at any moment under many different guises. Warfare was a metaphor commonly used by Protestants in pamphlets such as this one, which stressed the spiritual combat of individuals caught between the forces of good and evil in a Christian cognitive framework reliant on a logic of contrariety.[3]

The pamphlet also lays particular emphasis on the detection of evil and on what happens when evil is tracked down and named. It tells the story of one Richard Burt's encounter with an elderly woman and shows how Burt triggered an irreversible process when he lost his nerve and called her a witch. 'This was the first occasion (namely the tearming of hir a wit[c]h) of al poore *Richard Burts* future tragedie'.[4] Social historians and anthropologists would no doubt point out that it is precisely the naming of a person as a witch that creates the witch. In this sense the pamphlet enlightens us as to the fact that witches are cultural constructs and the symbolic vehicles of a system of thought which structured itself around the opposites of good and evil.[5]

Another distinctive feature of *A most wicked worke of a wretched witch* – which it shares with other similar works of the period – is its generic instability. Far from being a mere factual report, the narrative of the story of Richard Burt consciously *dramatizes* the events it purports to recount. Moreover, while the author claims to be dealing with moral issues, he strives hard to produce an entertaining 'tragedie', a piece of drama which borrowed some of its devices from theatre and which, as it happens, also inspired playwrights. Indeed, as Marion Gibson has shown, it is more than likely that the playwright Robert Greene seized on a number of situations and pithy elements from *A most wicked worke of a wretched witch* to pen his play on magic and witchcraft, *The Honourable History of Friar Bacon and Friar Bungay* (written *c*. 1592; printed 1594).[6]

Greene's was one of several plays on the subject born out of the troubled end of the 1580s, the years which saw the 'magic of Rome' – as some Protestant writers put it – attempt to tarnish Elizabeth I's charisma and political legitimacy.[7] The Queen's excommunication by the Pope, Mary Stuart's threatening presence on English soil and her alarming political aspirations, the Babington Plot and the menace of the Armada had created an atmosphere of almost constant unrest. At the outset of the 1590s, playwrights caught some of the *angst* of the period, mixing politics and the occult (a common blend in times of trouble) and history and matters of state with magic and witchcraft, as John Lyly had already done so powerfully in 1588 in *Endymion* (published 1591).[8] To a large extent, Shakespeare's *King Henry VI* plays, especially *Parts 1 and 2* – on which we wish to concentrate – embrace themes that emerged from the same climate.[9] There was a trend in the early 1590s for plays about politics and witchcraft, a fashion in which Shakespeare played his part, as we shall argue.

If these plays were influenced by the pamphlet literature of the period, the reverse was also true. Indeed, the early 1590s were a turning point for the pamphlet literature on witchcraft and magic. Works ceased to be simple reports of witchcraft cases and veered very much towards prose writings of a literary nature.[10] Writers used fictional and dramatic techniques to make the fate of their characters more vivid; what mattered was moral verisimilitude rather than circumstantial accuracy.[11] The fictionalization and dramatization of cheap print came from a will to make reporting more entertaining, but it also grew out of readers' need for real stories, addressing graver concerns, such as the apparent unintelligibility of the disturbed world around them. Beyond their entertainment value.

these narratives – a good many penned by clergymen – tried to make the purposes of the Almighty less mysterious by assigning a role to the presence of evil in God's Creation.[12] For most of these writers, the challenge was to restore people's faith in God's Providence by pointing, for instance, at the demonic origins of witchcraft and enabling people to rise above its material aspects and uncover the spiritual significance of evil. Much depended in fact on these writers' ability to 'spiritualize human experience by raising its significance beyond the plane where physical harm by witches and devils and physical punishments and remedies against them mattered most'.[13] This was a tall order, as we shall see.

Early Shakespeare and particularly *1 and 2 Henry VI* are fraught with allusions to magic and the influence of the supernatural. The world of these two plays – all too often neglected in studies devoted to magic on the early modern stage – is also one in which the characters are almost constantly tormented by doubt, in which religion and faith are terms marked by instability, and where characters seek answers to the mysterious unfolding of history through various forms of religious or magical practice. In this way, despite the explicit late medieval setting of these plays, Shakespeare's characters belong very much to that tense but rich moment of the early 1590s when dramatists and pamphlet writers competed for the attention of an Elizabethan public fascinated by the issues of magic, religion and politics.

Crises of faith and anti-Catholicism

> If we say that we have no sinne we deceive our selves, and there
> is no truth in us.
> Why then belike
> We must sinne, and so consequently die,
> I, we must die, an everlasting death.
> What doctrine call you this? *Che sera, sera:*[14]

One of these Elizabethans of the early 1590s is certainly Christopher Marlowe's Doctor Faustus. *Che sera, sera*, what will be will be, was the doctrine of those who were left disoriented or indeed disillusioned by official religion. Shakespeare also peopled *1 and 2 Henry VI* with characters who were sometimes at odds with the Christian system of belief. One notable exception is of course King Henry VI whose eye on events was no doubt perceived by audiences as being distinctly Christian, if not Catholic.

Yet the Henry VI who walked the Elizabethan stages was himself partly a product of early Tudor propaganda. If Henry's faith appears so commendable and yet if the King is shown in the course of the three plays Shakespeare wrote about his reign to be such a political misfit, it is because of Henry VII's tampering with history, as Keith Dockray explains, 'Once Henry VII ascended the throne in 1485, what he wanted for propaganda purposes was an ancestor worthy to have carried the precious blood of Lancaster: so, if Henry VI could not be portrayed as a successful ruler (as clearly he could not), then he must at least be a saintly one'.[15]

When Henry escapes from the pages of the Tudor chronicles to walk the planks of Elizabethan theatres, the propaganda does not quite translate to the stage and the King's attitude calls forth a series of fundamental questions on the place of religion in society and on the nature of faith. Henry's faith makes him appear incongruous and his religious zeal is repeatedly read by characters as being plain naiveté and blindness. In his hunger for power the Duke of York writes Henry off as someone 'Whose church-like humours fits not for a crown' (*2H6*, 1.1.244) and whose 'hand is made to grasp a palmer's staff / And not to grace an awful princely sceptre' (*2H6*, 5.1.97–8).[16] The King himself, as he is forced to part with his Lord Protector, claims that the only 'protector' he needs is his faith:

> Stay, Humphrey, Duke of Gloucester. Ere thou go,
> Give up thy staff. Henry will to himself
> Protector be; and God shall be my hope,
> My stay, my guide and lantern to my feet.

> (*2H6*, 2.3.22–5)

For all his religious zeal, however, Henry appears strangely and alarmingly misguided. Confronted with Jack Cade's violent rebellion, and as his own state could well totter, his reading of events is filtered through his unflinching faith: 'O, graceless men! They know not what they do' (*2H6*, 4.4.37). In a desperate situation, the only decision he feels he can take is to hand over everything to God: 'Come, Margaret. God, our hope, will succour us' (*2H6*, 4.4.54). The rebellion among his nobles is like a final straw, however – Henry appears suddenly stretched to his limits, almost beaten by a world in which he so clearly feels a misfit: 'O, where is faith? O, where is loyalty?' (*2H6*, 5.1.166). Queen Margaret, his spouse, had provided audiences earlier in the play with a mock-portrait of a king steeped in *contemplatio*, devoid of knightly qualities and resembling a pope (i.e. an impostor in the

eyes of Elizabethan anti-Catholic propagandists). The Queen makes this
disappointed depiction of her husband to Suffolk:

> I thought King Henry had resembled thee
> In courage, courtship and proportion.
> But all his mind is bent to holiness,
> To number Ave-Maries on his beads.
> His champions are the prophets and apostles,
> His weapons, holy saws of sacred writ;
> His study is his tilt-yard, and his loves
> Are brazen images of canonized saints.
> I would the college of the cardinals
> Would choose him Pope, and carry him to Rome
> And set the triple crown upon his head:
> That were a state fit for his Holiness.

> (*2H6*, 1.3.54–65)

Should we conclude from this that Shakespeare intended to suggest
the ills of Catholicism through his portrayal of Henry? Perhaps not.
Margaret's depiction of her husband stems largely from personal frustration and should not be taken too literally, especially in the light of
1 and 2 Henry VI's complex and sometimes puzzling use of anti-Catholic
propaganda. As we shall see, what certainly emerges in many scenes is
a crisis of faith, one, in particular, that challenges the over-zealous, but
also one which calls relentlessly, but somewhat hopelessly, for answers
in the domain of belief.

Answers are not readily available. Religion is either associated with
Henry's fervent but ultimately blind faith, or with the high clergy's position which is repeatedly denounced by a number of characters as being
politics in disguise. The opposition between the Cardinal of Winchester
and the Duke of Gloucester (the Lord Protector) runs through both *1 and
2 Henry VI*, and it is soon apparent that the Cardinal's say in political
affairs is resented and considered to be a meddling and unholy – if not
manipulative – interference in temporal matters.

In *1 Henry VI* the Duke of Gloucester is the character who most systematically denounces the Cardinal for diverting religion from its rightful aims:

> Name not religion, for thou lov'st the flesh,
> And ne'er throughout the year to church thou goest –
> Except it be to pray against thy foes.

> (*1H6*, 1.1.41–3)

Gloucester's criticism of the Cardinal has little to do, however, with the defence of religion itself: it is of a personal nature. Yet the accusations directed against this high prelate are often couched in anti-papal or indeed (for an Elizabethan audience) anti-Catholic invective, as Gloucester's clever pun at the end of this exchange clearly demonstrates:

> GLOUCESTER   Thou art reverend
> Touching thy spiritual function, not thy life.
> WINCHESTER Rome shall remedy this.
> GLOUCESTER   Roam thither, then.
>
> (*1H6*, 3.1.49–51)

Anti-papal or more generally anti-Catholic prejudice is the form that political bickering tends to adopt in *1 and 2 Henry VI*.

The play wields different types of arguments and discourses in a puzzling or disconcerting fashion. Religious zeal is synonymous with blindness, religion is a byword for ambition, political and military strife do not seem to furnish characters with a solution to their larger-than-life issues. In a world where those who are blinded by faith or ambition lead, it is little wonder that many characters who wish to shape their own destiny are left to grope in the dark, striving to decipher the potential signs of God's presence.

Reading the signs: revelation and the question of Providence

1 and 2 Henry VI multiply allusions to the supernatural and repeatedly point to apparent signs of God's presence. None the less, so-called expressions of divine Providence turn out to be misleading in most cases. Shakespeare in fact stages characters who are prone to interpret signs hastily, incompletely or superficially. A prominent example of superficial misreading is the so-called miracle scene of *2 Henry VI* when the King is hawking with Gloucester and Winchester at St Albans and a citizen interrupts them to call them to witness a miracle: one Simon Simpcox, who was supposedly born blind, has miraculously recovered his sight. Interestingly, as Ronald Knowles remarks, 'All three sources record that it is Gloucester who is overjoyed at the miracle . . . . Shakespeare transfers it to Henry's pious credulity and contrasts Gloucester's worldly astuteness here'.[17] The dramatist thus consciously strayed from his historical sources to underline Henry's blind faith which makes him read the falsely blind as truly blind. Indeed, the nation's leader mistakenly attributes to God what is in fact mere trickery – he swiftly falls for the false miracle:

> Now God be praised, that to believing souls
> Gives light in darkness, comfort in despair!
> . . .
> Poor soul, God's goodness hath been great to thee.
> Let never day or night unhallowed pass,
> But still remember what the Lord hath done.
>
> (*2H6*, 2.1.65–6; 81–3)

It is tempting to interpret Gloucester's ensuing exposure of the false blind man as a proto-Protestant gesture. The source for this story, however, is Thomas More's *Dialogue of the Veneration and Worship of Images* (1529).[18] Moreover, the Duke of Gloucester himself hardly has time to reap the fruits of his spectacular exposure of the false miracle. He too is blind to the political machinations around him; these are revealed to us as Buckingham arrives just after the Duke's triumph to announce that the Duchess of Gloucester has just been arrested and charged with sorcery and high treason. Thus, the man who set out to expose the false miracle is himself exposed because of his wife's occult practices, leaving the audience to wonder at the dramatic irony of an episode which has blurred reference points somewhat and shattered confessional certainties. The episode is not a denunciation of the crudeness of Catholic providentialism, neither does it seem to be a vindication of a Protestant interpretation of Providence.

A passage which ties in with this one is the scene of the trial by combat (2.3) between an apprentice by the name of Peter Thump and an armourer called Thomas Horner, the former having brought a petition against his master 'for saying that the Duke of York was rightful heir to the crown' (1.3.26–7). During this scene, which is not devoid of humour – were it not for the ensuing death of the accused – much drinking is done by the supporters of each contestant and by the contestants themselves. Peter, who kills his master in the fight, is much relieved to be alive and is certain that he 'prevailed in right' (2.3.100). Henry is also convinced that the outcome of the duel reveals God's will and that divine justice has been done (*2H6*, 2.3.101–6).

Henry thinks he has detected the finger of God in these events and yet York – who is no innocent party in the play – offers the hint of a conflicting interpretation. Were it not for the effects of alcohol, the armourer would perhaps have prevailed over his apprentice: '– Fellow, thank God and the good wine in thy master's way' (2.3.97–9). The Duke thus questions in passing the reliability of the interpretation of signs in the play.[19] Yet this is not systematically the case in *2 Henry VI*. There are scenes where Shakespeare seems to cast all ambiguity aside and plays rather with the possibility that signs can sometimes reveal a divine nemesis at work. This is the case when Sir William Vaux comes on stage to tell the King that Winchester is dying and that the Cardinal is delirious, tormented and somewhat blasphemous. Henry interprets this in a moral light almost immediately: 'Ah, what a sign it is of evil life / Where death's approach is seen so terrible!' (*2H6*, 3.3.5–6). For once, what we have been shown of the character on stage does not conflict with the King's interpretation. At the Cardinal's bedside, Henry (ever hopeful) tries to find signs of repentance and it does not come as much of a surprise when Winchester does not produce the sign that would indicate either his contrition or God's forgiveness: 'He dies and makes no sign. O God, forgive him!' (*2H6*, 3.3.29).

As these various passages suggest, Shakespeare is in fact sending conflicting signals. He seems more concerned about opening a debate on the possible interpretation of signs and on God's degree of involvement in human affairs than about promoting a specific confessional agenda.

Indeed, the interpretation of signs is like a recurrent obsession in the play – whether signs can be read, whether they signify something, whether God's will can be known. It is a problem which is both theological and doctrinal, but which is also at the heart of the problematics of theatre. Theatre is entirely reliant on signs, and signifies not only through voice, but through a whole array of visual and aural signs. Moreover, these signs are never fixed and have to be reinvested with meaning at every performance so that what the play can *reveal* to us is at once unpredictable and endless.

Thus, through its very functioning theatre raised questions which were at the heart of the religious controversies of the time. Some Protestant writers, for instance, considered that the Revelation had happened once and for all, that the spirit of God would no longer speak and that one should not seek to know God's intentions, or try to read the signs of any further Revelation of his divine will.[20] This was a view defended by the Elizabethan theologian Richard Hooker: 'His [God's] surceasing to speake to the world since the publishing of the Gospell of Jesus Christ, and the deliverie of the same in writing, is unto us a manifest token that the way of salvation is now sufficiently opened, and that wee neede no other meanes for our full instruction, then God hath alreadye furnished us withall'.[21]

Reginald Scot defended similar views well before Hooker in a more popular and accessible work: *The Discoverie of Witchcraft* (1584). For Scot also, miracles and prophecies were things of the past because everything had been revealed and all the elements of faith were there for the Christian believer to discover.[22] According to this view, any miracle, or any so-called sign of God's will, was a fabrication, or a misinterpretation of the 'true' Protestant doctrine:

> Indeed it pleased God heretofore, by the hand of *Moses* and his prophets, and speciallie by his sonne Christ and his apostles, to worke great miracles, for the establishing of the faith: but now whatsoever is necessarie for our salvation, is conteined in the word of God: our faith is alredie confirmed, and our church established by miracles; so as now to seeke for them, is a point of infidelitie. Which the papists (if you note it) are greatlie touched withall, as in their lieng legends appeareth. But in truth, our miracles are knaveries most commonlie, and speciallie of priests, wherof I could cite a thousand.[23]

Yet even a sceptic like Reginald Scot had to admit that exposure of a miracle as fraud did not necessarily preclude belief in miracles, nor did it invalidate the idea that, in the eyes of the populace, God's will could be known.[24] The rational and the irrational can coexist, as in Shakespeare's *2 Henry VI* when the discovery of Simpcox's false miracle does not stop characters from believing that God may still send signs to them. For Scot, it was an endless source of wonder that 'reason', or the unmasking of fabricators, could not defeat the belief in miracles or crude providentialism: 'It is also to be woondered, how men . . . will not suspect, but remained unsatisfied, or rather obstinatelie defend the residue of witches supernaturall actions: like as when a juggler hath discovered the slight and illusion of his principall feats, one would fondlie continue to thinke, that his other petie juggling knacks of legierdemaine are done by the helpe of a familiar . . . '.[25]

One explanation for the lasting hold of this hope for a sign from God is of course psychological – it is more reassuring for human beings to believe that God can speak to them and change their lives through revelation. Another explanation is furnished by George Gifford who, in *A Discourse of the subtill Practises of Devilles by Witches and Sorcerers* (1587), suggested that the Devil could induce human beings to believe in miracles and so-called signs of the supernatural so as to lead them into error: 'In like manner there are straunge woonders reported of Witches and Conjurers, they have bene believed, as also many counterfaite things, because he [the Devil] hath power at many times given unto him to torment men, and because he doth make his vaine apparitions'.[26] Thus, from a theological point of view, argued Gifford, the Devil was not God's mighty opposite, but merely a master of lies and illusion. Moreover, Satan had a specific function in the Christian universe – his presence was a reminder to the good Christian of what should be eschewed. Indeed, the nonconformist George Gifford has 'Daniell', one of the characters in a later work – his *Dialogue Concerning Witches and Witchcraftes* (1593) – declare that if the Devil seduces human beings and repeatedly strives to make them believe in false miracles and signs from God, it is because God *allows the Devil to do so*:

> It is peculiar to God alone, to know what shall come to passe hereafter. But the Lord God hath reuealed by his Prophetes, and Apostles many thinges that after should be fulfilled. Satan can giue a nere coniecture when these come to be fulfilled. Hee is a most subtill observer of thinges, and will gesse at many: but especially, where hee hath power giuen him to worke and to bring any matter about, he can and will tell it aforehand. Finally, God in his iust iudgement giueth him power to seduce the wicked.[27]

It is doubtful whether Gifford's efforts at educating the masses in these matters were fully effective. What many people experienced in their everyday life was far removed from Gifford's doctrinal subtleties. It was easier to believe that evil was at work in the universe and that Satan had real powers, against which one had to seek protection – not by putting one's trust in some inscrutable divine Providence, but by resorting to white magic and exorcisms.[28] Gifford's arguments did, none the less, find their way into the polemical debates of the time. Indeed, it was a short step from such views to the idea that the theatre was a house of sin and illusion and that it was not surprising that the Devil should resort to it to stage false miracles. In turn, this view could lead to the suggestion that through magic or the supernatural one could gain knowledge of God's will and that the Revelation was not ended. Later in this chapter we shall come back to these arguments as we examine their full implications.

Suffice it to say for the moment that the history play, almost by essence, invites conjectures about time and destiny and that particularly in *1 and 2 Henry VI* Shakespeare's characters seem to have embarked upon a quest for meaning, an anxious form of questioning of time, God's Providence and their own destiny. It is no mere coincidence that in *2 Henry VI* the Duke of Gloucester's wife Eleanor, who has hired exorcists to know more about her husband's future, couches her intentions in terms which associate destiny and theatre very closely: 'I will not be slack / To play my part in Fortune's pageant' (1.2.66–7).

Both *1 and 2 Henry VI* are riddled with prophecies and attempts at reading the future. This is no doubt because the world they stage is plagued by deep-seated uncertainty and is also longing for brighter perspectives. In *2 Henry VI* the Duke of Gloucester has an ominous dream 'Methought this staff, mine office-badge in court, / Was broke in twain; by whom I have forgot' (1.2.25–6). Later, in the same play, a witch by the name of Margery Jourdain and a conjuror called Roger Bolingbroke, with the assistance of John Southwell, a (Catholic) priest, promise Eleanor, Gloucester's wife, that they will disclose the secrets of the future with the help of sorcery, or so says John Hume, their accomplice:

> This they have promised, to show your highness
> A spirit, raised from depth of underground,
> That shall make answer to such questions
> As by your grace shall be propounded him.
>
> (*2H6*, 1.2.78–81)

In *1 Henry VI*, the French appear to be sensitive to the possible influence of the planets and the cosmos. Indeed, Charles the Dauphin regrets that for the moment, 'Mars his true moving, even as in the heavens / So in the earth, to this day is not known' (*1H6*, 1.2.1–2). The lack of a decisive military victory and the resulting political stalemate make the French (as well as the English) desperate for some sign of hope. They thus become obsessed with the future. Sceptics like Reginald Scot warned that conjurers and sorcerers had no real powers and that soothsayers and prophecies were not to be believed. It was blasphemous to maintain the contrary as, '*Peter Martyr* saith, that onelie God and man knoweth the heart of man, and therefore, that the divell must be secluded, alledging these places; *Solus deus est scrutator cordium*, Onelie God is the searcher of hearts'.[29] For Scot, oracles and spirits had been silenced by Christ himself, and such practices belonged to the pre-Reformation world, which was peopled by men who may remind us of the characters of Robert Greene's plays – those friars, monks and priests, who made their living, argued Scot, out of practices which fooled the populace:

> These cousening oracles, or rather oraclers used (I saie) to exercise their feats and to doo their miracles most commonly in maids, in beasts, in images, in dens, in cloisters, in darke holes, in trees,

in churches or churchyards, &c: where preests, moonks, and friers had laid their plots, and made their confederacies aforehand, to beguile the world, to gaine monie, and to adde credit to their profession.[30]

Scot's rhetoric reaches the apex of its demonstration with the argument that not only have the Reformation monarchs (the reign of Mary I goes unmentioned) rid England of such characters, but also no trace of their existence is left. This is, of course, where Scot's speech is closest to wishful thinking:

> But if those doctors had lived till this daie, they would have said and written, that oracles had ceased, or rather beene driven out of *England* in the time of *K. Henrie* the eight, and of Queene *Elizabeth* his daughter; who have doone so much in that behalfe, as at this houre they are not onlie all gone, but forgotten here in this English nation, where they swarmed as thicke as they did in *Bœotia*, or in any other place in the world.[31]

One is left to wonder what Scot would have made of Shakespeare's prophecies, those staged omens which – through the agency of drama – often turn out to be true, especially in *2 Henry VI*, but not solely.[32] The latter play offers perhaps the best example of what might be called the *poetic* fulfilment of a prophecy. In the course of the 'conjuring' scene (1.4), the spirit called forth by Bolingbroke and his helpers had been prompted to make a prediction regarding the Duke of Suffolk: 'By water shall he die and take his end' (1.4.33). This prediction is taken up later in the play and reaches its fulfilment as we hear these words spoken:

> WHITMORE And so am I; my name is Walter Whitmore.
> How now! Why starts thou? What, doth death affright?
> SUFFOLK Thy name affrights me, in whose sound is death.
> A cunning man did calculate my birth
> And told me that by water I should die.
> Yet let not this make thee bloody-minded,
> Thy name is Gualtier, being rightly sounded.
>
> (*2H6*, 4.1.31–7)

The tragic punning on 'Walter' and 'water' gives dramatic resonance to the poetic truth of the prophecy. Here Shakespeare's theatre gives the lie to the words of the rationalists, those Protestants, like Reginald Scot, for whom words had no power *per se*: 'For by the sound of the words nothing commeth, nothing goeth, otherwise than God in nature hath ordeined to be doone by ordinarie speech, or else by his speciall ordinance'.[33]

Shakespeare likewise played with the idea that not all prophecies should be discarded, that it is perhaps simplistic to cast them aside as being things of the past, or to associate them systematically with remnants of the time when England was a Catholic nation. It is true that many visions and prophecies were used to support the Catholic cause in the 1530s and even later during Elizabeth's reign they served as propaganda for Mary Queen of Scots, but as social historians remind us, Protestants also had their own prophecies, despite claims to the contrary:

> It is less well known that similar prophetic power was attributed to the heroes of early English Protestantism. The Marian persecution was said to have been predicted by Hooper, Bradford, Latimer and other Protestant martyrs. The pages of John Foxe's *Acts and Monuments* abound in stories of the martyrs who foretold their own deaths or kept up the hopes of their supporters by correctly prognosticating Queen Mary's death and the end of persecution.[34]

What is more, in a recent study of Providence in early modern England, Alexandra Walsham shows that Protestant views on Providence were not clear cut and that it was not only a subject of discord between Catholics and Protestants, but also among Protestants themselves.[35] The view that 'miracles are ceased' may have been proverbial – so much so that the expression would appear in Shakespeare's own *Henry V* (1.1.67), placed somewhat anachronistically in the mouth of the Archbishop of Canterbury – it was nevertheless far from unanimously embraced by all Protestant writers. In fact it seems that the argument was often used by Protestant controversialists as an expedient way of disarming their Catholic opponents, at the snap of a finger as it were. Protestants were aware that the idea of God's miraculous intervention in human affairs was, after all, part of the Christian heritage they shared with Catholics – even if, of course, most clergymen insisted that real miracles were extremely rare. Yet to promote such argumentation was also to give a serious advantage to their Catholic adversaries who knew how to put the so-called miracles of divine Providence to use when required to prove that God supported their cause.

For Protestant theologians then, miracles had not quite ceased, even if the Protestant concept of miracle was "hedged about with a number of significant qualifications. 'Special providences' and miracles were not spontaneous or impromptu interventions; they were events for which God had foreseen the need and built into His plan for humanity before the beginning of time".[36] Still, the notion of 'special Providence' enabled Protestants to get themselves out of a tight corner and combat their opponents on an almost equal polemical footing, especially when they sought to win over those who wavered most in their convictions.[37] Many were indeed hesitant and remained so, like Shakespeare's Lord Lafeu, who in a much later play – *All's Well That Ends Well* – would seem to put his faith in 'special providences', or indeed miracles:

> They say miracles are past, and we have our philosophical persons to make modern and familiar things supernatural and causeless. Hence is it that we make trifles of terrors, ensconcing ourselves into seeming knowledge when we should submit ourselves to an unknown fear.[38]

Interestingly, as Lafeu utters these words, he is holding one of those broadsheet ballads which were used by Elizabethan controversialists and religious propagandists across the religious spectrum to influence opinion. The ballad in question is precisely one which seems to make much of the existence of 'special providences' – it bears a very revealing title, which Lafeu reads out to the audience: "'A showing of a heavenly effect in an earthly actor'" (2.3.24–5).

Witchcraft and questions left unanswered

The use and abuse of 'special providences' by Elizabethan controversialists led polemicists onto dire doctrinal ground and, rather than reassuring those who wavered in their faith and creeds, it actually gave cause for further reflection, or even doubt. Indeed, controversialists themselves quickly realized that 'adducing evidence of divine wrath against one's adversaries could not on its own convince people to embrace or retain a particular faith . . . '.[39] Furthermore, this did little to restore people's faith in God's Providence, as the Almighty appeared strangely factionalized. The exploitation of Providence ultimately went against the evangelical wish to spiritualize human experience by raising it above the level of the supposed harm and charms of witchcraft. People's reliance on exorcisms and white magic to ward off witchcraft was not going to go away easily, nor was the subject of witchcraft itself.

In fact, the regular reappearance of witchcraft on the Elizabethan stage remained tied to genuine concerns regarding the future and the meaning of life itself, whether these concerns were openly acknowledged or not. Witchcraft implied not only that supernatural agency was a reality, but also that such powers could be used and channelled in some way.

As Christina Larner explains, 'Witchcraft is the generation of supernatural power with or without particular performances'.[40] The emergence of witchcraft thus implicitly addressed the question of supernatural agency – its sheer existence, its meaning and interpretation, and its potential purposes or use. It is in fact remarkable that the subject of witchcraft and its implications has been overlooked or played down by critics of Elizabethan theatre, often because it was long thought that 'witchcraft was not very frequently touched on, and when it was it was treated more lightly and tolerantly than in the seventeenth-century plays'.[41]

One would hardly call 'light', however, the treatment given, for instance, to the conjuration scene of *2 Henry VI* (1.4), which stages an exorcism and ends with the arrest of a prominent member of the aristocracy – Eleanor, Duchess of Gloucester, whose arrest will trigger her husband's fall and ultimately his death. This is a complex scene, which works on several levels. John Hume, a priest hired by the Duchess to exorcize spirits in an attempt to know more about the future, gives away the plot – the whole is supposed to be a machination meant to ensnare the Duchess:

> Dame Eleanor gives gold to bring the witch:
> Gold cannot come amiss, were she a devil.
> Yet have I gold flies from another coast:
> I dare not say from the rich Cardinal
> And from the great and new-made Duke of Suffolk,
> Yet I do find it so. For, to be plain,
> They, knowing Dame Eleanor's aspiring humour,
> Have hired me to undermine the Duchess
> And buzz these conjurations in her brain.
>
> . . .
>
> Well, so it stands; and thus, I fear, at last
> Hume's knavery will be the Duchess' wrack,
> And her attainture will be Humphrey's fall.
> Sort how it will, I shall have gold for all.

> (*2H6*, 1.2.91–9; 104–7)

Magic and witchcraft appear to be treated like commodities. The Duchess purchases occult knowledge of the future to serve her political ends, but she is outbid by Cardinal Beaufort, the Bishop of Winchester, and William de la Pole, the Duke of Suffolk. Interestingly, the machination is something which Shakespeare invented: 'to interrelate historical materials for dramatic effect Shakespeare invented the enmity of the Queen and the Duchess, as well as Hume's agency for the Cardinal-Suffolk faction' and no doubt he also wished to imply that magic can easily become the instrument of the conniving politician.[42] He may also have been influenced by John Foxe's sympathetic depiction of Eleanor Cobham in the 1576 edition of his *Acts and Monuments* (and in all the ensuing editions) where Foxe suggests that Gloucester's wife was the victim of the Catholic prelates' malice and political ambition.[43] One is therefore led to believe that one is about to witness a cunning spectacle, a false ceremony, similar to that which Reginald Scot calls a 'publike confederacie' in his *Discoverie of Witchcraft*:

> Publike confederacie is, when there is before hand a compact made betwixt diverse persons; the one to be principall, the rest to be assistants in working miracles, or rather in cousening and abusing the beholders. As when I tell you in the presence of a multitude what you have thought or doone, or shall doo or thinke, when you and I were thereupon agreed before. And if this be cunninglie and closelie handled, it will induce great admiration to the beholders; speciallie when they are before amazed and abused by some experiments of naturall magike, arythmeticall conclusions, or legierdemaine.[44]

Scot also associates such ceremonies with those practised by the Catholic Church: 'The papists (I saie) have officers in this behalfe, which are called exorcists or conjurors, and they looke narrowlie to other cousenors, as having gotten the upper hand over them'.[45] While Margery Jourdain is 'a witch' and Roger Bolingbroke a necromancer, both John Hume and Southwell – who also take an active part in the exorcism – are described in the Folio stage directions as 'two [Catholic] priests'.[46] Furthermore, one of their secret benefactors is, as we know, none other than a cardinal. On the face of it, the scene could thus be read as an anachronistic denunciation of Catholic practices. When writing this scene, Shakespeare may likewise have been aware that a group of Catholic missionary priests had acquired quite a reputation in 1585–86 after a number of exorcisms which they had practised mainly in or around the town of Denham. Samuel Harsnett later famously exposed their activities in his *Declaration of Popish Impostures*, a book which influenced Shakespeare's *King Lear*.[47] Well before these events, Elizabethan law had changed significantly as a result of perceived threats to destabilize the Queen. Since the early 1580s a new set of laws had sought to impose silence around the question of the Queen's succession and a charge of 'Felonie' could be brandished to discourage those who 'shall by setting or erecting of any figure or figures, or by casting of nativities, or by calculation, or by any prophecying, witchcraft, conjurations, or other like unlawfull meanes whatsoever, seeke to knowe, and shall set foorth by expresse wordes, deedes, or writings, how long her Majestie shal live or continue, or who shal reigne as king or queene of this realme of England after her highnesses decease'.[48]

What Shakespeare found in his sources – especially in Hall's depiction of the episode – was material which would be far too dangerous to stage in a climate which had only worsened a decade after the aforementioned legislation.[49] In Hall's description, the sorcery is explicitly directed against the King and is thus tantamount to high treason: 'thei, at the request of the duchesse, had devised an image of waxe, representyng the kynge, which by their sorcery, a litle and litle consumed, entendyng therby in conclusion to waist, and destroy the kynges person, and so to bryng hym death ... '.[50] When adapting this scene for the stage Shakespeare significantly altered his source, turning the episode into a scene of exorcism and prophesying rather than of sorcery.

There is good reason to believe that the audience of *2 Henry VI* may well have expected a strong anti-Catholic undercurrent to run through the scene as it began to unfold before their eyes. After all, Act 1, scene 4 describes precisely the type of ceremony denounced by Scot and others as mere deception and there is much in Bolingbroke's stage management of his fellow exorcists which smacks of artifice: 'Mother Jourdain, be you prostrate and grovel on the earth; John Southwell, read you; and let us to our work' (*2H6*, 1.4.11–12).

Yet Shakespeare seemingly adds another level of meaning to this scene by going beyond the mere satire of the wiles of politics, or the so-called practices of the Catholic Church. Indeed, it is not often remarked that in both the Quarto and Folio version of the play the stage directions appear to authenticate the spirit's presence on stage: '*It thunders and lightens terribly; then the* Spirit *riseth*' (1.4.22.2–3).[51] As the scene progresses and the questioning carried out ceremonially by Bolingbroke centres on the fates of the King, the Duke of York and the Duke of Somerset, the audience seems poised between cynical manipulation and a true conjuring of spirits – a very delicate balance which Shakespeare appears intent on maintaining for a few minutes, until the arrival of the manipulative politicians, with the Duke of York's triumphant lines:

> Lord Buckingham, methinks you watched her well. –
> A pretty plot, well chosen to build upon. –
> Now, pray, my lord, let's see the devil's writ.

> (*2H6*, 1.4.55–7)

Interestingly, when York reads the spirit's prophecies, his cynicism and detachment make him comment on the so-called revelations in a way which sheds light (unwittingly) on the ambiguous nature of the whole scene – which can be read on several, sometimes conflicting, levels: 'Why this is just / *Aio te, Aeacida, Romanos vincere posse*' (1.4.61–2). Despite the obviousness of the manipulation, Shakespeare neither writes off the whole episode totally as mere trickery and foolery, nor does he fully embrace the magic of the scene. Thus, we, as an audience, are left with important questions unanswered – Is this genuine witchcraft? Can magic serve political ends? Is this the work of the Devil and what part does Satan play in the ills of society?

In the so-called war of religion which the English are fighting against the French in Shakespeare's later play on the reign of Henry VI – *Henry VI, Part 1* – such questions arise again, and again remain unanswered. In the masculine world of the play, a woman – one who, this time, is ready to transgress the barrier of the sexes – acts as a catalyst for a while, both absorbing and redirecting many of the tensions of the play's universe. Lord Talbot's first physical encounter with Joan of Arc is one during which she is immediately branded a witch:

> Devil, or devil's dam, I'll conjure thee.
> Blood will I draw on thee – thou art a witch –
> And straightway give thy soul to him thou serv'st.

> (*1H6*, 1.5.5–7)

In the epic discourse of the English, a woman's manly prowess can only be devilish, and if the French have gained the upper hand it has to be through the agency of the Devil, who, if one follows this dangerously Manichaean logic, has naturally sided with the enemy. The Duke of

Bedford is the one to denounce the unsavoury and unbecoming collusion of the Dauphin with the 'witch':

> Coward of France! How much he wrongs his fame,
> Despairing of his own arms' fortitude,
> To join with witches and the help of hell.
>
> (2.1.16–18)

In his chronicle of these events Hall also seems to credit Joan with supernatural powers. For the Tudor historian, there was no doubt that she was an instrument of the Devil: 'For surely, if credite maie be geven to the actes of the Clergie, openly done, and commonly shewed, this woman was not inspired with the holy ghoste, nor sent from God, (as the Frenchmen beleve) but an enchanteresse, an orgayne of the Devill, sent from Sathan, to blind the people and bryng them in unbelife'.[52] Not all Shakespeare's sources were agreed on the status of Joan of Arc.[53] Holinshed finds the monstrosity not in Joan, but in those who were eager to use her.[54] Whilst not denying the force of witchcraft and sorcery, nevertheless he dismisses it as a weapon of the weak and desperate, thus clearly calling into question the Dauphin's recourse to such practices: 'the Dolphin, whose dignitie abroad foulie spotted in this point, that, contrarie to the holie degree of a right christen prince (as he called himselfe), for maintenance of his quarels in warre would not reverence to prophane his sacred estate, as dealing in divelish practises with misbeleevers and witches'.[55]

As for Reginald Scot, he was no doubt conscious that lending true powers to witches and believing that they were instruments of an all-powerful Devil turned people away from the idea of an all-encompassing divine Providence. Ultimately, it could also lead to Manichaean visions of the world. He therefore scoffed at the idea that witches could be in charge of or indeed replace whole armies: 'One old witch might overthrowe an armie roiall: and then what needed we any guns, or wild fire, or any other instrument of warre? A witch might supplie all wants, and accomplish a princes will in this behalfe, even without charge or bloudshed of his people'.[56] Yet this is precisely the possibility which Shakespeare makes available to his audiences in several scenes of *1 Henry VI*, for dramatic purposes no doubt, but also perhaps to tempt them with the possibility of supernatural agency.

The playwright – as in *2 Henry VI* – leaves us to wonder at the Manichaean expressions of evil in the play and at the reality of Joan's supernatural powers. It seems that both the French and the English have had to believe in the reality of her magic, so as to exorcize their own quarrels. As the play demonstrates, 'the witch' is at first exploited and when she has ceased to fulfil her purpose, she is sacrificed on the altar of Christian reconciliation. Yet her disappearance, and even her desperate efforts at saving her life, cannot obliterate the powerful figure which Shakespeare has created. Theatrically, she has tempted us with the belief that supernatural agency exists and can be called upon, that spirits can be brought on stage and questioned.[57] Witchcraft in *1 and 2 Henry VI* is turned into a commodity by political power, but it also functions as a smoke screen to prevent more fundamental questions from emerging and being addressed. Still, Shakespeare – particularly during the brief conjuration scenes of both plays – lets these questions be aired as the characters strive to find answers through supernatural agency, official religion being seemingly incapable of providing satisfactory solutions.

Witchcraft and official religion

If witchcraft would not go away it was also because it was part and parcel of the ideological framework within which the different religious groups operated at the time. In the fight against evil, each religion was eager to prove that it was superior to the other. Like crude providentialism, exorcism was to become a central weapon in the ideological and religious warfare which raged during the whole of the sixteenth century. As D. P. Walker writes, 'It was not until the Reformation had got well under way that the possibility arose of exorcisms being used by one group of Christians as propaganda against another'.[58] Catholics used exorcisms to defend the practices and beliefs which Protestants denounced as magical superstitions, that is to say, exorcism *per se*, the use of relics, holy water, blest objects, the sign of the cross or the power of names.[59] Yet, for some Protestants, such as the dissident John Darrell – who was to become famous in the flurry of polemical literature about his activities in the late 1590s – it was a case of using exorcism to sanction a number of crucial Puritan practices and dogmas.[60] Ceremonies – not unlike the conjuration scene of *2 Henry VI* – were meant to prove the power of respective doctrines to conjure up spirits, exorcize them efficiently and combat the forces of evil. For those who practised exorcism it was, as has been suggested, only a short step to practising witchcraft, as witch and exorcist used almost the same language. It was again a short step to a Manichaean view of life, as the Devil could soon become, either expressly or not, a sort of anti-God.

Thus, Catholic exorcists and dissident Protestants who dabbled in magic shared a common ground to the extent that both represented a challenge to official religion. Darrell's exorcisms of the possessed culminating in the year 1597 were indeed regarded as being as much a threat as the Catholic exorcisms of 1587–88 conducted by the Jesuit William Weston and other secular priests. There is no proof that Darrell ever challenged the Catholic exorcists – his real target (like his Catholic predecessors) was the Church of England.[61]

Both John Bancroft, the Bishop of London, and his chaplain (who was none other than Samuel Harsnett), were to try to counter Darrell's growing influence. In 1599 Samuel Harsnett's *A Discovery of the Fraudulent Practices of John Darrell* was published. The work attacked both Catholic and Protestant exorcists and argued that there were 'no genuine post-apostolic possessions and that all the apparently supernatural symptoms of demonic possession actually had natural causes'.[62] Both the physical possibility of possession and its theological foundations were strongly challenged.

Yet in the light of James VI's imminent accession to the throne of England such arguments coming from the Bishop of London's corner could easily turn out to be a source of embarrassment. In 1597, in his *Daemonologie*, the King of Scotland had strongly opposed the opinion of those who did not believe in post-apostolic possession and the reality of witchcraft. James denounced the writings of Reginald Scot, whose arguments Harsnett had used to write his book against Darrell, *A Discovery of the Fraudulent Practices of John Darrell*. Bancroft and Harsnett therefore had to act prudently. In 1603 Harsnett published *A Declaration of Egregious Popish Impostures*, 'ostensibly an attack on the notorious exorcisms conducted by Catholic priests in the London area in 1585–86, but in reality an attack on the more recent Puritan exorcisms'.[63] Why indeed go back almost two decades to events which had little bearing on the political realities of 1603? Harsnett, it seems, in fact *used* the (then distant) threat posed by Catholic exorcism as a ploy to try to reconcile the King with the views of the Church of England.[64] But, as we shall see, too much was at stake for monarchs, who remained reluctant to denounce such beliefs.

Witchcraft and state secrets

John Lyly's *Endymion* – a fable and a probable veiled allegory of Elizabethan politics written in the year of the Armada (1588) just a year after the execution of Mary Queen of Scots – is a play which, like Shakespeare's

1 and 2 Henry VI, bears the distinct marks of its age. Written for the private stage, Lyly's piece is an apparently detached love comedy with more of a political undercurrent than Shakespeare would have allowed himself to use in writing for the public theatre. It also stages a witch – Dipsas – used by a character called Tellus to put a spell on Endymion, who may have been a thinly veiled allegory of the Catholic Earl of Oxford, Lyly's own patron.[65] Tellus, who stands as a representation of the recently executed Mary Queen of Scots is opposed to Cynthia, a not-so-disguised representation of Elizabeth and the only character able to lift Endymion's spell. As the piece draws to a close, Cynthia condemns Tellus to death for conspiring with a sorceress and she addresses Dipsas the witch directly in these words:

> Thou hast threatened to turn my course awry and alter by thy damnable art the government that I now possess by the eternal gods. But know thou, Dipsas, and let all the enchanters know, that Cynthia, being placed for light on earth, is also protected by the powers of heaven. Breathe out thou mayst words, gather thou mayst herbs, find out thou mayst stones agreeable to thine art, yet of no force to appal my heart, in which courage is so rooted, and constant persuasion of the mercy of the gods so grounded, that all thy witchcraft I esteem as weak as the world doth thy case wretched. (5.4.6–16)

In the play's world of ancient legend Cynthia/Elizabeth acknowledges the reality of witchcraft, so as to rise above it and appear untouchable. Lyly's eulogy of Elizabeth also subtly implies that Cynthia/Elizabeth should be ready to welcome and embrace those who have been estranged from her like Endymion/the (Catholic) Earl of Oxford. In other words, if they abandon the magic of Rome, Catholics should be allowed to return to the fold of a sovereign who, clearly, is 'protected by the powers of heaven' against magic and occult practices.

These arguments are redolent of James VI's self-fashioning as a ruler in the 1590s, the Scottish king wanting to be cast in a favourable light, especially as far as the English succession was concerned. James too was aware of the power of the so-called magic of Rome. The challenge for him (which no doubt was also a polemical strategy) was to use the fascination for magic and occult practices to establish himself as a sovereign with a religious aura strong enough for him to be regarded as an ideal successor to Elizabeth. This of course was the propaganda side of a far more subtle diplomatic and political game in which he was engaged during the whole of the 1590s. Be that as it may, James's propaganda warfare was an effort on the part of the Scottish sovereign not only to adapt to Elizabethan society but also to begin to influence it.

In 1592 a pamphlet appeared in London, the title of which is worth quoting in full, as it gives away most of the work's story line: *Newes from Scotland. Declaring the damnable life of Doctor Fian a notable Sorcerer, who was burned at Edenbrough in Ianuarie last. 1591. Which Doctor was register to the deuill, that sundrie times preached at North Baricke Kirke, to a number of notorious Witches. With the true examinations of the said Doctor and witches, as they vttered them in the presence of the Scottish king. Discouering how they pretended to bewitch and drowne his Maiestie in the sea comming from Denmarke, with such other wonderfull matters as the like hath not bin heard at anie time.*[66] The pamphlet was also said to have been 'Published according to the Scottish copie' and yet, as no such copy has ever been found, there is good reason to doubt that the Scottish edition ever existed.[67] The work was probably intended as propaganda for the English market only.

Between November 1590 and May 1591, mass trials had been held in Scotland against persons accused of raising storms while the King and his bride, Anne of Denmark, were at sea, returning to Scotland in the spring of 1590. In fact the anonymous author of the pamphlet took great care in his narrative of events to show that the Devil had no greater enemy in the world than the Scottish king: 'At which time the witches demaunded of the Divell why he did beare such hatred to the king, who aunswered, by reason the king is the greatest enemie hee hath in the world: all which their confessions and depositions are still extant uppon record'.[68] The author also used the testimony of one of the witches to insist that the King was saved only by his faith: 'and further the sayde witch declared, that his Maiestie had never come safely from the Sea, if his faith had not prevayled above their ententions'.[69] The conclusion of the pamphlet neatly summed up the moral to be drawn from the narrative – that the prospective claimant to the English throne was – like Elizabeth – virtuous, that he entertained a special relationship with God and that he was concerned about the welfare of his state and people:

> so long as God is with him, hee feareth not who is against him. and trulie the whole scope of this treatise dooth so plainely laie open the wonderfull providence of the almightie, that if he had not bene defended by his omnipotencie and power, his Highnes had never returned alive in his voiage from Denmarke, so that there is no doubt but God woulde as well defend him on the land as on the sea, where they pretended their damnable practise.[70]

James would later buttress his reputation as a holy king – or at least as one who would defend the 'true faith' – in the *Daemonologie* (1597), in which he was to argue that, while witches' spells, ceremonies and exorcisms were of little effect, sorcerers were nevertheless manipulated by the Devil whose power was not to be doubted or underestimated.[71] The main tenet of the treatise – the one which would later be a matter of embarrassment and preoccupation for Bancroft and Harsnett – was that the King's 'work' in this domain could not easily be contested, for to deny the existence of the Devil was to deny God's existence: 'Doubtleslie who denyeth the power of the Devill, woulde likewise denie the power of God, if they could for shame. For since the Devill is the verie contrarie opposite to God, there can be no better way to know God, then by the contrarie . . . '.[72] With this statement James showed that he was ready to fit himself into the constrictive system of contraries which was the hallmark of the early modern period. Evil was needed as much as good to make God's Creation perfect.[73] This, to some extent, was a perverse logic for it implied that God could only be known through evil. For a monarch so determined to argue that kings were God's representatives on earth, it was, however, a necessary and inevitable logic: indeed, it was 'precisely because there was a mystical dimension to politics that there was a political dimension to magic; both were modifications of the same world of thought'.[74]

* * *

As they looked back, some writers found that Shakespeare had fallen for the false magic of the Church of Rome in an age which had not yet fully acknowledged 'true faith', which devoted too much attention to witches and had a fascination for magical ceremonies which seemed quaint and not entirely rational.[75] Writing some fifty years after *The Tempest*, John Dryden's portrait of Shakespeare is of a dramatist still mesmerized – and somewhat imprisoned – by the magical powers of Catholicism which, Dryden suggests, permeate his art and also partly explain its uniqueness:

> But Shakespear's Magick could not copy'd be,
> Within that Circle none durst walk but he.
> I must confess 'twas bold, nor would you now,
> That liberty to vulgar Wits allow,
> Which works by magick supernatural things:
> But Shakespear's pow'r is sacred as a King's.
> Those Legends from old Priest-hood were receiv'd,
> And he then writ, as people then believ'd.[76]

Leaving aside the slightly condescending tone of these lines, there is a measure of truth in the view that Shakespeare was sensitive to the values of 'old Priest-hood', as Dryden puts it. Yet Shakespeare's obvious interest in magic, witchcraft and the supernatural is a complex issue, as complex and paradoxical as the links between politics, religion and magic during the decade in which the dramatist began writing.

As we hope to have demonstrated in this chapter, political power during this period needed a built-in enemy (witches, Catholics, Puritans...) to maintain and justify itself. It needed to create an all-powerful Devil to be able to show that its rulers were untouchable, but by adopting this logic it ran the risk of implicitly deconstructing its own argumentation. Indeed, what is interesting in Dryden's lines is that he has also clearly sensed that Shakespeare's so-called Catholic magic was akin to that used by sovereigns: 'But Shakespear's pow'r is sacred as a King's'. In other words, in Dryden's mind the difference between the magical aura of monarchs and the magic used by those who sought to conjure up supernatural forces was probably slight.[77] Within the Christian cognitive framework of the time, so reliant on the principle of contrariety, good and evil were morally opposed and yet these terms were indispensable to each other. James had to speak at length about witchcraft and the Devil in order to address the subject which mattered most in his eyes – God and his own powers as sovereign. There are moments when we may even wonder where his priority lies[78] – and this is also true of many of the pamphlets produced by religious controversialists. Another problem with this logic is that it does not provide individuals with access to meaning. This is something to which Shakespeare was no doubt sensitive in his depiction of characters who embark on a seemingly endless quest for meaning in the religious domain.

Meaning in the moral and religious domain seems to be suspended or deferred because of the way the logic of contrariety functions. In a world structured by the opposition between good and evil, 'the mind only settles on the meaning of one contrary by confronting the meaning of its partner; whereupon the semantic dependence of the second term becomes just as apparent, and the initial act of understanding is unsettled'.[79] In addition to this semantic problem, there were ideological difficulties which further blurred Christian values. Indeed, in order to affirm the superiority of good over evil, theologians and pamphleteers had to produce a solid sum of irrefutable Christian truth – but how could they do that, when the Catholic and the Protestant churches were arguing bitterly over the very nature of truth.

It is not an absurd or godless world that Shakespeare depicts in *1 and 2 Henry VI*, it is rather a universe where no single religion can be a source of certainty, but where opposing forces try to conquer ground through confessional overstatement and a measure of overinvestment. This paradoxically leaves us – and many characters in the plays – in doubt and indirectly continues to promote the occult as a possible source of knowledge. Elizabethan politics exploited religious concerns, but this does not mean that we should take this process at face value and read it from our perspective, that of a largely secularized Western world. We should bear in mind that religious concerns were genuine for many people and that in the hybrid culture of Elizabethan England, such concerns were rife and resurfaced repeatedly. Theatre is particularly well adapted to describe the processes by which politics use religion, especially when it adopts self-reflexive modes, such as meta-drama. Yet Shakespeare's theatre also points to what remains – it is not content to signal manipulation, it is also capable of looking beyond, of showing that politics can never totally extinguish the validity of religious concerns.[80] One should also try to look or read beyond, to understand that witchcraft was not simply used to validate political power, or as a denunciation of the Catholic Other; witchcraft signalled the need for answers in the religious domain.

2
Acting the Insubstantial in *King Richard III*

King Richard III[1] does not only depict the gross political manipulations of its main character, the late medieval king, who was to become such a popular tyrannical figure on the Elizabethan stage. There is much in the play which refers, alludes or appeals to another dimension that runs almost parallel to it. For Richard, at the beginning of the play, this other dimension is entirely fabricated, as it is part of the art of the so-called Machiavellian courtier to be able to create false belief in the supernatural: 'Plots have I laid inductions, dangerous, / By drunken prophecies, libels, and dreams' (1.1.32–3). Whether engineered by Richard or not, an otherworldly presence is felt at the highest levels of the kingdom. His brother Clarence, for instance, reveals that the King has fallen prey to superstitious fears which in fact permeate the corridors of power:

> But as I can learn,
> He harkens after prophecies and dreams,
> And from the cross-row plucks the letter G,
> And says a wizard told him that by 'G'
> His issue disinherited should be.
>
> (1.1.53–7)

While the King himself is influenced by this other world which is partly illusory, language also appears to work on two levels. For the audience it is increasingly clear that Richard's words and actions extend beyond the political world of the living. He is, after all, '*determinèd* to prove a villain' (1.1.30), as both a voluntary agent of evil and as an instrument of a higher purpose.[2]

The presence of the dead in the play is something the characters relentlessly comment upon. In *Richard III*'s morbid atmosphere they often seem poised between two states, two worlds or even two kingdoms, as in the Queen's speech of lamentation for her dead husband. As the play continues to unfold, it takes an ever-increasing number of souls on its dramatic journey:

> If you will live, lament; if die, be brief,
> That our swift-wingèd souls may catch the King's,
> Or like obedient subjects follow him
> To his new kingdom of perpetual rest.

(2.2.42–5)

Invoking the dead

In the second scene of the play, the burial of King Henry VI recalls the fact that *Richard III* marks the end of a series of plays covering the reign of the last Lancastrian monarch. The characters thus seek to lay the dead of the civil wars to rest and heal their wounds.

The presence of a coffin on stage is, however, a reminder of the weight of past quarrels, which impinge on the universe of the play. Funerals on stage have a disquieting effect, especially when they do not end a play but figure prominently at its outset. This was a device used by Shakespeare in *1 Henry VI*, which opened literally on the burial ceremonies of King Henry V, signalling the end of a heroic era and the beginning of political and religious turmoil. 'Funeral is the expected *end* of tragedy' and so *Richard III*'s displaced burial of King Henry VI alerts us to the fact that the play is not just the story of a tyrant's rise to power, it is also a piece set in 'a world intensely conscious of ending', a universe where the dead play their part, even if – and this is immediately brought to the fore by Richard's abruption of the rites accorded to the deceased sovereign – the place of the dead in such a universe is a source of deep uncertainty.[3]

In this way, *Richard III* anticipates in some respects many of the tensions present in *Hamlet*, 'a play obsessed with getting a decent burial', but also one which makes its audiences conscious of the difficult – or indeed imperfect – transition from Catholic rites of intercession between the living and the dead to Protestant commemoration of the departed.[4] The vast system of intercession – indulgences, prayers and masses for the repose of the souls of the deceased – had been contested by Protestant reformers and was officially condemned in Elizabethan England as 'popish'. Yet the scene in which Lady Anne accompanies the coffin of her father-in-law, King Henry VI (another victim of the War of the Roses), shows Shakespeare's conscious evocation of some ceremonies associated with the 'Old Religion'. Anne's apostrophe and eulogy of the dead king, as well as the ritualized language used in the scene are recognizably Catholic for an Elizabethan audience:

> Poor key-cold figure of a holy king,
> Pale ashes of the house of Lancaster,
> Thou bloodless remnant of that royal blood,
> Be it lawful that I invoke thy ghost
> To hear the lamentations of poor Anne,
> Wife to thy Edward, to thy slaughtered son
> Stabbed by the selfsame hands that made these holes.
> Lo, in those windows that let forth thy life
> I pour the helpless balm of my poor eyes.
> Cursed be the hand that made these fatal holes,
> Cursed be the heart that had the heart to do it.
>
> (1.2.5–15)

In Elizabethan England invoking the ghosts of the departed was not officially acceptable, hence Anne's anachronistic 'Be it lawful that I invoke thy ghost': it was certainly not 'lawful'. The dead could be remembered, but belief that one should pray for their souls or that one could enter into a dialogue with their ghosts was to be shunned. What the audience is witnessing here is a re-enactment of rites redolent of the Catholic religion. Invocations of saints (cf. 'a holy king') were probably still familiar to quite a few of Shakespeare's playgoers, but they had also been officially condemned early in the Queen's reign as 'popish' or 'Heathenish' by Protestant polemicists.[5] Yet Richard's arrival and his determination to put an end to these ceremonies add confessional complexity to the scene.

'And curst be he that moves my bones'

Open conflict has ceased in the play, but the ghost of former feuds has yet to be laid to rest. The diverting by Richard of Henry VI's coffin is emblematic of the painful journey the play takes to allow the past to be remembered and properly interred. As 'funeral itself constitutes a form of symbolic narrative', it can be argued that these maimed rites represent an unfinished story in a play which constantly unearths past narratives and calls forth an array of discontented ghosts from the past.[6]

Richard himself had pointed ironically at the apparent difficulty in remembering the dead in the play. The dead of the infra-dramatic world – those of the War of the Roses – are not fully honoured even though, for some of them, their death is very recent: 'Hath she forgot already that brave prince / Edward, her lord, whom I some three months since / Stabbed in my angry mood at Tewkesbury?' (1.2.224–6). Richard's cynicism is in many ways an extreme expression of the unease of the world around him. 'But first I'll turn yon fellow in his grave' (1.2.245): ritual is dismissed by Richard as a meaningless convention – the important matter being the prompt physical elimination of his adversaries, or, in his own words, that they 'be packed with post-haste up to heaven' (1.1.145). The burial rites of the past are thus rudely and spectacularly perturbed by the would-be tyrant.[7]

To a large extent, *Richard III* may remind us of a number of plays – most of them revenge tragedies – in which we sense that much stems from an initial failure (either deliberate or not) to honour the dead or indeed to give them a decent funeral. In Thomas Kyd's *Spanish Tragedy* much of the action appears to come from the vindictiveness of the ghost of Andrea in the play's Induction, while in Henry Chettle's *Hoffman* and the anonymous *The Revenger's Tragedy* the persistence of unburied human remains has dire consequences.[8] In the anonymous *True Tragedie of Richard The Third*, the ghost of George, Duke of Clarence appears on stage calling for revenge in the prologue of the play, which makes clear that Clarence's life was abruptly and violently cut short by his brother Richard.[9] Shakespeare himself seems to have held the belief that the proper preservation of mortal remains was a necessary condition for the soul's repose in the afterlife, judging by the stone epitaph which marks his grave in Holy Trinity church, Stratford: 'Bleste be the man that spares these stones, / And curst be he that moves my bones'.[10]

Richard III thus shares with many revenge tragedies a deep concern for death and its associated rituals. Interestingly, as a history play Shakespeare's piece also works partly as a ritual of remembrance of the dead. Alluding to Shakespeare's *1 Henry VI*, Thomas Nashe famously remarked in *Pierce Pennilesse*, a year before *Richard III* was first performed:

How would it haue ioyed braue Talbot (the terror of the French) to thinke that after he had lyne two hundred yeares in his Tombe, hee should triumphe againe on the Stage, and haue his bones newe embalmed with the teares of ten thousand spectators at least (at seueverall times) who, in the Tragedian that represents his person, imagine they behold him fresh bleeding?[11]

As a tragedy *Richard III* underlines the trauma of death, the necessity of ritual and the overbearing presence of the dead. As a history it resurrects the dead who, Lazarus-like, are brought back before us. By seeking to cut short the ritual of Henry VI's burial, Richard paradoxically also denies the theatrical ritual that has given him life again. Yet if the dead come back to join the living on the stage of history, they remain 'embalmed' and like Nashe's Talbot, come back to bleed somewhat painfully in the world of the living. Because he introduces a character who challenges the process by which the ghosts of the past are resurrected and remembered, Shakespeare enters a debate which is not only generic, but also cultural and metaphysical. The result, of course, is a play that unsettles, particularly because as early as the second scene of *Richard III* it mixes 'hornpipes' and 'funerals' as Philip Sidney put it when commenting on the unsavoury mixture of opposed genres.[12] Richard's sacrilegious wooing of Anne over Henry VI's coffin can indeed be described as a 'ritual of debasement', one which in some respects foreshadows Claudius's 'mirth in funeral' and 'dirge in marriage' in *Hamlet*.[13]

Richard's arrival in the midst of the funeral of Henry VI in fact complicates confessional issues. For Anne, his arrival is akin to the apparition of a fiend conjured up by an evil magician: 'What black magician conjures up this fiend, / To stop devoted charitable deeds?' (1.2.32–3). Richard arrests the progress of the King's body by threatening the pallbearers with what will become his hallmark in the play, the Pauline oath: 'by Saint Paul' (1.2.34). There may be a measure of irony in this oath in that Richard retaliates by naming a saint who was known for his exorcism of evil spirits at Ephesus which forced magicians to renounce their art: 'Many also of them which used curious artes, broght their bokes and burned them before all men'.[14]

The insistence in this scene is on the protection and preservation of Henrys 'soul' ('His soul thou canst not have, therefore be gone' (1.2.46)). Through the power of her rhetoric Anne manages to convey the impression that a quasi miracle has happened on stage: 'O gentlemen, see, see dead Henry's wounds / Open their congealed mouths and bleed afresh' (1.2.53–4). Henry's wounds are bleeding to voice Richard's guilt through a visual rhetoric that turns the dead king into a Christ-like figure. Anne toys with the idea that the dead can 'bleed afresh' and that they can still speak to us through 'congealed mouths'. Shakespeare lets grief be expressed in unorthodox idioms, those of the Catholic Church, or indeed those of Catholics or of unconforming Protestants who believed that the devil could be exorcized and that the ghosts of the dead could come back to haunt the living.[15]

Purgatory

'The belief in ghosts and unquiet spirits may be related to the incomplete eradication of purgatory from popular consciousness, long after its elimination from the official protestant religion,' wrote David Cressy.[16] Indeed, Shakespeare imported some of the cultural idioms of the pre-Reformation world into his work, especially when his play was set so clearly in late medieval England. At the same time, his views as a playwright seem to be embracing the world before and after the Reformation. His repeated and more often than not conscious anachronisms are the symptoms of a syncretic and interrogative mind.[17]

The position of Catholic polemicists on the question of purgatory was to criticize those who dared practise in these fields 'contentious reasoning of thinges vncertaine'.[18] This was William Allen's position, who called – in the name of faith – for a kind of willing suspension of disbelief regarding such matters. Allen also denounced Protestant arguments which used 'negative proof'. Just because the scriptures never mentioned purgatory, this did not mean that a place where souls eschewed the eternal pains of hell and awaited purgation to enter heaven did not exist: 'This negatiue faith hath no grownd nor confidence of things to be hoped for, nor any certayntye of suche thinges as doo not yet appeare, but it is an euident ouerthrowe of all our hope, and a very canker of thexpectation of thinges to coom. . . . mary by way of negative profe, they confirme theire negatiue and no faith'.[19] Faith had to produce hope and purgatory furnished people with something that could alleviate the sorrow of the bereaved.

Debates over the existence of purgatory had in fact become politicized, for behind purgatory lay the power of the Pope, which Protestant writers denounced as a sham: 'him that toke vpon him to commaunde not only men, but also the angels of God, to goe, to come, to leade soules into purgatory, & to bring them back againe when it liked him . . . '.[20] The emphasis for Protestants was on the remembrance of the dead, rather than on intercession between the living and the dead, which purgatory subsumed, as the living were supposed to pray for the benefit of the souls of those who awaited redemption in purgatory.[21] Even

though purgatory was a notion which had influenced several generations, its existence was officially denied and the belief was denounced
as folklore: 'For as touching that their ar wonte to boast them of their
Purgatory, althoe we know it is not very newly inuented: yet yt ys
nothing but mere foolish and an olde wiffes tale', wrote Bishop John
Jewel.[22]

By the 1580s belief in purgatory was on the decline. The bishops'
forty-two articles of 1553 had condemned the doctrine and called it
'a fonde thing vainlie feigned, and grounded upon no warraunt of
scripture, but rather repugnant to the woorde of God'. This was reiterated in the thirty-nine articles of 1563, which were ratified by Parliament in 1571.[23] In Protestant England the notion that the souls of the
departed underwent a process of purgation in a kind of middle state
and were partly dependent on the prayers of the living was fundamentally incompatible with one of the central tenets of Reformation theology – justification by faith alone.[24] Yet, contrary to what both Catholic
and Protestant polemicists affirmed, purgatory was less a doctrine, than
a highly creative mix. Purgatory was the least authoritatively defined
doctrine; it was in fact part of 'a nexus of objectified theological and
cultural values, visionary speculation, and calculating didacticism'.[25]
Purgatory and the notion of intercession had always been elastic enough
to combine the prescriptive and the speculative, so much so that 'within
its orbit, spiritual, social, economic, and political interests were endlessly
intertwined'.[26] While the decrees of the Church of England were prompt
to dismantle its outward forms, the cultural hold of the system did not
disappear immediately.

In Shakespeare's syncretic play of *Richard III* it is relatively easy to
detect the verbal presence of elements of this system. In the morbid
atmosphere of the play, characters often use these idioms to convey
their feelings and emotions. Interestingly, the post-Tridentine conception of purgatory insisted on the fact that purgatory was more 'a state of
being rather than . . . a specific location'.[27] Richard describes himself for
instance as being caught in a kind of intriguing middle-state, 'a living
death', which reminds one of purgatory:

LADY ANNE Would they were basilisks to strike thee dead.
RICHARD DUKE OF GLOUCESTER I would they were, that I might
die at once, For now they kill me with a living death. (1.2.148–50)

Henry VI's corpse on stage is also like the presence of an absence – so
is his wife, Old Queen Margaret, who died in France before the events of

the play, but whom Shakespeare brings back from the dead: 'Her presence is both ahistorical and ghostly'.[28] Indeed, the Margaret who speaks of her 'woeful banishment' in 1.3.190 is not the historical character, as Margaret of Anjou, Henry VI's wife, died in France in 1482 (a year before Edward IV's death). Margaret is a figure who is both inside and outside the play, in a kind of middle state; when she enters it is first at a distance before she joins the fray (1.3.109.2). Like Andrea in Kyd's *Spanish Tragedy*, who has journeyed into Hades and come back to haunt the living, she acts as a sort of revengeful Chorus to the tragedy.[29] Like many other ghosts of the Elizabethan stage, she remembers and calls for remembrance of the dead:[30]

> Out, devil, I remember them too well.
> Thou slewest my husband Henry in the Tower,
> And Edward, my poor son, at Tewskesbury.
>
> (1.3.118–20)

Margaret is Shakespeare's creation, someone who lives between heaven and hell in the symbolic or even verbal otherworld of the play.[31] She confirms her status as an outsider-insider, as someone whose spirit has haunted the characters because of her threats in a later scene of the play where she defines herself as a ghostly presence:

> Here in these confines slyly have I lurked
> To watch the waning of mine adversaries.
> A dire induction am I witness to,
> And will to France, hoping the consequence
> Will prove as bitter, black and tragical.
>
> (4.4.3–7)

Clarence's dream likewise tells a tale of in-betweenness. The verbal universe that Shakespeare creates for his character is one imbued with both Senecan and classical reminiscences and Catholic fears of the ghostly otherworld.[32] It brings to mind Andrea's opening description of his descent into the classical underworld in Kyd's *Spanish Tragedy*, both passages being partly adapted from Virgil's *Aeneid*. Andrea too describes how he craved 'a pasport for my wandring Ghost'.[33] Andrea's long and detailed account of his Underworld experiences reminds one of the traditional function of such narratives: 'the pains of Hell and Purgatory, far from being secret, had been graphically paraded as a warning to the living'.[34] Shakespeare's dream-vision is almost as vivid, even if of course it is conceived as oneiric. Clarence experiences the fate of those who are not quite dead, whose soul can have no rest. There can be no peace when the ghost cannot be fully yielded:

> for still the envious flood
> Kept in my soul, and would not let it forth
> To seek the empty, vast, and wand'ring air,
> But smothered it within my panting bulk,
> Which almost burst to belch it in the sea.

(1.4.34–7)

Amid references to Hades, there are figures who are closer to the ghosts of the Christian purgatory, however ambiguous these may be:[35]

> Then came wand'ring by
> A shadow like an angel with bright hair,
> Dabbled in blood, and he shrieked out aloud,

(1.4.49–51)

Clarence's 'like an angel' seems to indicate that the figure is construed by him as a victim who cannot rest in peace until justice is done. The Duke is himself aware that he has a heavy reckoning to make: 'O Brakenbury, I have done those things / Which now bear evidence against my soul' (1.4.63–4). Clarence's keeper speaks the words of consolation usually employed to allay the pains of tormented souls: 'God give your grace good rest' (1.4.68). Whereas Hamlet's father remains relatively silent about his otherworldly experiences (as if the ghost himself was ironically conscious of the official ban on such matters . . .), Shakespeare in this passage follows a long tradition of stories, particularly the popular genre of the 'news from Hell' and perhaps more distantly, medieval visions of Hell.[36] A burlesque example of the genre of the 'news from Hell' had been published a few years before *Richard III*. *Tarlton's newes out of purgatorie* (1590) uses Richard Tarlton's ghost (the most popular comic actor of the time had died in September 1588) for a fictional journey through purgatory. A number of ballads had also appeared with his name in the title and his ghost made other appearances in several works of the popular literature of the time.[37] *Tarlton's newes* employs purgatory as a literary device for social satire and also for criticism of Roman Catholicism. The narrator's dream-vision is a convention which enables him to meet the ghost of Richard Tarlton, who makes a comic defence of purgatory, one which, interestingly, shows how shreds of Christian theology, together with allusions to Dante's *Divine Comedy*, could find their way into popular works of literature – the piece is clearly another vivid example of the Elizabethan culture of 'bricolage':

> as soone as I heare the principles of your religion, I can say, oh there is a Calvinist: what doe you make heaven and hell *Contraria immediata*, so contrarie, that there is no meane betwixt them, but that either a mans soule must in post hast goe presently to God, or else with a whirlewind and a vengeance goe to the divell? yes, yes my good brother, there is *Quoddam tertium* a third place that all our great grandmothers have talkt of, that *Dant* hath so learnedly writ of, and that is Purgatorie.[38]

Despite its obvious critique of Catholicism, *Tarlton's newes* demonstrates the continuing circulation of notions which Protestant polemicists dismissed as things of the past. There was in truth 'an element of disingenuity about all this: polemicists professed to regard the arguments for purgatory as beneath their notice even as they continued to commit considerable resources to their confutation'.[39] Shakespeare's syncretic vision of life after death is a step removed from these debates – it is less theologically precise and the tonality of Clarence's dream is of course far more tragic. Yet both works use the same convention – the dream-vision – and both were partly inspired by the same popular tradition, that of the 'Newes from Hell'.

Acting the insubstantial

Whether they believed in purgatory or not, many Elizabethans continued to believe in ghosts. In fact, belief in ghosts was not denominational. Catholics were reluctant to defend the existence of ghosts openly and yet in many texts written for their coreligionists ghosts were used to prove that theirs was the true faith and to empower them with hope.[40] As for Protestants, they were often forced to recognize that ghosts had considerable emotional and cultural leverage and that they proved 'peculiarly intractable to the dictates of Protestant orthodoxy'.[41] This sometimes encouraged Protestant writers to tone down their arguments against ghosts. Protestant theologians never dismissed the possibility that God might send souls back into the world, they only claimed that in practice this hardly ever happened. The reality was that 'an openness to the messages of returning spirits was no peculiarity of a diehard Catholic remnant, but rather a shared cultural assumption with many of their conforming neighbours'.[42]

Only a small minority of sceptics were ready to dismiss the possibility of genuine apparitions altogether. The often quoted Reginald Scot was in fact far from representative of his era. Many considered Scot's *Discoverie of Witchcraft* (1584) to be dangerous for the Christian faith and with the rise of atheism at the turn of the following century some orthodox theologians even 'became more sympathetic to the idea of ghosts'.[43] Ghosts of dead persons were found sometimes in stories of Protestant providentialism. John Foxe in his *Book of Martyrs* unexpectedly told the story of an excommunicated bishop who returned after his death to beat up Pope Innocent IV; Philip Stubbes in a 1581 pamphlet recounted how an avaricious old lady was visited by a ghost who punished her. Such tales of Protestant providentialism continued well into the next reign.[44] Those who tried to educate people on the subject of ghosts were faced with a daunting task and could not always produce clear or consistent answers. An English translation of the Swiss Protestant reformer Louis Lavater's treatise on ghosts was published in London in 1572 under the title *Of Ghosts and Spirites Walking by Night*. In his treatise – to which Shakespeare would later be partly indebted for the writing of *Hamlet* – Lavater argued that visions and spirits are 'not the souls of dead men as some have thought', but 'either good or evill Angels'; the theologian added likewise that the devil has 'power to appeare under the shape of a faithfull man'.[45] The problem was that Lavater and other Protestant writers could not produce a truly effective method of distinguishing between good and devilish spirits and thus left large portions of the population at a loss. The result was that the belief in ghosts lived on, despite what polemicists maintained,[46] and that more often than not people were forced to construct their faith from a variety of different materials, as only these different elements enabled them to make some sense of the world around them. Their faith, in other words, was hybrid.[47]

Ghosts continued to form an integral part of popular culture, but belief in apparitions was common at almost every social level, as historians have shown.[48] One cannot quite argue therefore that the Elizabethan world had become secular and that in most cases ghosts were to be found only in fiction, as Stephen Greenblatt has recently contended: 'the ghosts who are increasingly labeled as fictions of the mind – these do not altogether vanish in the later sixteenth century. Instead they turn up onstage'.[49] It seems rather that the situation was more complex and certainly more ambiguous than the scenario of a gradually disenchanted world would lead to think. It is doubtful that Shakespeare's audience had any precise idea of what 'secular' meant, despite Greenblatt's elegant claim that, as far as ghosts are concerned, 'Shakespeare achieves the remarkable effect of a nebulous infection, a bleeding of the spectral into the secular and the secular into the spectral'.[50]

Indeed, it would be wrong to underestimate the cultural presence of ghosts in Elizabethan society at large. Theatre did not function in a vacuum, nor was it the final refuge of ghosts – it was one of the many places where ghosts appeared.[51] The important point was that theatre by essence entertained a special relationship with ghosts and apparitions – one which Shakespeare was evidently aware of.

It takes an actor playing the part of a quasi ghost to highlight the closeness between actors and spirits. Old Queen Margaret touches upon something fundamental through her use of the word 'shadow', with its dual attested meaning of 'actor' and 'ghost, or spirit':[52]

> I called thee then vain flourish of my fortune;
> I called thee then poor shadow, painted queen,
> The presentation of but what I was,
> The flattering index of a direful pageant[.]

> (4.4.77–80)

In the last act of the play when Richard wakes up from a dream where he has been haunted by the ghosts of his victims, the tyrant recognizes his fear of the spectral otherworld – whether it be the produce of a guilt-ridden conscience or not – by alluding to the insubstantial 'shadows' which he encountered in his nightmare: 'shadows tonight / Have struck more terror to the soul of Richard / Then can the substance of ten thousand soldiers' (5.4.195–7).[53]

But Margaret's use of the word 'shadow' is more meaningful in that it can be interpreted as a comment on the insubstantial nature of Elizabethan theatre conjuring up the dead past through the breath of its actors, as when Margaret enriches the metaphoric associations between dream and the living breath of actors: 'A dream of which thou wert a breath, a bubble – ' (4.4.83). From a meta-dramatic point of view, the actor suddenly appears behind the character in order to comment upon 'the direful pageant' of history.

The theatrical metaphor enables the characters to reflect on themselves and on their place both in history and in the play. The two queens (Old Queen Margaret and Edward IV's widow) mirror each other in Margaret's words – both are ghosts in the nightmare created by Richard. In this scene (Act 4, scene 4), where the women remember and invoke their dead, the boundaries between the living and the dead are slipping. The 'slippage' is also aesthetic as the meta-dramatic hints dropped in the course of the scene point to the aesthetic processes at work in the play. This may remind us of the dialogue between Poetrie and Truth in the prologue to *The True Tragedie of Richard The Third* where dramatic art (Poetrie on stage) admits that its function is to create insubstantial figures – 'shadowes' – while Truth (that is, historical verisimilitude) is there to give flesh to these figures ('adde bodies to the shadowes'). Thus, in the way they operate, Elizabethan history plays are themselves a comment on the frail imbalance of human existence both embodied in the flesh and yet also tending towards the insubstantial:

> *Poetrie.* Truth well met.
> *Truth.* Thankes Poetrie, what makes thou upon a stage?
> *Poetrie.* Shadowes.
> *Truth.* Then will I adde bodies to the shadowes,
>   . . .[50]

Prayers, curses and purgation

> Forbear to sleep the nights; and fast the days.
> Compare dead happiness with living woe.
> Think that thy babes were fairer than they were,
> And he that slew them fouler than he is.
> Bett'ring thy loss makes the bad causer worse.
> Revolving this will teach thee how to curse.
>
> (4.4.112–17)

Margaret's ritualistic verse in this scene creates the impression that a ceremony is taking place before our eyes. What is at stake is the release from the weight of past crimes by invoking the dead and cursing Richard. The release may be more psychological than effectual as Richard's queen herself admits; be that as it may, it is still worth attempting even if what is voiced is carried by human breath only: 'Poor breathing orators of miseries – / Let them have scope' (4.4.123–4).

As the women begin to voice the woeful litany of their dead, it becomes increasingly clear that this form of communal mourning is an effort to put an end to the long string of violent deaths brought about by the civil wars and perpetuated by Richard.[55] The repetitive and ritualistic aspects of the scene ('I had an Edward, till a Richard killed him' (37) and particularly the anaphora in Margaret's long and bitter speech in lines 77–109) all these effects create an unbearable atmosphere marked by remembrance of the numerous dead, verbally present to us and painfully present to the characters, who seem haunted by their memory. The women appear determined to intercede for the repose of the dead through their increasing appeals to divine justice. This is also what lends the scene its ambiguity. The mourners' remembrance of their dead brings them to curse Richard, their common enemy, in terms which are somewhat unorthodox. Their cursing implies that their words are charged with occult faculties.[56] Moreover, in their thirst for revenge, they seem willing to intercede with God in the name of their dead. According to orthodox Christian doctrine, the all-knowing and all-powerful God was supposed to compensate for the shortcomings of human justice, in the future if not in the present, in the next world if not in this one: 'Vengeance and recompense are mine' (Deuteronomy, 32:35).[57] Cursing one's enemies was thus, from a Christian point of view, both ineffective and unlawful.[58]

Yet the women's determination to wreak revenge remains inextricably tied to the remembrance of their dead. This is something which again makes us conscious of the fact that Shakespeare's *Richard III* is partly indebted to the popular genre of the revenge tragedy. To seek vengeance in a revenge tragedy is in itself an act of remembrance: 'Since revenge drama shows vengeance to be no more than memory continued by other means, the role of the revenger is essentially that of a 'remembrancer' in two senses of that once potent word: he is both an agent of memory and one whose task is to exact payments for the debts of the past'.[59] Like Shakespeare's *Richard III*, revenge drama bears witness to the fact that relations with the dead after the Reformation remain problematic and that more often than not 'its protagonists are haunted by ghosts because they are possessed by memory'.[60]

The women's resolve to seek vengeance for their dead adds another level of complexity to the scene, as their vengeance also implies that they believe in and call for a process of purgation. The release from the past and from the weight of these generations of dead people awaiting repair can only be obtained through the purgation of sins. Catholic and Protestant polemicists were, of course, divided over these issues.

For Protestants, broadly speaking, only divine intervention independent of human will could bring repair; for Catholics, prayers of intercession could have some effect on divine will and could bring about the purgation of sins. For a militant Catholic theologian like William Allen, there was no doubt that prayers could 'pierce the clouds and enter heaven', to use Margaret's revengeful words about the force of cursing (1.3.192): 'Praier is soueraigne, ioyned with almose and fastinge: the which being doone ether for the liue or dead, is with speede by angelles ministery, carried into heauen'.[61] It is crucial to note furthermore that the word 'revenge' is found in the writings of Catholic polemicists such as Allen or Robert Parsons. Interestingly, the word is used in Parsons' *Christian Directory* as well as in Allen's *Defense of Purgatory* to write about purgatory. Parsons writes of 'this fire revenge', while Allen is more explicit:

> If sin then be so revenged and thoroughly tried out of man's body, and all corruption out of these elements, for the glory of that new and eternal kingdom, shall we doubt of God's justice in the perfect revenge of sin in the soul, or purifying that nature which, as it was most corrupted and was the very seat of sin, so namely appertaineth to the company of angels and glory everlasting?[62]

Thus, the word 'revenge' is not associated here with a pagan nemesis, as is the case of course in Senecan tragedy. It refers to the belief that the effects of sin can be purified, or purgated, by divine will.[63] This went against the Protestant idea that only the elect could go to heaven, that prayer could not help the dead. Indeed, *The second Tome of Homelyes* of 1563 claimed that 'the sentence of God is unchangeable and cannot be revoked agayne'.[64] Its authors called upon everyone 'to take away the grosse errour of purgatory, out of our heades', adding significantly, 'neyther let us dreame any more that the dead soules are anye thynge at all holpen by our prayers'.[65] Yet even in this homily the word 'purgatory' would not go away easily; its Protestant authors were forced to use it, but strove to alter its meaning: 'the onely purgatory wherin we must trust to be saved is the death and bloud of Christ, which if we apprehende with a true and stedfast fayth, it purgeth and clenseth us, from all our sinnes, even as well as yf he were nowe hangynge upon the crosse'.[66] Nevertheless, there were many, like King Edward's queen in *Richard III*, for whom prayers for the repose of the dead helped to 'ease the heart', even when they knew that the efficacy of such rituals was contested: 'Let them have scope. Though what they do impart / Help not at all, yet do they ease the heart' (4.4.124–5). As late as the reign of Charles I, a good Protestant like the physician Thomas Browne confessed that he had wished that praying for the souls of the departed 'had been consonant to truth, and not offensive to my religion'; he further confessed that 'I could scarce contain my prayers for a friend at the ringing of a bell, or behold his corpse without an orison for his soul: 'twas a good way, methought, to be remembered by posterity, and a far more noble than an history'.[67]

It is noteworthy that Browne compares intercessory prayer for the dead to 'history', that is, the Protestant commemoration of the dead through monuments, speeches, books, etc. A tension of this nature is also felt at the heart of the women's lamentation scene, as Shakespeare's *Richard III* not only reawakens the dead of history, but initiates an anxious questioning on the relation of the dead to the living. This is possible because the play itself is a hybrid piece – mixing historical drama and elements of classical tragedy, or indeed of Elizabethan revenge drama. The lamentation scene is thus a complex one, consisting in an interweaving of different patterns of thought and belief. It also helps us understand the strange syncretic verbal confusion in the play between cathartic elements (the purifying of all evil thanks to the sacrificial killing of Richard at the end of the play) and the apparent belief of some characters in purgatory and in the effect of prayer for the dead.

Dreaming of ghosts

he tooke ill rest at nights, laie long waking and musing, sore wearied with care and watch, rather slumbered than slept, troubled with fearefull dreames, suddenlie sometime start vp, lept out of his bed, and ran about the chamber; so was his restlesse heart continuallie tossed and tumbled with the tedious impression and stormie remembrance of his abhominable déed. Now had he outward no long time in rest.[68]

The fame went that he had the same night a dreadful & terrible dreame, for it semed to hym beynge a slepe that he sawe diverse ymages lyke terrible develles whiche pulled and haled hym, not sufferynge hym to take any quyet or rest. The whiche straunge vision not so sodeinlie strake his heart with a sodeyne feare, but it stuffed his hed and troubled his mynde with many dreadfull and busy Imaginacions . . . . And least that it might be suspected that he was abasshed for feare of his enemyes, and for that cause looked so pitiously, he recyted and declared to hys famylyer frendes in the morenynge hys wonderfull vision and terrible dreame.[69]

These two passages, by Thomas More and Edward Hall respectively, are the only known *direct* sources for the so-called ghost scene in Act 5. In both, Richard is clearly portrayed as a tormented soul, More's *History of Richard III* being less specific than Hall's chronicle. For More the tyrant was continuously 'troubled with fearefull dreames'; for Hall he had this dream on the eve of the battle of Bosworth. There is a world of difference none the less between Hall's cautious and fairly unspecific phrase ('he sawe diverse ymages lyke terrible develles whiche pulled and haled hym') and the fact that Shakespeare actually brings a series of ghostly figures on stage.[70] The dramatist was protected by the dreamlike nature of the scene. But the fact remains that, to this day, theatre directors almost inevitably use actors to play the ghosts on stage and that as a consequence they are physically present, and not just abstract figments of Richard's or Richmond's imagination.[71]

In this scene Shakespeare 'embodies' the dead and gives them 'objective power'.[72] Whereas Clarence's dream tended to internalize the ghosts, the dreams here have the effect of externalizing them and of establishing clearly who the victor will be.[73] The ghost of Buckingham, who ends the visitation, finishes on a proleptic couplet: 'God and good angels fight on Richmond's side, / And Richard falls in height of all his pride' (5.4.154–5). In many ways, as Emrys Jones points out, 'In stage terms the procession of ghosts *is* the battle of Bosworth'.[74]

Shakespeare also toys a little with orthodoxy, as has already been suggested. What is remarkable – and rather ironic – in this scene is that the dramatist is able to conjure such a powerfully meaningful array of spectral figures from the forbidden purgatory of the 'Old Religion' to bolster a dynastic line which will, with the exception of Mary Tudor's reign, embrace the Protestant religion. With a measure of irony and ambiguity Shakespeare thus probes the origins of the Tudors, that allegedly 'happy race of kings', as the ghosts of Edward IV's sons would have us believe (5.4.131). For a moment Richard seems to credit a piece of Elizabethan ghost lore when he notices that 'The lights burn blue' (5.4.159), a traditional sign of ghostly presence. Even the founder of the Tudor dynasty is shown clearly embracing the belief in ghosts, thus potentially subsuming the existence of Catholic purgatory. Richmond also alludes to the ghosts in ways which are unambiguously pre-reformed: 'Methought their souls whose bodies Richard murdered / Came to my tent and cried on victory' (5.4.209–10).[75] It is amusing to consider that Richard – although shaken – is the one who shows himself most sceptical: 'Have mercy, Jesu! – Soft, I did but dream. / O coward conscience, how dost thou afflict me!' (5.4.157–8). The difference for us as an audience is that this visitation has been no dream – the ghosts acquired a *visible, tangible* existence when they appeared before us on stage.[76]

*   *   *

Despite its main character's histrionics and its pervasive meta-theatricality, *Richard III* is far from being a play set in a disenchanted world. The insubstantial *is* acted (to go back to the title of this chapter) in a profound and provocative fashion. Shakespeare's apparently secular play cuts through realms of the uncertain, posing essential questions, mimicking the rituals of the Catholic religion, confronting the old (the pagan world, the Roman Catholic world) and the new (Protestantism), creating a hybrid piece, so wonderfully attuned to the 'hybrid' religious culture of the England of the early 1590s. Shakespeare's *Richard III* bears witness to the fact that the boundaries between reality and illusion, between the literal and the figurative in the Word of God, between the living and the dead, were constantly renegotiated in early modern England.[77]

Ghosts were part and parcel of the fabric of society, so much so that a writer like Thomas Nashe could denounce their politicization. 'Spirits of the aire', wrote Nashe, commonly speak with 'politique statesmen', whom 'they privily incite, to bleare the worlds eyes with clowdes of common wealth pretences, to broach any enmitie or ambitious humor of theire owne, under a title of their cuntries preservation'.[78] The Stuart pamphleteer John Gee also denounced the so-called manipulations of the Jesuits, whose staged apparitions of ghosts from purgatory were supposed to induce Protestants to convert to Catholicism. Such sights were entertainment of the sort that a popular art-form like theatre could provide, argued Gee. Shakespeare's stage ghosts were cheap entertainment for people who enjoyed such thrills: 'Representations and Apparitions from the dead might be seen far cheaper at other Play-houses. As for example, the *Ghost in Hamlet, Don Andrea's Ghost in Hieronimo*'.[79] Yet these sectarian, secularized or indeed functionalist approaches to the phenomenon of ghostly apparitions do not tell the whole story. If belief in Purgatory was on the decline, it had not become a mere 'poet's fable', as William Tyndale had famously written.[80] It still remained – at the

beginning of the seventeenth century – a subject of debate for polemicists and a reason for apostasy for men like Theophilus Higgons, who
in a tract published in 1609 explained that his belief in purgatory had
prompted him to abandon the Protestant faith and become a Catholic.[81]
At all events, the decline of purgatory – or what one contemporary
writer called the 'hunting of purgatory to death' – had not really affected
beliefs in revenants, spectres or other apparitions of the deceased, which
continued often independent of any mention of purgatory.[82] Yet, to a
large extent, the *idea* of purgatory was something which remained a
modality of the human psyche, as it seemed 'more 'realistic', emotionally as well as cognitively, to subdivide the world and posit a place
between Heaven and Hell rather than to imagine nothing at all'.[83]

Theatre was not the 'Last Frontier' of ghosts; it was a place where some
of the deepest anxieties of Elizabethan society came to be voiced, often
in ambiguous fashion as in *Richard III*, where death is on everyone's lips
and where many characters have trouble dealing with the dead, despite
their pressing need to exorcize the past. Even the advent in the play of
the first Tudor monarch seems marked by ambiguity and a measure of
irony, as we have seen. The dead remain present almost to the very end,
regardless, it seems, of the play's apparent resolution. Ultimately, the
insubstantial in *Richard III* also resists concrete definition. The insubstantial is a felt presence, which is often voiced through the otherworldly
idioms of angst-ridden characters. It is, however, never totally metaph-
orized, as many of these idioms no doubt retained their associations
with religious or indeed confessional issues for Shakespeare's audience.
The insubstantial is likewise part and parcel of the fundamental aesthetic
fabric of Elizabethan historical drama and of its frail attempts to bring
the dead to life again on its ephemeral and 'unworthy scaffold'.[84] Its full
meaning, none the less, remains forever 'fragmentary, contested and
uncertain'.[85] How could it have been otherwise in a world which was
being remade and where religious and metaphysical beliefs were being
restructured in ways which, to many, never ceased to be mysterious.[86]

3
Religious Conscience and the Struggle for the Succession in *Richard II*

Well before the staging and first publication of Shakespeare's *Richard II* in 1597, the story of the unfortunate Plantagenet king had been on the shelves of Elizabethan stationers, available to almost every cynic and malcontent of the period.[1] Indeed, when Shakespeare completed the writing of *Richard II* in or around 1595[2] the life of Richard of Bordeaux and the allusions to his reign had already been used by historians and law specialists to discuss the terms under which a king might be deposed. The theme had also been repeatedly appropriated by polemicists and malcontents to point to the moral of the story, in ways which sought to confront the so-called Elizabethan status quo.[3] Polemical tracts which warned Elizabeth to beware the fate of Richard II (and other weak English sovereigns) had been in circulation since the 1580s.[4] In other words, allusions to Richard II had become commonplace when commenting on the realm of politics. The tale of an ambitious courtier of royal blood who was to challenge and depose his lawful king might also have had a peculiar ring to some ears, especially to the ears of those who regarded the rise to prominence and influence of such young and eager royal favourites as Robert Devereux, Earl of Essex, as a threat.[5] Evidently, the reception of such stories could prove as dire as it was unpredictable. Plays were volatile material within a fast-changing context which called for caution, especially when, as a dramatist, one had very limited control over events.

A Christian moral dilemma

Given the particularly tense political and religious climate of the mid-1590s, it is then little wonder that, as Shakespeare's *Richard II* opens, the issues at the heart of the first scenes of the play are slightly obfuscated. The initial tensions in the play are channelled by Richard through a court of chivalry and then, as a last resort, through a trial by combat. We quickly encounter a debate on treason and the trial opposing Henry Bolingbroke and Thomas Mowbray, Duke of Norfolk, highlights betrayal as being crucial to the unfolding of the plot.

Shakespeare maintains an equal degree of obfuscation when the two contestants come close to implicating the King in matters which are not altogether wholesome. By finally pronouncing a sentence of exile on both parties, Richard seeks to put a physical bar between him and those who might seek another type of justice that would circumvent the King's justice. Mowbray pays a heavy price for what his conscience cannot quite reveal. The way in which he and Bolingbroke are forced to swear an oath never to meet abroad and plot against Richard is intriguing, especially if one adopts an Elizabethan perspective. The question of the oath of allegiance had been a moot point ever since the Papal Bull *Regnans in Excelsis* (1570) in which the Queen was declared excommunicated and deprived of political authority. In this scene, however, Richard gets the two prospective exiles to swear to God and not to Richard – God's deputy on earth – that they will not plot against him. While, on the face of it, this oath adds strength to Richard's sentence (both men swearing directly to God) it also – from an Elizabethan point of view – greatly weakens his position, since it severs the link between subject and king and dissociates God from the English monarchy:

> Swear by the duty that you owe to God –
> Our part therein we banish with yourselves – [6]
> To keep the oath that we administer:
> . . .
> Nor never by advised purpose meet
> To plot, contrive or complot any ill
> 'Gainst us, our state, our subjects or our land.

(1.3.180–2, 188–90)

In Elizabethan terms such a statement could be read as meaning that Bolingbroke and Mowbray were free to alter their allegiance once they had left the country. There are other elements in the history of these events which Shakespeare does not mention – perhaps because they did not serve his artistic purpose directly, or perhaps because the playwright thought he had gone far enough. Indeed, the chronicles reveal that when Bolingbroke came back to England in apparent breach of his oath, his decision had the backing of the Pope. What is more, the Archbishop of Canterbury, Thomas Arundel, 'preach[ed] against king *Richard*, who also shewed a Bull procured from Rome, promising remission of sinnes to all those which shoulde aide the saide Henry, in conquering of his enemies, and after their death to be placed in paradise, which preaching mooued manie to cleaue to the Duke'.[7] In or around 1595 the inclusion of these historical facts in Shakespeare's play would certainly have had a disquieting effect on audiences. After all, Elizabeth and her Privy Council lived in constant fear of attacks from abroad orchestrated by Catholic powers, with the backing of the papacy.

On closer scrutiny, however, Shakespeare did not altogether shy away from these sensitive matters. As a dramatist, he appears to have been interested in exploring the plight of the malcontented subject who was left with a difficult choice to make between quietist modes and more radical means of redress. This choice usually expressed itself through the familiar Elizabethan alternatives of action and contemplation, dissidence and patience. It is crucial to note that, in the play, Shakespeare translates this dilemma into religious terms – we find it in the opposition between militant crusade and peaceful pilgrimage, alternatives which in fact form a running motif, not only in *Richard II*, but also in the rest of Shakespeare's second tetralogy.

As Andrew Gurr remarks, 'There are several verbal hints which link the alternatives of the militant journey to Jerusalem and the peaceable pilgrimage with the opposition between Christian patience and militancy in resisting an unlawful king'.[8] Moreover, the image of the crusade is one which brings to the fore the question of England's place within Christendom. Indeed, since the Henrician schism the English Church had been insular and the nation no longer took part in the defence of the Holy Land because – as English Protestants pointed out – the Protestant Church had cast away the 'popish misbelief that some lands were holier than others'.[9] These underlying confessional tensions – and contradictions – are well expressed in John of Gaunt's speech, which contains both a celebration of English separatism and insularity ('This fortress built by Nature for herself', 2.1.43) and a singular nostalgia for the heroics (and implicit internationalism) of the crusade:

> Renowned for their deeds as far from home,
> For Christian service and true chivalry,
> As is the sepulchre in stubborn Jewry
> Of the world's ransom, blessed Mary's son,

(2.1.53–6)

Gaunt's speech (anachronistically) epitomizes the paradoxes of the English nation: proud of its separatist religious and political identity, but also nostalgic for a time when it formed an active part of Christendom.

In Shakespeare's England this contradictory pull was also felt by Elizabeth I's Catholic subjects – there were some who considered the Elizabethan regime to be tyrannical but advocated patience, and others who looked towards other Catholic nations and contemplated joining the Spanish crusade against the 'Infidel'. For many, this was a true moral dilemma.[10]

In the mid-1590s several works of Catholic polemic used the crusading metaphor as a means of rallying Catholic nations to free England from heresy. These authors' view of European affairs was simple – they argued that the wars of Spain against England, against the Dutch and in France amounted to a crusade. The crusading metaphor was particularly apt. Indeed, William Rainolds devoted a huge book, printed in 1597, to pointing out the similarities between Calvinism and Mohammedanism. Some English Catholics also denounced Elizabeth's foreign policy, especially the diplomatic relations which the Queen entertained with the Turkish Sultan.[11]

It is interesting to follow the trail of the crusading metaphor in Shakespeare's *Richard II* and its more peaceful metaphoric alternative, the pilgrimage. The string of metaphors found in the play signals the dramatist's concern about these matters and, as we shall see, his awareness that confessional issues were not devoid of contradictions.

When Bolingbroke is about to vindicate his cause before his banishment, his language is first that of the pilgrim: 'For Mowbray and myself are like two men / That vow a long and weary pilgrimage' (1.3.48–9). But then it is the chivalrous crusader – the man who feels he has God on his side – who speaks: 'Add proof unto mine armour with thy prayers, / And with thy blessings steel my lance's point' (1.3.73–4). When Richard stops the trial by combat and pronounces his sentence, Gaunt points out to him that kings have only seeming control over time – they can 'stop no wrinkle in his pilgrimage' (1.3.230). Life for the Christian is a pilgrimage over which kings can have little control. Despite Gaunt's covert warning, Richard decides to turn Bolingbroke into a pilgrim because of his potential dissidence. Bolingbroke will have to seek God through peaceful means even if this is not his personal choice. It is something which is imposed on him for political reasons: Bolingbroke 'finds it an enforced pilgrimage' (1.3.264).

To some extent Bolingbroke and Mowbray are in a similar position to that of Elizabethan Catholic exiles. Both feel the instinctive need to hold on to their Englishness. Bolingbroke, who is about to be estranged from his native land, suddenly reverses his perspective and constructs his Englishness outside England itself: 'Where'ver I wander, boast of this I can, / Though banished, yet a true-born Englishman' (1.3.308–9). Gaunt's son has chosen one of the polarities constitutive of Englishness which his father had outlined in his speech on English identity, without totally negating the other. He will need to go overseas and become a pilgrim in the wide world of Christendom to be able to come back and reclaim the fortress. Shakespeare does *not* go as far as to suggest that Bolingbroke will come back to oust the Infidel, but it is nevertheless clear that when he returns Bolingbroke is closer to the crusader than to the pilgrim.

As we know, the historical Bolingbroke returned with the explicit support of the papacy. In *Richard II* both Mowbray and Bolingbroke (who can no longer fight for their king) choose to fight for God only – their choice is ultimately that of militancy like many Catholic exiles. But of the two men, only Bolingbroke returns. Carlisle will later make the dramatic revelation of Mowbray's death abroad as a hero of the Christian faith. He died in Italy after his fight for a godly cause:

> Many a time hath banished Norfolk fought
> For Jesu Christ in glorious Christian field,
> Streaming the ensign of the Christian cross,
> Against black pagans, Turks and Saracens,

> (4.1.93–6)

Yet if Bolingbroke had not gone overseas and returned to break the bounds of 'This blessed plot, this earth, this realm, this England' (2.1.50) in order to supplant King Richard II, England would not have been exposed to further threats of invasion in later ages. For Samuel Daniel, in Book II of his *Civil Wars*, sees the troubles of Richard II's reign as the starting point of England's ensuing troubles, especially with Catholic nations like Spain. Had Richard II's reign been settled and had Boling-broke not deposed his king, the Catholic enemy would not have over-stepped his own bounds to threaten the self-contained English nation:

> Then proud *Iberus* Lord [i.e. Spain] not seeking how
> T'attaine a false-conceiued Monarchie,
> Had kept his barraine boundes and not haue stood
> In vaine attempts t' inrich the seas with blood.[12]

In *Richard II* Bolingbroke is aware that he has severed the link between the land and its king. But Shakespeare focuses more on Bolingbroke's plight and moral dilemma than on the supposed consequences of his actions for Elizabethan England. The dramatist shows that whenever the characters attempt to shape their destiny, the question of England's place within Christendom resurfaces. The irony is that, on his return, Bolingbroke destroys his own father's image of an England free from outside invasion and that he has to live with this contradiction.[13]

Yet Shakespeare has further ironies in store for his audiences. Bolingbroke never quite becomes the image of the Catholic hero-king returning to his native land to oust Richard the tyrannical heretic. If Shakespeare seems to toy briefly – and anachronistically – with this idea, he soon dispels it through an ironic and pregnant reversal of perspective (one of many such reversals, as we shall see). As the wheel begins to turn in the play, the image of the pilgrim is one which Richard, the so-called tyrant, adopts, while Bolingbroke the former pilgrim returns in the guise of a crusader. Sensing defeat, Richard quickly adopts a quietist mode:

> I'll give my jewels for a set of beads,
> My gorgeous palace for a hermitage,
> My gay apparel for an almsman's gown,
> My figured goblets for a dish of wood,
> My sceptre for a palmer's walking staff,
> My subjects for a pair of carved saints
>
> (3.3.147–52)

With these images of *vanitas*, it is now Richard who becomes the Catholic pilgrim that Bolingbroke once was. When all is lost for Richard the fallen king advises his queen to go back to her native country and make the choice of many an exiled Elizabethan English Catholic:

> Hie thee to France,
> And cloister thee in some religious house.
> Our holy lives must win a new world's crown,
> Which our profane hours here have thrown down.
>
> (5.1.22–5)

Far from intimating that his play should be interpreted as a straightforward allegory of the situation of English Catholics, Shakespeare in fact complicates matters by making an ironical use of religious metaphors.

His purpose seems to be an exploration of how characters deal with situations within a Christian religious framework which tends to pull individuals in different, sometimes conflicting directions. Bolingbroke is a case in point: the pilgrim turned crusader promises, when the play is about to close, to become a pilgrim again: 'I'll make a voyage to the Holy Land / To wash this blood off from my guilty hand' (5.6.49–50).[14] Shakespeare shows how characters come to be entangled in a Christian dilemma from which it is increasingly difficult, if not impossible, to escape.

In staging King Richard II's demise and the rise of Bolingbroke, the playwright is not simply content to point to the moral and religious predicaments at the heart of the play. In a scene which is no doubt the ideological and dramatic high point of the play, he also focuses, on Parliament, an institution which nourished the hopes of many Elizabethan malcontents – especially Catholics and Puritans – who, like Shakespeare's Bolingbroke, were tempted to project their fantasies of political and religious change onto it. Shakespeare's depiction of and obvious interest in this institution also underlines many of the religious and political predicaments identified so far, as we shall see.

The 'Parliament Sceane'

With the 'Parliament Sceane' of Act 4, scene 1, Shakespeare consciously went well beyond his sources by having King Richard deposed in Parliament. This was a deliberate artistic choice, which makes the scene stand out in the play in more ways than one. Not that ideology is fully in the open of course – it is more that the scene is traversed by oppositional discourses. These – like powerful undercurrents – create a persistent ripple of which the audience becomes gradually aware during the process leading to Richard's demise. This 'ripple', as we shall see, also accounts for the scene's very special place in both the stage and publishing history of the play itself.

Indeed, none of the editions printed during Elizabeth's reign (1558–1603) contained the scene at the heart of Act 4, scene 1 (ll. 155–318) in which King Richard is deposed by his own Parliament.[15] It was only in 1608 that *King Richard II* was advertised by a publisher on the title-page of the fourth quarto edition (Q4), as a version containing 'new additions of the Parliament Sceane, and the deposing of King Richard'.[16] The publisher was Matthew Lawe, who had obtained the copyright to three of Shakespeare's plays in 1603: *Richard II*, *Richard III* and *1 Henry IV*.[17] The last two were printed the following year (1604), but Lawe waited until 1608 to publish *Richard II*, which could suggest caution on the part of a man who may well have known that he was handling politically sensitive material.

Lawe probably relied on a transcription which was, at least in part, dictated to him. But perhaps the scene was not cut from the stage version of the play and only the printed versions were affected. There are arguments which support this hypothesis. The presence of the deposition scene in the stage version of *Richard II* would probably have made the play a far more appealing choice for the Earl of Essex's supporters, who, on the afternoon before their failed *coup* of 8 February 1601, had paid Shakespeare's own company – the Chamberlain's Men – to perform what appears to have been the playwright's own *Richard II* at the Globe theatre.[18] Lawe would thus have been able to obtain his transcription fairly easily if the scene was still staged. It might well have been the case, as it is important to distinguish between the two separate systems of censorship which applied on the one hand to stage-plays and on the other to printed books: 'The bishops who descended on the verse satirists in 1599, the Archbishop of Canterbury in particular, had a sharp and sophisticated eye for anything dangerous in theology or politics . . . . Not so the censor of stage-plays. Edmund Tilney's record as censor is undistinguished and that of his understudy from 1597 and eventual successor, George Buc, not much stronger'.[19] Lastly, in Elizabethan times there is no example of a cut made by a censor in a printed book being restored a few years later. Andrew Gurr thus concludes that 'it seems likely that the deposition scene never was cut from the stage version', and this view is also supported by another recent editor of the play.[20]

Interestingly, what critics now refer to as the 'deposition scene' was originally described in 1608 by Matthew Lawe as 'the Parliament Sceane, and the Deposing of King Richard' – a phrasing which strongly emphasizes the sensational relation of cause and effect between Parliament and the fall of the Plantagenet sovereign. The subtitle itself is followed by the mention 'As it hath been lately acted by the Kinges Maiesties Seruantes, at the Globe', which may lead us to think (despite its ambiguity) that the stage version contained the censored scene.[21] If this scene was known to theatre audiences, but had hitherto remained unavailable in print, Lawe's gamble no doubt was that this new, enlarged edition would gain rapidly in market value. It is probably no accident that the scene only reached print in 1608, well after Elizabeth's death. Printed texts were more carefully screened than plays and as printed matter they sometimes ran the risk of being compared, or even associated with other printed books which were works of polemic. The publisher had apparently waited for the associations between Elizabeth's reign and that of

Richard II – which, as we know, had become common in the polemical literature of the latter end of the Queen's reign – to lessen.

In advertising the scene which served as a marketing device for his new edition of *Richard II*, it is significant, as we have suggested, that the publisher referred to it primarily as 'the Parliament Sceane' and not simply as the deposition scene. This, we shall argue, is of some importance. Indeed, it was already clear from the stage directions in the first quarto that the emphasis was on the proceedings of Parliament: '*Enter Bullingbroke with the Lords to Parliament*'.[22] In fact the full implications of this scene begin to emerge for the audience in Act 5, scene 2, when the Duke of York professes unconditional loyalty to the new regime in spite of a strong element of pathos attached to the evocation of Richard's fate: 'To Bolingbroke are we sworn subjects now, / Whose state and honour I for aye allow' (5.2.39–40). Moreover, the Duke's statement in the same scene when mentioning his pledge to Parliament regarding the loyalty of his son, Aumerle, can be considered a passing comment on what has just happened: 'I am in Parliament pledge for his truth / And lasting fealty to the *new-made* king' (5.2.44–5; italics mine). The implication here is that Bolingbroke has been *made* king by Parliament and that he has not inherited the crown by birth or succession. That Parliament had such powers and that it could summon a king to appear before it and force him to abdicate (cf. ll. 155–318 of Act 4, scene 1) was an extremely bold statement to make given the context in the mid-1590s.

When the play was composed (in or around 1595) Elizabeth was an ageing queen, who was slowly losing her grip on power and whose succession remained dangerously unsettled.[23] Her own conception of the role of Parliament had never fundamentally wavered: she refused to have her attitude dictated by an institution which had primarily a legislative role and which, at all events, she convened infrequently during her reign. In theory she had absolute power to summon and dissolve Parliament at her own discretion and thus in many ways Parliament could not exist without her.[24]

It is then interesting to notice that in the two Jacobean quartos where the 'additions' appear for the first time (Q4 of 1608 and Q5 of 1615) – the very scene which, as we have argued, was probably cut in the Elizabethan quartos of *Richard II* – the Earl of Northumberland's cue starting at 4.1.151 runs down uninterrupted to line 158. Only later, in the folio text, are these lines (156–8) given to Henry Bolingbroke:[25]

NORTHUMBERLAND Well have you argued, sir; and for your pains,
Of capital treason we arrest you here.
My Lord of Westminster, be it your charge

> To keep him safely till his day of trial.
> [*Bishop of Carlisle is taken into custody.*]
> May it please you, lords, to grant the commons' suit?
> BOLINGBROKE Fetch hither Richard, that in common view
> He may surrender. So we shall proceed
> Without suspicion.
>
> (4.1.151–8)

If one hears this as a continuous speech on the part of Northumberland, one is under the distinct impression that 'the commons' have ordered Richard's deposition.[26] As we shall see, such powers were closer to those envisaged by religious controversialists intent on curbing the prerogatives of tyrannical or otherwise impious monarchs than to Elizabeth's conception of the role of Parliament.

In fact, Shakespeare compressed his historical material considerably and somewhat recomposed the events leading to Richard II's deposition. The immediate result is an inversion of the sequence of events narrated in the sources. None of the main chroniclers gives us to understand that Parliament met first and that Richard then agreed to be deposed as a result of their decision.[27] Holinshed, for instance, tells us that Richard consented to be deposed in the Tower and that the question was subsequently submitted to the Commons:

> the archbishop of Yorke, and bishop of Hereford, according to the kings request, shewed vnto them the voluntarie renouncing of the king, with the fauour also which he bare to his cousine of Lancaster to haue him his successour. And moreouer shewed them the schedule or bill of renouncement, signed with king Richards owne hand, which they caused to be read first in Latine, as it was written, and after in English. This doone, the question was first asked of the lords, if they would admit and allow that renouncement: the which when it was of them granted and confirmed, *the like question was asked of the commons*, and of them in like manner confirmed.[28]

Shakespeare's conflation leaves us thinking that the 'commons' suit' was that they called for the King's deposition. All the chronicles (especially those in favour of the Lancastrian Henry Bolingbroke) make it clear, however, that the agreement was made in the Tower and that news of Richard's decision was conveyed to Parliament, which then voted *to decide whether it accepted the King's decision*. In Holinshed, Bolingbroke's supporters ensure that Parliament only has to vote on what remains the King's prerogative, even if the renunciation is naturally somewhat forced upon him and that it is Bolingbroke who calls Parliament in the King's name.[29] This is what lends an implicit ambiguity to the role of Parliament in the chronicles, because, as Richard Dutton explains, 'it had indeed been a marked feature of Henry IV's entire Lancastrian settlement . . . that it was conducted with the assent of Parliament in the absence of other forms of legitimation'.[30]

The historian John Stow is the only chronicler who appears more outspoken in his account of the deposition, especially in the crucial role he assigns to Parliament. Even before Richard's renunciation, Parliament had set out of its own accord to determine the succession: 'the parliament that beganne the first Wednesday of October in Westminster hall, which they had hung and trimmed sumptuously, and had caused to be set up a royall chaire, in purpose *to choose a newe king* . . .'.[31] Furthermore, Stow only mentions Richard's resignation in passing and this then becomes another step in the succession process which is stage-managed in Parliament by the Archbishop of Canterbury: 'This instrument being read, the Archbishop perswaded them to proceede to the election of a new king . . .'.[32] Stow is unique among the chroniclers in the stress he appears to lay on the deciding role of Parliament and on the notion of 'election', which may remind us of some of the tenets of Elizabethan oppositional discourse.[33] It may not be entirely fortuitous that such a bold account of these events should be found in the work of a historian who had been persecuted in the late 1560s for owning 'a fairly complete library of the up-to-date Catholic literature of the English Counter-Reformation' and – early in the next decade – for his so-called Roman Catholicism and his alleged sympathies towards Spain.[34]

Shakespeare no doubt had his artistic reasons for handling the historical material in the way he did to compose this scene. In seemingly following Stow's version of events and in bringing Parliament to the fore in this way the dramatist may have wished to incorporate elements of Catholic political ideology into the debate about Richard's deposition to arouse his audiences' interest. Indeed, he compressed and conflated various episodes in his dramatization of the events leading to the deposition and strayed substantially from his main source for the play, Raphael Holinshed's *Chronicles*.

Whatever his exact reasons for proceeding in this fashion, the result could – in the eyes of some – be deemed controversial or even polemical. Elizabeth's succession was a burning issue at the time. The theme had become a popular topic of oppositional discourse. In the field of religious polemic, Elizabeth's unsettled succession was a seemingly endless source of conjecture for authors who used this question as a means of calling for religious change in the not so distant future. Among the different writers who broached this issue, the English Jesuit Robert Parsons was the author who voiced the arguments of the polemic most strongly in his *Conference About the Next Succession to the Crowne of Ingland* (1594).[35] Indeed, few tracts in the polemical history of Elizabethan England have attracted more attention and prompted more indignation than Parsons' *Conference*.

One of the many points which were deemed scandalous in the work of the English Jesuit father, was Parsons' insistence that King Richard II's deposition was legal. To promote the Lancastrian line of succession for political-polemical reasons,[36] Parsons was in fact forced to emphasize and validate the role of an institution which was to acquire an unprecedented importance in his tract – Parliament.

The English Jesuit had a distinct ability for controversy. With the *Conference* Parsons called into question the so-called objectivity of former historians. For him it was clear that no field – and certainly not that of history – could be void of polemic: 'And truly', he wrote, 'if we looke into diuers histories recordes and authors which haue written of this matter, vve shal find that euery one of them speaketh commonly according to the tyme wherin they liued . . . '.[37] For Parsons, events acquired a value beyond themselves especially when they were politicized by historians. Historiography could thus be construed as a form of political discourse, while history itself was nothing else, for Parsons, but a vast ideological battlefield.[38]

In this light, circumstantial events such as the Duke of York's implicit support for the Lancastrian Henry Bolingbroke were highlighted by Parsons and used in a demonstration that had immediate bearing on the Elizabethan succession issue: 'that king Richard vvas vniustly deposed . . . the howse of Yorke can not iustly saye this, for that the chiefe prince assistant to the deposing of king Richard, vvas lorde Edmond hymselfe duke of Yorke and head of that familie . . . '.[39] Given this ideological context, it might have been a matter of prudence for Shakespeare to cloud the issue of the Duke's support for Henry Bolingbroke slightly: 'But heaven hath a hand in these events, / To whose high will we bound our calm contents', says York cautiously (5.2.37–8). Bent on vindicating the rights of a Catholic successor to Elizabeth at all costs, Parsons delved into the work which provided Shakespeare with most of the material for his play, to extract what Elizabeth and her ministers did not wish to be reminded of. The Jesuit made a point of stressing the Englishness of what he unearthed at all times – he sought to appear a patriot (despite his hidden agenda) and enrolled Holinshed to demonstrate in passing that the coronation oath in England traditionally implied allegiance to the 'Catholique church'.[40] In fact Parsons tried to use some of the ideological polarities which we identified in John of Gaunt's speech and which were expressions of Elizabethan England's confessional crux.

Among the ancient English institutions which were so dear to Parsons – and which could be so useful to his polemical argument – was of course Parliament. Bolingbroke, as the English Jesuit sought to persuade his readers, was no usurper because his deposition of King Richard was condoned by the people and the entire commonwealth, who authorized and ratified the act: 'king Henry the fourth, first king of the house of Lancaster, entred vvithout bloodshedd as hath bin shewed, beinge called home by the requestes and letters of the people and nobility, and his election & admission to the crowne, vvas orderly, and authorized by general consent of parlament, in the doing thereof'.[41] In other words, Parliament, which was the mouth of the commonwealth, had the power to *make* kings. This argument – which was used, incidentally, by all sixteenth century resistance theorists – took Parsons even further than he had wished, for it implied that much of the political power was handed over to Parliament, leaving aside that 'crowning glory of Catholic resistance theory, the doctrine of papal political power'.[42]

Parliament as an institution in fact crystallized the hopes of those who called for urgent religious and political changes. Another oppositional voice, from the other side of the religious spectrum – the Puritan side – was trying to make itself heard in the mid-1590s. Peter Wentworth had got into considerable trouble in 1593 as he tried to petition Parliament for a debate on the Queen's succession. This caused the imprisonment of the Parliamentary leader. In 1587 he had drafted *A Pithie Exhortation to her Maiestie for Establishing her Svccessor to the Crowne*, which was circulated in the following years. It was in the Tower in 1595–96 that Wentworth wrote the sequel to the *Pithie Exhortation*, his *Discovrse containing the Authors opinion of the true and lawful svccessor to her Maiestie for Establishing her Svccessor to the Crowne*,[43] a work which is in open disagreement with Parsons' *Conference* whose genealogical claims are dismissed summarily: 'it seemeth a thing altogether needlesse, yea voide of common sense and reason, to fetch with so great adoe the branches and pedegrees . . . '.[44]

Wentworth argued the need for a debate on the succession. Indeed, settling the question once and for all (especially in favour of the Protestant James VI whose cause Wentworth clearly supported) would, in his view, be the best way to 'break the neck of the Popishe hope of their golden day'.[45] Such sectarian statements should not delude us into thinking that Wentworth's oppositional stance differed radically from Parsons'. Despite obvious differences, the *Pithie Exhortation* was not far from the Jesuit's *Conference*, especially in its vindication of the rights of Parliament: 'for the safetie of the kingdomes of England and Scotland, and of the Religion professed in them, it is absolutely necessarie that al the claimes and titles to the crowne of this Realme be tried by Parliament . . . '.[46] When it came to Richard's deposition, Wentworth appeared to be walking a very dangerous tightrope, especially in his analysis of the reasons which determined Parliament to support Bolingbroke: 'his nobility and commons shewed, that they liked rather to haue an vsurper to raigne over them, that would preserue the crowne & them, then a righfull king, that would perill the crowne and state also'.[47]

No doubt conscious that his definition of the role of Parliament was dubious enough to conjure up associations with Parsons, Wentworth was later keen to drive home the point, in his *Discovrse containing the Authors opinion of the true and lawful svccessor to her Maiestie*, that Parliament was really there to ensure that the law of primogeniture was not misinterpreted or travestied. Going back on his previous argumentation, he affirmed that Bolingbroke in fact relied more on a fabricated genealogical claim than on the actual assent of Parliament: 'So Henrie the fourth did more rest vpon the blind pretence of a claim by Edmond crook-back, then vppon the voice of the Parliament . . . '.[48] To counter Parsons' opportunistic use of Parliament, Wentworth was also forced to affirm that, as an institution, Parliament could not be swayed by the whims of individuals: 'But the meanest & simplest in al the land knowes this much I hope, that the wisest men of the Realme are chosen out and sent to the Parliamentes, not to determine or establishe whatsoever they will, but to advise, dispute and discerne what in reason & conscience they ought & should determine and conclude'.[49] Even so, Parliament again 'determined' and 'concluded' the fate of who should reign, and this was as unacceptable at the time as the tenets of Parsons' claim.

In expounding the arguments of these pamphleteers, we do not wish to suggest that Shakespeare had *direct* access to either Parsons' or Wentworth's tracts; what we should like to argue is that given the polemical context and the increasing sensitiveness of the authorities to the subject of the Queen's succession during the same period, it is more than likely that the dramatist knew very well that he was handling sensitive material. As for the Elizabethan publishers of

Richard II, they had no doubt been unwilling to take the risk of illegally printing a passage which the press censors could easily have marked for deletion. There is likewise good reason to believe that, as Cyndia Susan Clegg points out, 'the so-called 'deposition scene' was perceived as dangerous and was absent from the Elizabethan quartos not because it represented usurpation or deposition but because, as the 'Parliament Sceane', it corroborated late sixteenth-century resistance theory'.[50]

The 'Parliament Sceane' of Act 4, scene 1 is also rendered particularly dramatic because of the simultaneous onstage presence of an empty throne, a fallen king and a king to be.[51] No equivalent of Shakespeare's staging of the deposition *in Parliament* can be found in the chronicles.[52] If – historically – Richard II did perhaps ask for a hearing in Parliament *before* his deposition, Lancastrian propaganda saw to it that no trace of this request remained.[53] The King had *abdicated* – he had not been deposed – was the official version. Parliament was subsequently summoned in the King's name by Bolingbroke, but the throne remained unoccupied.

Shakespeare's Duke of York is the character who gives Bolingbroke the long-awaited cue designed to enable him to fill the visually vacant seat: 'In God's name I'll ascend the regal throne', is Bolingbroke's answer (4.1.114). Yet Shakespeare has Carlisle stall Bolingbroke's ambitions immediately. The Bishop undercuts the pretender with a long diatribe marking the difference between Bolingbroke – referred to as 'this noble presence' – and 'this royal presence', the royal seat. The effect produced is striking and ironic: indeed Carlisle emphasizes the uncanny opposition between the man who so wants to fill the throne and the empty seat which must remain unfilled, according to Carlisle, for fear of sacrilege (cf. 4.1.126–32).

In the course of his speech Carlisle also prophesies civil war – which, of course, Shakespeare had already depicted in his sequence of three plays on Henry VI's reign and in *Richard III* (1593). For an Elizabethan audience, these allusions to civil war could well have been associated with the then more immediate threat of seeing the wars of religion spread to England – a threat which was no fantasy and which Shakespeare's spectators had to learn to live with:

> The blood of English shall manure the ground,
> And future ages groan for this foul act.
> Peace shall go sleep with Turks and infidels,
> And in this seat of peace tumultuous wars

> Shall kin with kin and kind with kind confound.
> Disorder, horror, fear and mutiny
> Shall here inhabit, and this land be called
> The field of Golgotha and dead men's skulls.

(4.1.138–45)

It is, however, Carlisle's symbolic marking of space which really creates the possibility of a topical reading: 'O, if you raise this house against this house / It will the woefullest division prove' (146–7). Carlisle naturally alludes to the two noble Houses of York and Lancaster, to the Parliament house (thus creating a sense of occasion), but also possibly to the theatre itself – that house full of spectators around him.[54] Thus, in the midst of this 'Parliament scene', which is largely the fruit of the dramatist's imagination, we sense that Shakespeare is exploring the full dialogic potential of the moment to reach out to his audience and make it aware of the different dramatic and ideological levels of the scene.[55] In doing this, he no doubt ran the risk of being deemed dangerously topical.

Bolingbroke wished to create a spectacle out of Richard II's abdication ('that in common view / He may surrender...' (4.1.156–7), but it is precisely the staging of this abdication which escapes him – despite the fact that he had prepared the ground for it – because Richard finally upstages Bolingbroke by playing the tragic victim. Against all odds, the irony of *Richard II* is that its eponymous king ultimately conducts his own deposition ceremony and holds the attention of a Parliament of which we as an audience are also members: 'Now mark me how I will undo myself' (4.1.203). Such is the extraordinary power of Shakespeare's Parliament scene.

Northumberland may well insist on the (undramatic) reading of the articles of accusation – Richard remains adamant that he will not comply with what is untheatrical. As an audience, our sense of unease grows steadily from this point as Richard turns us into accomplices in his deposition and the linguistic arms he wields are those of the Christian, or indeed Catholic, martyr:[56]

> Nay, all of you that stand and look upon me ...
> Though some of you, with Pilate, wash your hands,
> Showing an outward pity, yet you Pilates
> Have here delivered me to my sour cross
> And water cannot wash away your sin.

(4.1.237, 239–42)

Strangely, as Bolingbroke rises in authority the roles are reversed and Richard, who is now in the opposition, uses familiar idioms which could be associated with the English Catholic discourse on martyrdom and resistance to tyrannical power,[57] even though he feels a traitor to his own cause ('I find myself a traitor with the rest' (4.1.248)), because he too is a sinner. As we know, this is one of many reversals in a play which explores the ambivalence and sometimes the contradictions of religious discourses.

Richard stage-manages his own exit from the Parliament scene, finishing on a passing comment on how the succession is carried out. As Andrew Gurr points out, 'Richard develops the principal sense of the word 'convey' as to 'escort' with its two other meanings, 'to transfer property', and 'to steal".[58] Despite the parliamentary process of destitution, Richard suggests that political power has in fact been stolen from him:

> BOLINGBROKE Go, some of you, convey him to the Tower.
> KING RICHARD O, good – 'Convey'! Conveyers are you all
> That rise thus nimbly by a true king's fall.

> (4.1.316–18)

Henry Bolingbroke wished to make a spectacle out of Richard's fall from power. Yet playing with theatre is like playing with fire. In its last few moments the deep irony of the 'Parliament Sceane' becomes fully available when Shakespeare leaves us to wonder if the player-king has not in fact managed to defeat the Parliamentarians theatrically.

* * *

Shakespeare's audience cannot be but divided between Bolingbroke's political ambition and thirst for justice and Richard's histrionic martyrdom. Within the Christian framework of the play, the playwright also suggests that the identities of these characters are, to a large extent, dependent upon the set roles and mighty opposites constructed and put forward by Elizabethan religious polemics (martyr/tyrant; heretic/sacred king). As the dramatist's repeated changes of perspective demonstrate, the play is as much about the tragic and ironic reversal of these roles, as about the rise to prominence of the future Henry IV. *Richard II* indirectly addresses the issue of Elizabeth's succession and points to the many unresolved confessional cruxes brought up by this unsettled question. Shakespeare is likewise conscious that in a nation which sits uneasily between two conflicting images of itself (England which pictures itself as being both inside and outside Christendom), the road to political, or indeed religious, unity can be a troublesome one. It is only with *King John* that Shakespeare will fully confront these issues and that religious ideology and propaganda will be anatomized on the open stage, as it were. In *King John* the painful religious and moral predicaments of *Richard II* are out in the open, as the nation as a whole is torn by its religious contradictions.

4

'So mak'st thou faith an enemy to faith': Religion, Propaganda and Dreams of National Unity in *King John*

King John constitutes an implicit oddity for many critics, even an embarrassment. The play stands alone and lacks the appropriate historical context – unlike Shakespeare's previous historical dramas, which are well set in their period and benefit from Shakespeare's apparent intention to explore English history through a series of plays on similar themes. *King John* seems to float awkwardly in time, as scholars have so far failed to agree on its date and because it is also said to be a piece 'in which the past does indeed seem a foreign country'.[1] With its abrupt beginning and its sharp ending, the play is adrift in a sort of historical vacuum, a disconnected world of its own, presenting 'an isolated series of episodes that are linked to the reign of one king'.[2]

This, however, is only superficially true, especially if we pause for a moment to consider that – not unlike the events of Richard II's reign – the story of King John had in fact been told and retold, exploited and used, and that the main lines of its plot were thus readily available to audiences when Shakespeare set out to write *King John*.[3] Its eponymous monarch needed no introduction – he came, like Richard II, with quite a (mixed) reputation.

The reputation of King John

> I am a scribbled form, drawn with a pen
> Upon a parchment, and against this fire
> Do I shrink up.
>
> (5.7.32–4)[4]

If Shakespeare had King John reflect in this way on his status as an historical character, this was no doubt because the pens and quills of many before him had attempted to sketch the King. But John's words also acknowledged the frail and necessarily short-lived attempts of theatre to bring him back to life. All writers, dramatists and chroniclers are 'scribblers' of some kind, spilling their ink to exhume those whose life has long been extinguished.

The reign of King John contained many elements which were deemed emblematic to those writers, artists, historians and propagandists who looked back to find the vindication of their Protestant and Reformist present in history. Thus, his reign was repeatedly appropriated in the name of a new kind of historiography bent on constructing another narrative, which took on board John's moral failings only to promote the King as a proto-Protestant, one who had paved the way for Henry VIII's Reformation, but one who had fallen short of this great mission and had been trampled to the ground by Catholic writers and historians.

William Tyndale inaugurated this influential Protestant tradition of seeing John as a martyr-king who had defied the tyranny of Rome. In *The obedience of a Christen man*, first published in 1528, Tyndale denounced the Church's supremacy over rightful sovereigns and urged his readers to consult the chronicles of England to seek examples of Rome's tyranny, but he also warned them against Catholic readings of these events:

> Reade the cronycles of Englande (out of which yet they have put a greate parte of their weckednisse) and thou shalt fynde them all wayes both rebellious & disobediente to the kynges & also churlysh & unthankfull so that when all the realme gave the kynge some what to mayntene hym in his ryghte they wolde not geve a myte. Consider the story of kynge John where I doute not but they have put the best and fayrest for them selves and the worst of kinge John for I suppose they make the cronycles them selves.[5]

Inspired by the story of King John, Tyndale also voiced fears of a foreign invasion in a kind of visionary passage: 'And veryly I se no other lykelyhode but that the lond shalbe shortly conquered. The starres of the scripture promyse us none other fortune in as moch as we denye Christ with the weked Jewes and will not have hym regne over us...'.[6] This type of prophecy would later be voiced relentlessly during the reign of Elizabeth, as propaganda writers perpetuated the myth of a nation whose mission was to defend the 'true religion' and thus imagined England as a fortress to be defended.

Well before Shakespeare's *King John*, the story of John's tumultuous reign had also been appropriated by dramatists. Likewise, John Bale's *Kyng Johan* conveyed a revisionist message – one which had an obvious political and religious agenda. Indeed, the play was acted in 1538–39 before King Henry VIII under the auspices of Thomas Cromwell; it was later revised between 1547 and 1560, a revision indicative of the longevity of the work. Like Tyndale, Bale denounced the fact that the writing of history had been in the hands of the Catholic clergy – Bale's play was there to set the record straight:

> You pristes are the cawse that Chronycles doth defame
> So many prynces, and men of notable name,
> For you take upon yow to wryght them evermore,
> And therfore Kyng Johan ys lyke to rewe yt sore
> Whan ye wryte his tyme, for vexyng of the Clargy.[7]

Bale in fact practised a typological exegesis of history which enabled him to see King John foreshadowed in Moses' confrontation with Pharaoh, and David as a forerunner of Henry VIII, who 'Clerely brought us into the lande of mylke and honye'.[8] Thus Bale's Kyng Johan only delivers his crown to Pandulph and submits to the Pope in order to save England from destruction – the King himself appears almost morally flawless, but warns that his reputation will be tarnished by his enemies: 'There is no malyce, to the malyce of the clergye.... / For doynge justyce, they have ever hated me'.[9] From a theatre history point of view, it seems that Bale had wanted, with this and other moral interludes penned by him, to build on the popularity of late medieval plays of the East Anglian dramatic tradition (such as the *N-Town* plays) 'to construct something like a reformed version of the cycle plays'.[10] His idea was no doubt to establish a form of drama which put forward the Word of God, did not concentrate too much on Christ's incarnation and physicality, and sought to establish a less affective relationship with its audiences.[11] Shakespeare, who had probably read Bale's piece,[12] never went so far with his *King John* – even though his play clearly contains elements of Protestant propaganda; his project, as we shall see, seems to have been different in intent.

At all events, the story of King John was also filtered through Tudor and Elizabethan chronicles. With his *Book of Martyrs* (1583), John Foxe's will was to alter people's perception of English history and to foreground a number of proto-Protestant figures as models to counter the Catholic Church's array of saints and martyrs. This was a cultural as well as an ideological battle, and King John was also embarked on Foxe's crusade and turned into a Protestant hero. Foxe in turn influenced Raphael Holinshed's account of the reign of King John.

As regards John's direct responsibility for Arthur of Brittany's death, Holinshed was more circumspect than Shakespeare would later be. The chronicler also implicitly condoned John's defiance of the Pope, whom he described vividly as 'that beast, whose hornes were pricking at everie christian prince that he might set himselfe in a seat of supremasie above all principalities... '.[13] The author of Shakespeare's main source for *King John* could not deny, however, that the King was somewhat of an ambivalent character – one who was 'not verie fortunate' and 'tasting of fortune both waies'.[14] For the Tudor historian, however, John's ill reputation was the result of the medieval Catholic Church's bias against him, an argument which only reiterated Tyndale's so-called revisionist criticism of Catholic historiography:

> Verelie, whosoever shall consider the course of the historie written of this prince, he shall find, that he hath beene little beholden to the writers of that time in which he lived; for scarselie can they afoord him a good word, except when the trueth inforceth them to come out with it as it were against their willes. The occasion whereof (as some thinke) was, for that he was no great freend to the clergie.[15]

When Shakespeare set out to dramatize his reign, King John was thus a loaded subject ideologically – to say the least. The theme was very much at the heart of the religious and political controversies of the time. But Shakespeare's play was also born out of its more immediate dramatic context – a context equally marked by ideological controversy.

Shakespeare and George Peele

'One need no longer hedge or leave an escape route in assuming that *King John* derives ultimately from *The Troublesome Raigne*', wrote Guy Hamel confidently in 1989.[16] A year later, however, L. A. Beaurline, in his New Cambridge edition of *King John*, was to draw totally opposite conclusions.[17] The case is still not settled as we write, for critics do not agree definitively on the date of *King John* and on its relationship to the two-part play *The Troublesome Raigne of John King of England* first published in 1591, then in 1611 with the indication 'Written by W. Sh.', and finally in 1622 in a Quarto edition advertising the play as 'Written by W. Shakespeare'. The ascription to Shakespeare is puzzling but so far no one has been able to show conclusively that this play was composed by the author of *King John*.

One of the first editors to support the 'early start' theory for the composition of Shakespeare's plays was E. A. J. Honigmann in his 1954 edition of the play. He believed the piece had been written in the winter or spring of 1590–91 and that the author of the *Troublesome Raigne* had in fact been influenced by *King John* and not the reverse.[18] Convinced that *King John* had been written no later than 1590, Beaurline followed Honigmann's conclusions regarding the order of composition of the two plays, adding that the '*Troublesome Reign* is not an imitation of Shakespeare's play but an adaptation. It is a quasi-independent work, not exactly a bad quarto but a propaganda piece awkwardly draped over Shakespeare's structure'.[19]

There are, none the less, substantial arguments against this theory. Some are not new. Geoffrey Bullough noted, for instance, that the resemblances between the situations of Hubert de Burgh in Shakespeare's play (who is forced to obey John's order to execute Arthur in order to protect the former's throne) and Elizabeth's Secretary Davison (who had been made a scapegoat in the aftermath of Mary Stuart's execution for having allegedly persuaded the Queen to sign Mary's death warrant) would have made the play seem 'most inopportune', as Davison had just been released from prison thanks to the Earl of Essex's intervention in 1589.[20]

More to the point perhaps, Robert Smallwood remarked that while any date of composition between 1591 and 1598 was possible, a 'date of 1593 or 1594, just before *Richard II*, seems likely'.[21] Indeed, the stylistic and verbal parallels between *King John* and this play cannot be easily dismissed and if the date of *Richard II* is equally uncertain, it is a far from easy task to demonstrate that it was penned before 1595–96.[22] What is more, arguing cautiously for a 1595–96 composition of *King John*, A. R. Braunmuller found indeed that the play shares with *Richard II* 'an exclusive or almost exclusive use of verse and the absence of a subordinate action that parallels the royal political action'.[23]

Part of the problem also lies in the assessment of the relationship between the two plays – *The Troublesome Raigne* and *King John*. Implicitly and sometimes expressly, there is often the assumption in the arguments of those who consider Shakespeare as the author of the original play and the anonymous writer of *The Troublesome Raigne* as an imitator that the genial Shakespeare could never have stooped so low as to imitate or even be inspired by such poor work. This view stems in fact from a double assumption – first, that the anonymous author was an incompetent playwright and second, that Shakespeare, whose superior artistry is an established fact, could never have gleaned anything from the work of an unskilled dramatist. Indeed, Beaurline remarks that it is difficult to believe that *King John* was a 'derivative', as the play was undoubtedly 'original theatre of a high order, expressing historical and political ideas of continuing value'.[24]

More recently, Brian Boyd has appeared convinced that the inexperienced anonymous author of *The Troublesome Raigne* could never have wrestled with Holinshed to extract material and turn it into a play: 'Nor is there any indication in any other aspect of the play that he has the literary skill and strength to perform such a complex and subtle task. But where he has neither means nor motive, Shakespeare has both'.[25]

Was the anonymous author of *The Troublesome Raigne* so inexperienced and who could he have been? Such questions which remain delicate to determine are, as we shall argue, crucial if we wish to set Shakespeare's *King John* in its historical and artistic context.

New evidence has in fact recently come to light which points to a number of similarities between *The Troublesome Raigne* and George Peele's (*c*. 1557–96) *Edward I* (1593). Brian Vickers has convincingly argued, on the basis of a series of linguistic tests examining the use of alliteration, vocatives, the use of Latin and the metrics, that both plays are the work of the same author.[26] What is more, it is now almost certain, thanks to the work of a series of scholars – including P. W. Timberlake, John Dover Wilson, J. C. Maxwell, MacDonald Jackson and Brian Boyd – that Peele and Shakespeare collaborated on the writing of *Titus Andronicus* (*c*. 1593), Peele being almost certainly the author of Act 1, Act 2, scenes 1 and 2; Act 4, scene 1.[27]

It is not surprising to discover affinities between *The Troublesome Raigne* and *Edward I*, both plays being deeply imbued with anti-Catholic sentiment and particularly with anti-monastic satire. 'A possible scenario', to cite Vickers, would be that Shakespeare learned from and was influenced by a more experienced dramatist, who had written a history play in 1591 on the reign of King John (*The Troublesome Raigne*) and another (*Edward I*), which also contained elements of anti-Catholic propaganda, in 1593. Peele was far from being an inexperienced or a clumsy dramatist. In the early 1590s he was a dramatist and writer who had ventured into more literary genres than most. Although admittedly proving more limited than Shakespeare in his art, he was none the less a 'university wit'.[28] That Shakespeare, who was not much older but who had probably begun his theatrical career later than Peele, could find a model in the older dramatist should not surprise us. Vickers even suggests that in the year of Peele's death – 1596 – Shakespeare may have taken over the plot of *The Trouble-some Raigne* 'from his former partner, perhaps in emulation, perhaps in tribute, totally transforming its language and characterization, and fully realizing the story's dramatic potential'.[29]

Creating a Protestant Super-hero

TO THE GENTLEMEN READERS
You that with friendly grace of smoothed brow
Have entertaind the Scythian Tamburlaine,
And given applause unto an Infidel:
Vouchsafe to welcome (with like curtesie)
A warlike Christian and your Countreyman.
For Christs true faith indur'd he many a storme,
And set himselfe against the Man of Rome . . . [30]

Thus wrote George Peele, the probable author of the anonymous *Trouble-some Raigne*.[31] This opening is interesting on different counts and first because it seeks to profit from the huge success of Christopher Marlowe's two-part play about the Scythian shepherd who becomes a formidable warrior and ruler and cuts such a heroic picture. Marlowe's *Tamburlaine*, written *c*. 1587 and published shortly after in 1590, was, however, as Peele writes in the opening, a heathen hero, whereas this new play seeks to build on audiences' patriotic fervour and on their thirst for heroic figures by presenting a *Protestant* super-hero, one who is both 'Christian' (i.e. a proto-Protestant) and English ('your Countreyman').[32] Beyond the religious and indeed sectarian agendas, there is also on the part of Peele a deliberate will to entertain and write an engaging play, by opportunistic imitation of a successful model.

The Troublesome Raigne itself is divided into two parts, thus replicating Marlowe's diptych, and its hero fashions himself clearly as a Chris-tian Tamburlaine and also – anachronistically – as a champion of the Reformation. Peele has adopted for his King John the magniloquent and threatening tone of the conquering Scythian, as in this striking and defiant address to Pandulph, the Pope's legate:

Tell thy Maister so from me, and say, *John of England* said it, that never an Italian Priest of them all, shall either have tythe, tole, or poling penie out of *England*, but as I am King, so wil I raigne next under God, supreame head both over spirituall and tem[p]rall: and hee that contradicts me in this, Ile make him hoppe headlesse.[33]

Shakespeare seems to have been influenced by Peele's efforts at creating a national figure of heroic stature – at times he too uses Marlovian bombast to lend King John a dramatic aura, as in this defiant nationalistic diatribe, using imagery closely resembling that of a number of passages in *Tamburlaine, Part 1*:[34]

> France, I am burned up with inflaming wrath,
> A rage whose heat hath this condition
> That nothing can allay, nothing but blood,
> The blood and dearest-valued blood of France.
>
> (3.1.340–3)

To some extent, it is also true that, as Honigmann has noted, 'in *King John* . . . Shakespeare's anti-papal rhetoric fires on all cylinders, with astonishing ferocity . . . '.[35] Possibly in imitation of Peele and Marlowe again, Shakespeare uses all the available sectarian rhetoric to heighten the tension of many of his scenes, even if, as we shall see, this rhetoric is closer to empty bombast and is not to be taken at face value.

King John's answer to Pandulph, for instance, is close to Peele's (cited above). It is also straight out of the propaganda pamphlets of the period and carries with it words resounding with the sound of religious controversy. John's magniloquent speeches at 3.1.147–60 and 162–71 had no doubt a familiar ring to audiences through their use of the standard or indeed clichéd expressions of sectarian and anti-papal rhetoric, such as 'the free breath of a sacred king', 'Italian priest' or 'this meddling priest' to refer to the Pope, 'Purchase corrupted pardon of a man / Who in that sale sells pardon from himself', to denounce the practices of indulgences, or again 'This juggling witchcraft' to speak of Roman Catholicism.[36]

Shakespeare's King John – like Peele's – fashions himself as a Reformation hero alone against all others, denouncing the moral corruption of the Church of Rome, despite the fact that his own sense of right and wrong is equally corrupt, especially in his breach of promises, or in his determination to have his rival Arthur physically eliminated. Shakespeare was perhaps fascinated by Peele's King John – the Protestant super-hero with a weakness, the morally imperfect or rather incomplete sovereign, one who prepared the way for King Henry VIII:

> Thy sinnes are farre too great to be the man
> T'abolish Pope, and Popery from thy Realme:
> But in thy Seate, if I may gesse at all,
> A King shall raigne that shall suppresse them all.[37]

Despite critics' disparaging comments against Peele's *Troublesome Raigne* and beyond its opportunistic propagandist rhetoric, there are moments, especially near the end of the play, when John becomes a true tragic hero in passages where the style and sheer poetic value of the lines are commendable:

> Set downe, set downe the load not worth your pain,
> For done I am with deadly wounding griefe:
> Sickly and succourles, hopeles of any good,
> The world hath wearied me, and I have wearied it.[38]

At such times, it is easy to see how Shakespeare created his own King John, the bombastic proto-Protestant figure but also the doomed and introspective king of the latter half of the play. The difference between Shakespeare and Peele is that the latter seldom looks beyond the sectarian rhetoric he employs, unlike Shakespeare, who makes it resonate loudly but not deafeningly and points at once to its origins and to its contradictions.

Post-Armada trauma and propaganda: an invading Catholicism

Some critics have been tempted to read *King John* in the light of Anglo-French relations in the early 1590s. It is true that 'in the play England has ultimately to yield to the Pope because of France, a danger ever near them if Henry leagued himself with Spain to complete a circle of Catholic enemies around English Protestantism'.[39] Yet there is another context which corroborates the scenario of the 1596 composition of *King John* more consistently. The Spanish context is one which has been insufficiently explored by critics and which deserves some attention. Indeed, Shakespeare's *King John* seems to be part of a wave of plays conveying anti-Spanish sentiment in the aftermath of the Armada and well into the 1590s – many of these plays being written by Shakespeare's partner, George Peele. The year 1596 also saw the publication of a wealth of pamphlets on similar themes, written in a moralizing tone and playing likewise on the fear of the great Other, at a time when the Spanish navy was raiding Cornwall and the urgent recruitment of troops had become a necessity.

In Act 2 of *King John* Shakespeare gives the Duke of Austria – a foreigner – a speech in which the formidable (and false) image of England as an impregnable fortress set upon an island is conjured up.[40] No doubt for maximum dramatic effect the playwright places this

English fantasy in the mouth of a foreigner, a mythical image which, as Austria develops it in front of the Breton Arthur, appeals to English patriotism, but also plays on fears of invasion and of ensuing foreign succession to the throne of England:

> Even till that England hedged in with the main,
> That water-wallèd bulwark, still secure
> And confident from foreign purposes,
> Even till that utmost corner of the west
> Salute thee for her king. Till then, fair boy,
> Will I not think of home, but follow arms.
>
> (2.1.26–31)

English myths uttered by foreigners are to be found in other plays of the period, such as George Peele's *The Battle of Alcazar* (composed 1588–89, earliest text 1594) or the anonymous *The Famous History of Captain Thomas Stukeley* (written *c*. 1589; printed 1605).[41] Shakespeare was certainly familiar with a string of other plays, whose themes were patriotic and/or anti-Spanish. Robert Greene's *The Honourable History of Friar Bacon and Friar Bungay* (written *c*. 1590; printed 1594) stages, for instance, the events leading to a dangerous match between Henry III's son, Edward (the future Edward I) and Elinor, daughter of the King of Castile. These events are continued in another play of the same period, George Peele's *Edward I* (composed 1590–93; printed in 1593) probably also performed, like *The Troublesome Raigne*, by the Queen's Men. Peele's work is markedly anti-Spanish and part of the play depicts the ills of having a Spanish Infanta as Queen Consort, even though xenophobia is couched in pseudo-moralistic argument.[42]

In *King John*, interestingly, it is perhaps not a coincidence that Shakespeare's (French) King Philip compares the English monarch's successful attack to a storm at sea and his defeated army to a scattered armada of ships:

> KING PHILIP So by a roaring tempest on the flood
> A whole armada of convected sail
> Is scattered and disjoined from fellowship.
>
> (3.4.1–3)

This may well be a reference to the Spanish Armada of 1588, but if our date of 1596 for the play is correct, there is reason to believe that Shakespeare had more recent threats in mind. As England was living in the fear of an imminent foreign invasion, other lines may have had an equally topical ring, such as the ones spoken by the Messenger in Act 4:

> MESSENGER From France to England. Never such a power
> For any foreign preparation
> Was levied in the body of a land.

> (4.2.110–12)

The Bastard, a few lines later, appears to echo the tone of pamphlets capitalizing on the fear of foreign invasion in 1596:

> But as I travelled hither through the land,
> I find the people strangely fantasied,
> Possessed with rumours, full of idle dreams,
> Not knowing what they fear, but full of fear.

> (4.2.143–6)

Act 5, scene 2 constituted no doubt an important moment in the play when Elizabethan audiences were given the opportunity to witness the arrival of foreign troops on English soil, *King John* being after all the only Shakespearean history play in which England is actually invaded by a foreign power. Not only this, but audiences also witnessed English noblemen turning against their king, swearing fealty to the enemy and setting these oaths on paper, a dramatic gesture which arrests the action of the play for a tense and fraught moment, while the English are seen to collaborate with the enemy:

> Return the precedent to these lords again,
> That having our fair order written down,
> Both they and we, perusing o'er these notes,
> May know wherefore we took the sacrament,
> And keep our faiths firm and inviolable.

> (5.2.3–7)

Post-Armada England is often wrongly figured as a relatively peaceful era, the Spaniards having been supposedly brought to a halt by their defeat. Yet, as historians have shown, this was not quite the picture. In fact, the English had only narrowly escaped an invasion in 1588 and, what is more, 'the defeat of the Armada did not change the balance of sea power in Europe. Within a decade Philip had rebuilt his fleet and he was able to launch three future armadas against England in 1596, 1597 and 1599, all of which were menacing since Ireland was then in rebellion'.[43]

A number of pamphlets published in 1596 bear witness to the fact that, for some, the memory of 1588 was still vivid and that the fear had not subsided. Roger Cotton, in a tract entitled *An Armor of Proofe*, plays consciously on this parallel to bring people back to the 'true' religion, with of course a pinch of sensationalism in his moralized depiction of the Spanish threat:

> His sworde thou knowest, he threatened fore to draw,
>   in eightie eight; but then he did thee spare:
> yet since that time, in thee great sinnes he saw:
>   wherefore for thee great plagues he did prepare.
> The Pestilence through out thy coastes hath bin,
>   and now with sworde, to threat he doth begin.[44]

Another pamphleteer, Thomas Nun, used a telling title – *A Comfort against the Spaniard* – to sell his tract. Nun, a 'Minister of the Word, at Weston', sets out to discuss the Armada of 1588 in his work, as well as the English expedition against Portugal in 1588. He is, however, quickly brought to speak of the present state of affairs. Again the tone is sensational, playing on people's fears, as the author pretends to be repeating a somewhat obsessive rumour, which so far no one has been able to deny: 'Is it true that the Spanyardes will com this spring? And is it not as true that we are ready to receive them?'[45]

Charles Gibbon penned a work in the same vein ominously entitled *A Watch-worde for Warre*. Gibbon's work in fact thrives on rumours which, with a hint of (false) naivety he takes as foreshadowing dismal events, namely, the arrival of the Spaniards. Despite the author's evident exaggeration, it is easy to imagine the climate of fear and unrest which so-called newsmongers such as Gibbon nourished. Indeed, his address to the reader is telling:

> The mutabilitie of reports had almost dismaide mee in proceeding: for one while they runne nothing but rumors of warre, an otherwhile there passe manie speeches of peace; the same mouth that saith at one time, the Spanyard will come, another time affirmeth, we neede not expect his comming. There may be many that wish warrs because they cannot thrive with peace, and others that speak of peace, because they love not to heare of war; but (good Reader) as there is no smoke

without fire, so there ariseth no rumor without some original, for rumors are commonly fore-runners of warre.[46]

When Shakespeare composed his *King John* it is our belief that the dramatist was inspired and influenced by the atmosphere created by the so-called writers of news, who have just been described. Douglas C. Wixson also argues that 'Elizabethan audiences' response to *King John* was more likely to have been conditioned by pamphleteering rather than the traditional John material appearing in the chronicles. In employing the Armada rhetoric of certain pamphlets Shakespeare distanced the rhetoric through dramaturgical open form, thus assuring that the propaganda content would remain outside his play'.[47]

Playing fast and loose with faith (Hubert's impossible neutrality)

Strangely enough, Shakespeare is seen by many critics as having withdrawn from religious issues in *King John* and this has been deemed an imperfection, particularly because the play appears to lose its unity, especially when compared to *The Troublesome Raigne* with its strong stage figures and its fairly obvious anti-Catholic agenda. 'We may wonder', wrote Virginia Mason Carr, 'if Shakespeare did not lose something when he chose to minimize the religious issue'.[48] But did Shakespeare really minimize religious issues in his play, is *King John* truly devoid of debate and reflection on these matters? It seems that, as we shall argue, we need to go deeper into the play's fabric to realize that a debate on these issues is really at work.

It has often been the fortune of the play's sectarian readers to find no religion in it, or rather none of the kind that would fully satisfy their personal tastes. Colley Cibber was famously astonished that Shakespeare 'should have taken no more Fire at the flaming contest between his insolent *Holiness* and *King John*' and it was thus 'this coldness', added Cibber to justify his own adaptation of the play, 'that first incited me to inspirit his King John with a resentment that justly might become an *English* Monarch'.[49]

Readers on the other side of the religious spectrum have tended almost instinctively to minimize Shakespeare's use of anti-Catholic rhetoric in the play. Comparing *The Troublesome Raigne* and Shakespeare's play, Henry Sebastian Bowden – a nineteenth-century Roman Catholic writer and apologist – found that 'Shakespeare, in so far as he follows the original piece, uniformly expurgates it of any anti-Catholic virus'.[50] Evidently one near-contemporary of Shakespeare was not of the same opinion. Indeed, a mid-seventeenth-century Jesuit by the name of William Sankey – who was in charge of expurgating a 1632 folio copy of Shakespeare's complete works destined to be used by students of the English College of Valladolid in Spain – considered a fair number of passages of Shakespeare's *King John* to be unsuitable for reading by his students. Sankey thus crossed them out conscientiously.[51]

Some more recent commentators have found Shakespeare's treatment of the religious issues in *King John* even-handed and have endeavoured to discuss the place of religion in the play, a topic which many other contemporary critics had been reluctant to tackle.[52] One notable exception is, of course, Ernst Honigmann, who finds that 'Shakespeare does his utmost to arouse anti-papal fury' even if the dramatist's fury, argues Honigmann, may not necessarily mean that Shakespeare was himself anti-Catholic: 'Shakespeare detested Rome's intrigues and abuses, but nowhere stoops to rabble-rousing against English Catholics'.[53]

From the outset a disconcerting ambivalence seems to be at work in the play. In the opening scene, our dramatic interest is sparked at once when Queen Eleanor in an intriguing aside tells John that God is witness that he is an unlawful king:

> KING JOHN Our strong possession and our right for us.
> QUEEN ELEANOR (*aside to John*) Your strong possession much
>   more than your right,
> Or else it must go wrong with you and me;
> So much my conscience whispers in your ear,
> Which none but heaven, and you, and I, shall hear.
>
> (1.1.39–43)

Does this mean that God is not on the King's side? Or does it mean that it is God's will that an illegitimate king should reign? As we know, these differences were touchy issues when Shakespeare wrote his play. The dramatist was thus, from the beginning, on slippery terrain.

More prudently (and half-jokingly) the Bastard hands over to God all knowledge of truth in the uncertain universe of the play: 'But for the certain knowledge of that truth / I put you o'er to heaven and to my mother' (1.1.61–2). Falconbridge would rather voice his one solipsistic certainty: 'And I am I, howe'er I was begot' (1.1.174). He also seems convinced that earthly matters require latitude and a large measure of tolerance – an unusual statement in a play where so many characters are inclined to impress their often sectarian comments on situations: 'Some sins do bear their privilege on earth, / And so doth yours. Your fault was not your folly', says the Bastard to his mother (1.1.261–2).

Hubert is perhaps the one character, however, who desperately and somewhat tragically strives not to give in to polarized sectarian discourse. His speech to defend the town of Angers is clearly an anomaly, in that its neutral premise is so alien to the rhetorical and ideological world of the play. Confronted with John and Philip's requests for allegiance he chooses not to choose – or rather he chooses to swear momentary allegiance to both sovereigns, which of course is a way of not choosing:

> Both are alike, and both alike we like.
> On must prove greatest. While they weigh so even,
> We hold our town for neither, yet for both.

> (2.1.331–3)

Hubert refuses to enter the political fray and cleverly uses God's ultimate judgment as an argument against those potentates who claim to have Heaven's support. In short, he hands over to God and to divine Providence the choice of the rightful sovereign:

> A greater power than we denies all this.
> And till it be undoubted, we do lock
> Our former scruple in our strong-barred gates.
> Kings of our fear, until our fears resolved
> Be by some certain king, purged and deposed.

> (2.1.368–72)

Whether it be through the Bastard's choric comments (Act 2 ends with Falconbridge's famous speech on 'commodity', which lends a particular moral colour to this first part of the play and sets the scene for the rest of the play) or through the desperate cries of the play's victims – often female, like Constance – we are gradually under the impression that *King John* is a story of broken faith in which religion is often intrumentalized. The Bastard is giddy – and so are we – with the moral paradoxes of the play, as France 'Whom zeal and charity brought to the field / As God's own soldier...' (2.1.566–7) has swiftly turned its back on its alleged holy mission and England has done no better – both having broken 'the pate of faith' (2.1.569).

It is perhaps not so much religion that is at stake in the play as faith, in its several senses of trust, social bond and belief in God. While the so-called victors speak the language of propaganda pamphlets the victims show how meaning has come to be warped, how faith is tossed and tumbled as powerful instances move semantic boundaries around and exchange words and their meaning to suit the occasion to the necessities of the action.[54] Through Constance's use of antanaclasis, a device implying the repetition of a word or phrase the meaning of which changes in the second instance, we realize how trust, belief and faith have become traumatically unsure notions in the world of the play:[55]

> I trust I may not trust thee, for thy word
> Is but the vain breath of a common man.
> Believe me, I do not believe thee, man;
> I have a king's oath to the contrary.
>
> (3.1.7–9)

Faith has been adulterated according to Constance – hollowed out, as it were, by falsehood: 'This day all things begun come to ill end; / Yea, faith itself to hollow falsehood change'. (3.1.94–5). 'Shakespeare's theater empties out the center that it represents', wrote Stephen Greenblatt, suggesting that theatre secularizes the world it stages.[56] Yet on closer scrutiny it seems that the universe of the play has not been emptied out of all Godly hope – God (not the God of propaganda pamphlets) still remains individuals' last, desperate hope of repair:

> Arm, arm, you heavens, against these perjured Kings!
> A widow cries, be husband to me, heavens.
> Let not the hours of this ungodly day
> Wear out the days in peace, but ere sun set,
> Set armèd discord 'twixt these perjured Kings.
> Hear me, O, hear me!
>
> (3.1.107–12)

There is a glimmer of hope when a little later, King Philip – one of the 'perjured Kings' – appears to have moral scruples and seeks answers from Pandulph – an ecclesiastic who should know about faith and such matters. Can faith be made to mean everything we wish it to mean?

This is Philip's urgent question which no doubt resonated in the ears of
Shakespeare's religiously hybrid audience:

> Play fast and loose with faith? So jest with heaven,
> Make such unconstant children of ourselves,
> As now again to snatch our palm from palm,
> Unswear faith sworn, and on the marriage-bed
> Of smiling peace to march a bloody host,
> And make a riot on the gentle brow
> Of true sincerity? O holy sir,
> My reverend father, let it not be so.
>
> (3.1.242–9)

Philip is reluctant to let go – after all he has pledged his word to seal
a peace with King John – but Pandulph too uses figures of repetition
(antanaclasis in the following example), like Constance, even if his aim
is rather to blur, obfuscate and deny access to meaning in order to win
the rhetorical battle by false logic and bend Philip's will.[57] His punning
game does indeed leave the impression that faith is in fact many-faceted
and can be accommodated to suit the occasion:

> KING PHILIP I may disjoin my hand, but not my faith.
> [*He releases John's hand*]
> CARDINAL PANDULPH So mak'st thou faith an enemy to faith,
> And like a civil war sett'st oath to oath,
> Thy tongue against thy tongue. O, let thy vow
> First made to heaven, first be to heaven performed;
> That is, to be the champion of our church.
> What since thou swor'st is sworn against thyself
> And may not be performèd by thyself.
>
> (3.1.262–9)

Pandulph continues to twist meaning around with a series of paradoxes which makes him sound like an equivocating Jesuit or at the very
least an adept of casuistry, as the ecclesiastic now broaches the subject
of religion which – like faith – undergoes a similar semantic process:

> It is religion that doth make vows kept,
> But thou hast sworn against religion:
> By what thou swear'st against the thing thou swear'st,

> And mak'st an oath the surety for thy truth,
> Against an oath the truth; thou art unsure
> To swear, swears only to be forsworn,
> Else what a mockery should it be to swear?
> But thou dost swear only to be forsworn,
> And most forsworn to keep what thou dost swear.
> Therefore thy later vows against thy first
> Is in thyself rebellion to thyself.

(3.1.279–89)

Beyond the anti-Catholic satire Shakespeare's players anatomize sectarian discourse, as the linguistic traits of their characters reveal how such argumentation functions, how it can be incredibly opportunistic, how it manages to turn words around, how it can leave people with a feeling of helplessness and how this insecurity can be ultimately destructive for the more exposed victims of power politics. *King John* anatomizes sectarian discourse at its worst – appropriating religion, truth and faith and destroying individuals.

Blanche, like Constance, is another victim of the politics of the play and of the wars of religion between England and France; like Hubert she is one of the few characters who have tried to express an impossible neutrality, one which – sadly – can only lead to destruction:

> The sun's o'ercast with blood; fair day, adieu!
> Which is the side that I must go withal?
> I am with both; each army hath a hand,
> And in their rage, I having hold of both,
> They wirl asunder and dismember me.

(3.1.326–30)

Thus Shakespeare's *King John* looks at the mechanisms of propaganda and apologetic discourse.[58] Not only does it point out the semantic and social dangers of these discourses but it thrives, for entertainment purposes also, on its gross absurdity. This is language 'so used that it stipulates polarized values while it also obscures polarity'.[59] It is a type of discourse which uses faith and belief to speak about other things – power politics, legitimacy, influence, kingship, leaving individuals or even whole nations disorientated. Moreover, as Donna B. Hamilton has argued, anti-Catholic discourse itself could function as a coded language which furnished a medium for the expression of church-state controversies between Protestant conformists and nonconformists – the word Catholic could in this perspective signify that someone did not conform and could thus potentially be accused of disloyalty to the state.[60] There were more agendas than met the eye when a dramatist deployed anti-Catholic discourse, especially when that discourse was anatomized, as is the case in Shakespeare's *King John*.

Dreams of unity

King John is a history play with a twist.[61] The twist is perhaps not only in its unusual structure, its wordplay and its critical imitation of pamphlet literature, it may also be in its last act where according to one critic Shakespeare has so much trouble putting 'Humpty Dumpty together again'.[62] Indeed two striking images of England are presented in the last Act, one by the Bastard in the final speech and one by the English rebel Salisbury. These two views of the same nation, we shall argue, deserve to be studied in parallel as their analysis may considerably enlighten our understanding of the play's religious politics.

King John ends with what looks like a patriotic set-speech calling for national unity as a condition for the preservation of the country (England being pictured as a fortress threatened on all sides by an exterior menace) and also underlining the necessity for the nation to remain true to itself. Much has been made of this ending by various critics, who have contended that the Bastard's speech puts forward 'the image of the ideal state with its dissident elements safely contained', 'the nation's survival through the common bond of patriotism', concluding that 'Without patriotism the character is nothing'.[63]

Yet none of these critics has commented on the somewhat ambiguous last line of the Bastard's speech – 'If England to itself do rest but true' – what truth are we talking about here? Whether England has to abide by a so-called 'true' religion is not clear and may have been left as an open question deliberately. Nevertheless, it is one of the central questions the play poses:

> BASTARD O, let us pay the time but needful woe,
> Since it hath been beforehand with our griefs.
> This England never did, nor never shall,
> Lie at the foot of a conqueror
> But when it first did help to wound itself.
> Now these her princes are come home again,
> Come the three corners of the world in arms

> And we shall shock them! Naught shall make us rue,
> If England to itself do rest but true.

(5.7.110–18)

Curiously enough, it seems that Shakespeare went to look at a specific episode in Holinshed's *Chronicles* to compose this speech, as a number of intriguing parallels between the chronicler's description of Jesuit activities around the Campion-Parsons mission of 1580–81 and the last lines of *King John* appear to indicate. In fact – to be precise – Shakespeare recycled some of the argumentation used during the 1581 trial for treason and rebellion of the Jesuit Edmund Campion:

> *This little Lland,* God having so bountifullie bestowed his blessings upon it, that *except it proove false within itselfe, no treason whatsoever can prevaile against it* [. . .] Secret rebellion must be stirred here *at home* among our selves, the harts of the people must be obdurated against God and their prince; so that when *a foren power* shall on a sudden invade this realme, the subiects thus seduced must ioine with these *in armes*, and so shall the pope atteine the sum of his wish.[64]

Shakespeare appears to have thought in terms of contemporary parallels when looking for material for his *King John*. The dramatist, however, does not go as far as to make the Bastard claim that foreignness and especially Roman Catholicism are synonymous with disunion and civil strife, although others had propounded this idea. Anthony Munday in his unabashed *Watch-woord to Englande* repeated to his advantage the government line that held the Pope and Roman Catholicism responsible for the destruction of civil peace and for England's internal strife. Towards this end, King John was naturally the example he used to start off his repetition of the Protestant government's 'revisionist' version of English history:

> So many foughten fieldes within the Realme, so long and so great uncertaintie, which side were true men and which were Traitours, and for how many dayes or howres they should be so esteemed: such desolation and miseries, to whome are they to be imputed, but to the Popishe Clergie and Papists . . . [65]

In 1596, probably the same year that Shakespeare composed his *King John*, Charles Gibbon in *A Watch-worde for Warre* also wrote on national unity and on the threat of civil war. Gibbon was a more subtle interpreter than Munday, especially in his moralization of domestic and international politics. For him the war abroad was a symptom of the war within England – the enemy within explained why the enemy without was so aggressive: 'God would never sende outward enemies to afflict the bodie, but that hee perceives the inward enemies doe prevaile with the Spirit'. Gibbon also came to almost the same conclusion as Shakespeare's Bastard and this, he claimed, was a common saying at the time: 'Thys is the common saying: if we be true within our selves, we neede not care or feare the enemy'.[66]

What is also noteworthy is that, in the name of national unity no doubt, Gibbon tried to rally Catholics – a rare attempt in the polemical literature of the time, so prone to ostracize 'papists' and exclude them from the fold. The author in fact tried to instil the fear of the foreign enemy in the hearts of those English Catholics who might have been ready to support the Spaniards in the event of an invasion. Foreigners were disloyal, they would not keep their word and would be ungrateful to their English supporters:

> let the Papists thinke, if the worst should fall (as God defend,) the Spaniard will deale as *Nabuchadnezer* did, he wil not spare a Papist though he be a Papist: (but he will rather suppose it is done of policie to possesse life) and therefore in this regard they should arme themselves against the enemie, because they are like to speed no better then we, if he prevaile.[67]

A similar situation is found in *King John* when Viscount Melun, a French nobleman, makes a stunning revelation to the English rebels – one which is like an echo of the anti-Catholic propaganda of the time as the threat of an invasion was thought imminent – far from being thanked, the English rebels will in fact all be killed by the Dauphin's henchmen. To make matters worse, Melun reminds the audience of the oath which the French and English rebels had sworn 'Upon the altar at Saint Edmundsbury', intimating that the French have perjured themselves and that their faith (i.e. their loyalty and their religion) is worthless and hypocritical:

> MELUN Fly, noble English; you are bought and sold.
> Unthread the rude eye of rebellion
> And welcome home again discarded faith.
> Seek out King John and fall before his feet,
> For if the French be lords of this loud day,
> He means to recompense the pains you take

> By cutting off your heads. Thus hath he sworn,
> And I with him, and many more with me,
> Upon the altar at Saint Edmundsbury,
> Even on that altar where we swore to you
> Dear amity and everlasting love.

(5.4.10–20)

It is interesting that Hubert – and thus indirectly the memory of Arthur, whom Hubert tried to save – is brought back in at this stage as Melun admits that his confession has been prompted by Hubert for whom he has the uttermost respect. Indeed Hubert is a figure of integrity in the play, a character who also fought against the odds to maintain a neutrality (during the siege of Angers) which the world of the play constantly denied him.

> MELUN ... Commend me to one Hubert with your King.
> The love of him and this respect besides,
> For that my grandsire was an Englishman,
> Awakes my conscience to confess all this.

(5.4.40–3)

Hubert's final decision not to execute the King's sentence and blind Arthur in Act 4, scene 1, turns him in fact into a figure of resistance and disobedience to the King's sacred authority, especially if one interprets this decision in the light of the biblical story of Abraham and Isaac, 'the proto-typical case of Christian obedience'.[68] It seems that the play validates this act of resistance and thus goes against governmental propaganda on these matters.[69] The point is that Hubert does the right thing – an obvious fact which stares everyone in the face but which complicates the ideology of obedience and loyalty to the sovereign (prerequisites to national union) which the play also voices, especially in the final speech.

Hubert thus plays an important part in the play's politics and this has not always been recognized, no doubt because the Bastard's role has been exaggerated.[70] It is perhaps not a coincidence that such an ambiguous and complex character as Hubert – one who is an example of civil disobedience – is present at almost every stage in the transition towards the new reign of Henry III. Indeed Hubert is brought on stage to announce that the King has been poisoned by a monk (5.6.23–7) and a few lines later he points towards a possible reunion of the nation by mentioning King John's heir – Prince Henry, who has decided to pardon and not chastise the rebellious lords: 'The lords are all come back / And brought Prince Henry in their company' (5.6.33–4). In the next scene (5.7) it is Prince Henry who is given the opening lines which announce King John's imminent death.[71] Shakespeare has carefully laid the ground for the royal, but also moral, succession – from Arthur to Hubert, from Hubert to Henry III.

This does not necessarily mean that Shakespeare supported Arthur's claim as far as the genealogical debates of the polemicists were concerned. Arthur is more of an icon in the play. Indeed Shakespeare's *King John*, when compared to its sources, makes much of him. The dramatist focuses on Arthur's fate in the long scenes devoted to him and to the nobles' reaction to his death (4.1; 4.2.47–105 and 182–269; 4.3). In fact, much of Act 4 is about Arthur. The pouring out of emotion around his plight culminates in a scene where he seems to have become, in the Bastard's choric comment, the dead embodiment of true royalty and innocence:

> I am amazed, methinks, and lose my way
> Among the thorns and dangers of this world.
> How easy dost thou take all England up!
> From forth this morsel of dead royalty,
> The life, the right, and truth of all this realm
> Is fled to heaven, and England now is left
> To tug and scramble, and to part by th' teeth
> The unowed interest of proud-swelling state.

> (4.3.140–7)

Arthur has been a pawn in the power struggle, a pretext, and this was the case from the very outset of the play. His memory is safe, as it is now above the ugly fray – he has become almost an ideal of royalty – 'heaven' (neither English nor French, neither Catholic nor Protestant) ensures that he remains an unadulterated icon. There is a kind of idealization of Arthur in the play – perhaps the fantasy of a monarch who would be able to unite the hybrid nation beyond its political and religious differences.[72] It will be Prince Henry's mission, in the words of the former rebel Salisbury, to try to live up to this fantasy:

> Be of good comfort, Prince, for you are born
> To set a form upon that indigest
> Which he hath left so shapeless and so rude.

> (5.7.25–7)

Salisbury too has journeyed in the play. His tortured speech as he is about to betray his country to join the French puts forward a vision of England which is quite different from the Bastard's final speech which we examined previously. This is a strong, dramatic moment imbued with pathos when Salisbury dreams of another England, in a vision which conjures up an image of civil war and another extraordinary image of England sailing away from European troubles to a 'pagan shore', where she would find a new religious purpose and could be united with the rest of Christendom:

> And is't not pity, O my grievèd friends,
> That we, the sons and children of this isle,
> Was born to see so sad an hour as this
> Wherein we step after a stranger, march
> Upon her gentle bosom, and fill up
> Her enemy's ranks? I must withdraw and weep
> Upon the spot of this enforcèd cause,
> To grace the gentry of a land remote
> And follow unacquainted colours here.
> What here? O nation, that thou couldst remove,
> That Neptune's arms who clippeth thee about
> Would bear thee from the knowledge of thy self
> And grapple thee unto a pagan shore,
> Where these two Christian armies might combine
> The blood of malice in a vein of league,
> And not to spend it so unneighbourly.

> (5.2.24–39)

One can perhaps hear in this poignant speech the cry of those whose divided faiths forced them into an impossible position and required them to join arms with strangers, with the feeling of being strangers in their own land. This was a type of sufferance which many English Catholics felt, especially those who were the most hostile towards the so-called new religion. Writing from London in a letter to his General dated April 1596, the Jesuit Henry Garnet showed how painfully conscious of this paradox he was; it was for him a strange fact indeed 'that, though we have outside of England so many Fathers and Brothers and foundations of our Order, there is nowhere where we can be more in exile than in this kingdom'.[73]

'Fractured and fragmented – radical at times – *King John* is Shakespeare's postmodern history play', wrote Virginia Mason Vaughan.[74] There is reason, as we have tried to argue, to disbelieve this judgment. *King John* is eminently of its time, which does not mean of course that it cannot speak to us across the centuries. If it appears fractured and tormented, it is because it is an open wound that bleeds into the last decade of Elizabeth's reign. Shakespeare in fact anatomizes this wound and in doing so gets his hands into the sometimes unsavoury matters of his time – acrimonious sectarian debate, opportunistic propaganda, nationalism and xenophobia. In doing so, he also gives a voice to those whom sectarian discourse and quarrels destroy, while his overall purpose is still to entertain against all odds. As Jeffrey Knapp writes, 'Shakespeare attempts, Robin Hood-like, to steal religion back from the prelates and preachers who had stolen it from the people in the first place'.[75] This is why the play lets us see through the propaganda and bombast of religious and nationalistic discourse so clearly. This is no doubt also because Shakespeare 'does not want his audience to mistake England for anything other than the latest prison in which Christians have tried to confine God's supranational church'.[76] If only England could drift away and drop its anchor of hope in less troubled waters – Salisbury's dream vision resonates throughout the final act, in a complex interplay with the Bastard's final speech which in fact could be construed as an open question: 'If England to itself do rest but true'?

Shakespeare had not finished trying to find answers to questions of this nature, which involved the nation and the whole issue of religion. With *Henry V* the dramatist would again look at the workings of propaganda, at how religious motives can be found to justify war and unite the nation at all costs, even if this means sacrificing those who will not fit the mould. Shakespeare and his company of players would also personally experience the effects of propaganda with their entanglement in an ideological battle and their partial implication in a failed rebellion – indeed they accepted to revive one of Shakespeare's old plays about a kingly succession (not *King John* but very probably *Richard II*), in support of a man who had set out to make the most of the mounting wave of discontent which had gathered in all quarters of society, Catholic, Protestant and Puritan. Robert Earl of Essex like Shakespeare's rebellious Salisbury was, for a brief moment, the man with a dream of reform.

5
The Discovery of a 'Popish Plot'? The Chamberlain's Men and the 1601 Essex Rising

> The prating tavern haunter speaks
> of me what he lists; the frantic libeller
> writes of me what he lists;
> they print me and make me speak
> to the world, and shortly they will
> play me upon the stage.
>
> (Robert Devereux, Earl of Essex
> to the Queen, 12 May 1600)[1]

> Littel Cecil tripps up & downe,
> He rules bot[h] court & crowne,
> With his brother Builie clowne,
> In his great fox-furrd gowne;
> With the long proclamation
> Hee swore hee sav'd the towne,
> Is it not likelie?
>
> (Anonymous ballad, 1601)[2]

Robert Devereux, Earl of Essex, was not only a leading patron of the arts, he was the man who received more works dedicated to him than any other leading figure of the 1590s, including the Queen herself.[3] By the turn of the next century, however, the nobleman who had managed to stir so much enthusiasm and gather around him so many followers – soldiers, writers or aristocrats – had lost the Queen's favour and was no longer in odour of sanctity with the prominent members of Elizabeth's Privy Council. This, however, had seemingly not tarnished the earl's popularity – he had in fact become something of a 'dangerous image'.

Early in 1600, Rowland Whyte reports indeed that an engraving was creating a sensation both at court and in the city, as 'some foolish idle ballad maker of late cawsed many of his [Essex's] pictures to be printed on horsback, with all his titles of honor, all his services, and two verses underneath that gave hym exceeding praise for wisdom, honor, worth; that heaven and earth approve yt, Gods elected'.[4] God's elected – or 'God's anointed' as Shakespeare's Richard II would have it – was a title usually applied to lawful sovereigns. On 30 August of that same year the Privy Council reacted and put a stop to expressions of this cult of honourable personages. The Archbishop of Canterbury received the following instructions from the Privy Council:

> There is of late a use brought up to engrave in brasse the pictures of noblemenn and other persons and then to sell them printed in paper sett forth oftentimes with verses and other circumstances not fytte to be used. Because this custome doth growe common and indeed is not meete such publique setting forth of anie pictures but of her most excellent Majesty should be permytted yf the same be well done, wee have for divers good respects thought good to praie your Grace that you will give direccion that hereafter no personage of any noblemann or other person shalbe ingraven and printed to be putt to sale publiquely, and those printes that are already made to be called in, unlesse your Lordship shall first be made acquainted with the same, and thincke meete to allowe them.[5]

Essex's partisans needed such impressive images of glory and honour. These were notions around which they could easily assemble in spite of their differences in the religious domain. Essex could pride himself in the fact that he managed to unite around him 'a few Puritans, a strong Catholic element, and a religious centre best described as made up of politique Anglicans'. Thus, 'the tendency of the group to articulate its solidarity in terms of honour was strengthened by the fact of its religious fissiparity, and the lack of any single unifying bond of religious allegiance'.[6]

An interest for the theatre appears also to have been another bond uniting a not so negligible number of persons in Essex's entourage. Theatre was no doubt a social occasion which provided the group with further opportunities for meeting and strengthening its ties. Robert Whyte reports that on 14 February 1598 prominent members of the earl's circle had supper and appeared to have been quite passionate about watching two shows until late. These were 'my Ladies Leicester,

Northumberland, Bedford, Essex, Rich, and my Lords of Essex, Rutland, Mountjoy, and others. They had two plays which kept them up till 1 o'clock after midnight'.[7] A year later, in the autumn, as Essex had returned from his unsuccessful campaign in Ireland and caused a political crisis, two of his closest followers were said to have been passing their time at the theatre, hoping no doubt for better days while the Privy Council was deciding what to do with Essex: 'My Lord of Southampton and Lord Rutland come not to courte . . . They pass away the time in London merely in going to plays every day'.[8]

Essex was tried by a special court in June 1600 on charges of treason and of abandoning his command in Ireland. He was found guilty and condemned to lose all offices of state, but was eventually freed in late August. In July, however, he was accused not only of betraying his country, but also of having condoned a work which was dedicated to him – John Hayward's *History of King Henry IV* (published in February 1599), which examined the deposition of King Richard II. The latter charge was almost certainly a false accusation, but it served, nonetheless, to buttress the authorities' case against the earl.[9] Essex's love of theatre was made to serve a similar purpose, as it was alleged that the earl had repeatedly attended performances of a play on the same topic:

> The Erle of Essex is charged with high Treason, namely, That he plotted and practised with the Pope and king of Spaine for the disposing and settling to himself Aswell the Crowne of England, as of the kingdome of Ireland . . . . His vnderhand permitting of that most treasonous booke of <John Hayward's> Henry the fourth to be printed and published, being plainly deciphered not onely by the matter, and by the Epistle itself, for what ende and for whose behoof it was made, but also *the Erle himself being so often present at the playing thereof, and with great applause giving countenance and lyking to the same* . . .[10]

The phrasing of the accusation implied that theatre was sometimes used as an instrument of propaganda for the Essex circle and could easily become a means of dissent. There are no known accounts of these performances attended by Essex. The allegation could well be a distorted exaggeration or even an amalgamation with Hayward's work. The historian Blair Worden has recently argued, partly on the evidence of the above reference, that Hayward's book had been dramatized, that the earl had endorsed this play and that 'the play performed at the instigation of Essex's followers in February 1601 was the dramatization of Hayward's book'.[11] Yet Worden has trouble explaining away the fact that one of the actors in the company – Augustine Phillips of the Chamberlain's Men – refers to it as 'so old and so long out of use', a description better suited to Shakespeare's *Richard II*, which was composed in or around 1595.[12]

A degree of prudence needs thus to apply when considering the staging at the Globe Theatre of 'the play of the deposyng and kyllyng of Kyng Rychard the Second'[13] on the eve of the Earl of Essex's famously ill-fated *coup* of Sunday, 8 February 1601. The play performed in the afternoon of 7 February need not necessarily have been Shakespeare's, even though, of course, it is true that it was performed by his own company, that the description given by Augustine Phillips in his deposition[14] before the authorities seems to fit Shakespeare's *Richard II*, and that we know of no other extant play which fits the description. It is on the grounds of what Samuel Schoenbaum calls a 'plausible assumption' that we shall proceed.[15]

A very special audience – Essex's followers at the Globe

The performance of what was almost certainly Shakespeare's *Richard II* was apparently arranged on Friday, 6 February and given the next day. On the day of the performance Essex received a summons to appear before the Privy Council and this may have 'interrupted his plans for securing possession of the Queen's person and arresting her ministers, and precipitated his futile outbreak of February 8'.[16]

The evidence we have for the 1601 staging is more substantial than for most of the other performances attended by the Essex circle, even if it remains frustratingly patchy. The only direct witnesses who testified during the inquest which followed the rebellion were William Constable, Gelly Meyrick (Essex's steward) and the player Augustine Phillips. The Earl of Essex did not attend the performance of Saturday, 7 February.

However scanty, the evidence allows us to paint a picture of those present and venture a few informed guesses as to these individuals' political and religious agendas. Of the party of ten or so who actually attended the play, three were executed after the failed *putsch*: Christopher Blount, Gelly Meyrick and Thomas Lee. All three were soldiers who were armed and active during the brief uprising. Even if the main leaders of the rebellion were not present at the Globe on Saturday afternoon, those who attended were still considered to be dangerous by the authorities.[17]

About half of those who did attend the play had Catholic leanings: Christopher Blount, Lord Monteagle, John Davies and the Percies (Sir Charles and Sir Josceline who came from a staunchly Catholic family). In this way, the small group which went to the Globe that afternoon was representative of the inner circle of Essex's supporters: 'The Puritans were the weakest . . . By contrast, Catholics, both converts and those of recusant descent were numerous. Thus of the seven present at, or in the secret of, the conference which, early in 1601, discussed the proposed Whitehall *coup d'état* against the court, four were Catholics (Davies, Danvers, Blount and John Lyttleton)'.[18] Furthermore, the majority of those who attended the play – whether Catholic or not – had been knighted by Essex himself (Monteagle, Meyrick, Davies, Constable and the two Percies) and 'To those who received it, knighthood implied a special relationship' with the earl.[19] This suggests that religious faith and political allegiance to Essex were fairly closely intertwined among those who were at the play on the afternoon of 7 February.

Among the Essexian spectators was Christopher Blount. 'There can be no doubt that Blount, as an enthusiastic young convert, sympathized with an attack on the existing government', wrote Sidney Lee in the *Dictionary of National Biography*.[20] Blount had recently returned to the Catholic faith and had also confirmed in the faith another of the theatre-goers of that day, John Davies. Blount and the Earl of Southampton, Henry Wriothesley, had been Essex's chief advisers in Ireland. He had very close and particular ties with Essex: although roughly of the same age he was the earl's stepfather by marriage (Blount had married the Countess of Leicester, Robert and Penelope's mother). He was imprisoned in the Tower with some of the more dangerous leaders of the rebellion and was executed on 18 March 1601 on Tower Hill.[21]

Edward Bushell was among those who got off fairly lightly after the prosecution of the plotters. On 14 February he was said to be imprisoned in the Marshalsea and on 26 February his name appeared on the list of those 'not yet indicted, but fit to be indicted'. Later the same day, he was called before the Star Chamber and fined.[22] Ellis Jones had pretty much the same fate: imprisoned in the Compter prison in Wood Street, 'not yet indicted, but fit to be indicted', he was called before the Star Chamber on 15 May 1601 and fined.[23]

William Constable, whose deposition is among the precious few accounts of the performance of 7 February, was also called before the Star Chamber (on 13 May 1601) and fined. Constable had been imprisoned in the Compter prison, and released on bail on 16 March 1601 owing to the Queen's 'gracious inclination to mercy and favour'.[24] Constable had seemingly actively collaborated with the authorities and his deposition of 16 February allows us to know who was present at the Globe. He had served in Ireland under Essex and was knighted by him at Dublin on 12 July 1599. Ironically, the authorities had released someone who was going to go down in history as a regicide. Indeed, the House of Commons was to appoint Constable as one of the King's judges and he was to be among those who signed the warrant for the execution of Charles I.[25]

Henry Cuffe, Essex's secretary, was not present at the play, but attended the midday meal before it. He was said to have had a bad influence on the earl, who later charged him. He was imprisoned in the Fleet and hanged with Meyrick on 13 March 1601.[26] Just before his death, he apparently wrote aphorisms inspired by the recent events – one of these is a direct comment on Elizabeth's declining years: 'Old Princes are more dangerously offended then younger, because feelinge the declynacon of nature they apprehend the declynation of Majestie'.[27]

John Davies held an office in the Tower of London, and was entrusted by Essex with the task of guarding the hall of the Queen's palace at Whitehall as soon as her attendants were overpowered. His confession shows that he was much in Essex's confidence. He was imprisoned in Newgate prison and, although convicted and sentenced to death on 5 March 1601, he was subsequently pardoned.[28] Davies was a sincere Catholic, as William Camden noted in his firsthand account of the trial of Essex's partisans:

> *Davies* being conuicted with his owne conscience and confession, in a manner held his peace; and being taxed by the way, that hee was Popish, hee denyed it not; that hee had beene instructed by his Tutor in the Vniversity of *Oxford*, in the Popish Religion, and confirmed in the same by *Blunt* whilest hee serued in the warres in *Ireland*. At which word when hee saw *Blunt* was moued, hee soone appeased him, saying, that hee was confirmed in that Religion, not by *Blunts* perswasion, but by the example of his christian and sincere life.[29]

Thomas Lee, who was a Protestant and had been a captain in Ireland during Essex's campaign, did not attend lunch apparently on the Saturday before the uprising, but joined Essex's followers afterwards at the Globe.[30] He was arrested on 12 February, imprisoned in the Tower and charged with attempting to secure the release by force of the Earls of Essex and Southampton. He was executed two days later at Tyburn.[31]

Gelly Meyrick arrived late at the play according to the statement he made to the authorities.[32] After the failed coup, during which he was in charge of the defence of Essex House and held members of the Privy Council as hostages, he was jailed in Newgate prison. He did not disclose much during his trial and was hanged at Tyburn with Cuffe on 13 March 1601.[33] Meyrick had close links with Welsh recusants at Wigmore Castle, his seat along the border, in Herefordshire.[34] These links provided Meyrick's master with a fairly extensive territorial network in those parts, but his hold on the rest of the country was limited compared to other nobles.

Henry Parker, fourth Baron Monteagle – also present at the Globe that afternoon – had been commissioner for the trial of Queen Mary Stuart in 1586 and of Philip, Earl of Arundel in 1589. But Parker's grandmother, Anne, Lady Monteagle, was a staunch supporter of the English Jesuits and both his parents, despite their apparent conformity, had strong Catholic leanings. Through his marriage to Elizabeth, daughter of Sir Thomas Tresham, Lord Monteagle was in contact with the chief Roman Catholic families in the country and supported their cause. He joined the Earl of Essex in Ireland in 1599, and was knighted there on 12 July. Following his involvement in the 1601 rebellion he was released after payment of a fine.

His involvement with Catholic circles continued none the less, and Monteagle even frequented Robert Catesby, the more militant among English Catholics, who was later to take part in the Gunpowder Plot. According to the *DNB*, 'Monteagle was as desirous as any of his Catholic friends and kinsmen that a Catholic should succeed Elizabeth on the throne, and with that object he aided in the despatch in 1602 of Thomas Winter and Father Greenway to Spain; these envoys carried an invitation from English Roman Catholics to Philip III to invade England'.[35] It was only on the accession to the throne of James I that Monteagle gave up his perilous activities.

The presence at the Globe Theatre of Charles and Josceline Percy – respectively fourth and seventh sons of Henry Percy, 8th Earl of Northumberland – is interesting on many counts. The brothers, after the coup, were put on the list of prisoners 'Already indicted and to be forborne to be arraigned, but yet fined' (26 February). Both had been imprisoned in the Fleet.[36] The two men came from a family which had a history of recusancy. Their father had been repeatedly involved in plots to free Mary Queen of Scots. In December 1584 he was sent to the Tower for a third time. Six months later, on 21 June 1585, Henry Percy was found dead in his cell. He had been shot through the heart. A jury was at once summoned and returned a verdict of suicide. Sir Christopher Hatton, the Vice-Chamberlain, had probably contrived his death and a few years later Walter Ralegh, in a letter to Robert Cecil, referred to Hatton's guilt as proved. The allegations made against him were that he not only sought to free Mary, but also wanted to extort from Elizabeth full toleration for the Catholics.[37]

Their elder brother, Henry Percy, who had inherited his father's title of Earl of Northumberland, finally managed to secure their release on bail on 16 April 1601.[38] Henry Percy's title gave him the right to stand eighth on the list of presumptive heirs to the Crown. Many Catholics desired him to marry Arbella Stuart to make his claim to the throne stronger. Instead, he married one of Essex's sisters, Dorothy, which made him part of yet another network. Yet he still tried to ensure, through his secret correspondence with James VI, that Catholics would be well treated when the time came for the Scottish sovereign to succeed. So as to get James interested in his plea for toleration, he tried to reassure him that Catholics would not represent a threat to his future rule, because the majority of them were moderates: 'vnles it be by some of them that are Puritane papistes that thirst after a spanish tytle', adding, 'Somme papists I have in my famylie, who serve me as watches how others are affected, and some that I am acquainted with, but yet I never heer any of them say but that they all of them wished your Maiesty the fruition of your right . . . '.[39] Henry Percy had much to do to convince James after Essex's rebellion – in which so many Catholics had been involved – that the earl's disastrous coup was not a 'popish plot', what the authorities wanted it to be, as we shall see. Percy, none the less, never really convinced James who remained guarded – in 1606 Northumberland was accused by the King of trying to become head of the Roman Catholics in England. He was tried, imprisoned and finally released only to die in disgrace.[40]

These were the people who attended a performance of what was probably Shakespeare's *Richard II* on the afternoon of 7 February 1601. In the group of men who hired Shakespeare's company of players there were thus noblemen, soldiers and people who had family ties with Essex, or who had served under him – and many of them were Catholics.

Who hired the Chamberlain's Men?

Why, indeed, were the Chamberlain's Men chosen and whose idea was it? Examining what evidence is extant, it seems that it was Charles Percy, third son of Henry Percy, 8th Earl of Northumberland, brother to the 9th

Earl, Henry Percy. Like many of the other theatregoers, he had fought in the Low Countries and in Ireland (with his brother Josceline) where he and Josceline had been knighted by Essex.[41]

That it was Charles Percy's idea to hire Shakespeare's company is something which is seldom mentioned, and yet this detail is not without interest, as will be argued. According to later accounts of the event which are misleading, the responsibility for the choice of the players would appear to go to Gelly Meyrick. Yet the depositions of Meyrick himself and – more importantly – of the actor Augustine Phillips seem to concur. For Meyrick, it was clearly Charles Percy: '& *at the mocyon of* S' *Charles Percy* and the rest they went all together to the Globe over the water wher the L. Chamberlens men vse to play and were ther somwhat before the play began, Sr Charles tellyng them that the play wold be of Harry the iiij[th]'.[42] The deposition shows that Meyrick apparently could not remember who decided on the play – Meyrick paused and hesitated in his statement and then cited Charles Percy: 'He can not tell who procured that play to be played at that tyme except yt were S' Charles Percye, but as he thyncketh yt was S' Charles Percye'.[43]

Augustine Phillips' deposition the next day (18 February 1601) names Charles Percy again and shows that his choice had seemingly been premeditated: 'He sayeth that on Fryday last was sennyght or Thursday S' Charles Percy S' Josclyne Percy and the L. Montegle with some thre more spak to some of the players in the presans of thys examinate to have the play of the deposyng and kyllyng of Kyng Rychard the second to be played the Saterday next'.[44]

On 5 March 1601 a report on Meyrick's trial states that he was mainly responsible for the hiring of the players. The Attorney-General Edward Coke charged him thus: 'And the story of *Henry IV* being set forth in a play, and in that play there being set forth the killing of the King upon a stage; the Friday before, Sir *Gilly Merrick* and some others of the Earl's train having an humour to see a play, they must needs have the play of *Henry IV*. The players told them that was stale, they should get nothing by playing of that, but no play else would serve; and Sir *Gilly Merrick* gives forty shillings to *Philips* the player to play this, besides whatsoever he could get'.[45] That Meyrick was part of the business transaction was one thing; that this was his idea was another.

To establish Meyrick's guilt further, the prosecution clearly decided to load him with this accusation, despite his own declaration and that of a presumably direct witness, the actor Augustine Phillips. The historian William Camden seems to allow for a slight doubt in the responsibility, even if, in the magistrates' rationale, the man who had defended Essex

House and had sequestered Privy Councillors could only have construed the play as a prelude to – or a rehearsal for – the rebellion: 'which the Lawyers interpreted to be done by him, as if they should now behold that acted vpon the stage, which was the next day to be acted in deposing the Queene'.[46] Again, Francis Bacon, in *A declaration of the practices and treasons attempted and committed by Robert late Earle of Essex* (1601), insisted that Meyrick mainly was responsible for hiring the player and even that this had been *premeditated* on his part: '*Merricke*, with a great company of others, that afterwards were all in the Action, had procured to bee played before them, the Play of deposing King *Richard* the second. Neither was it casuall, but a Play bespoken by *Merrick*'.[47] Evidently, it was more important to charge Meyrick (even wrongly) and thereby prove that his part in the rebellion had been well and truly premeditated, than to emphasize the responsibility of Charles Percy, who – unless Augustine Phillips was lying, or could not really remember – *was* responsible.

The authorities were interested only in the political responsibilities (whose money was spent and to what end)[48] and it was easy for the prosecution to use Meyrick to establish Essex's guilt further; this is what happened when the judges compiled evidence against him. A previously unpublished document preserved in the Public Record Office shows clearly how Coke's mind seemed to be working. In rough notes which Coke took as he was gathering evidence for the trial, he lists, among the four or five depositions destined to confound Gelly Meyrick, Augustine Phillips' testimony: 'phillips for the play of h 4'.[49] The Chamberlain's Men's performance had thus become just another item on the list of accusations meant to incriminate Essex's right-hand man (see Figures 1 and 2).

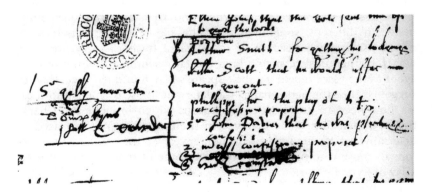

Figure 1 Extract of PRO SP12/278/98

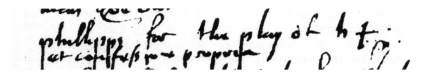

Figure 2   Close-up of allusion to the play [Henry IV]

In this way, it is also noteworthy that Coke – consciously or not – transformed the title of the play to 'h 4' [Henry IV] whereas Augustine Phillips, who must have been one of the persons most acquainted with the play (apart from Shakespeare himself), twice refers to it in his deposition as being of 'Kyng Rychard'.[50] Coke had probably still in mind the July 1600 accusations against Essex, which alleged that John Hayward's *History of Henry IV* had served the earl's political purposes. A play on 'Henry IV' performed by players who were hired by one of the earl's closest supporters, Gelly Meyrick, thus enabled the authorities to tie in all the accusations rather nicely.

Who was Charles Percy?

The authorities thus turned the performance of what was probably Shakespeare's *Richard II* into a mere item in a list of accusations. Such an idea is no doubt difficult to admit for Shakespeare scholars and yet this is what the primary sources seem to indicate. There is much here to disappoint the critics who construe this staging solely as an 'attempt to use the theatre to subvert authority', forgetting that literary artefacts are complex material, that their cultural value is endlessly reassessed and modified and that they can be manipulated in different, sometimes opposing ways.[51] It is precisely such mechanisms which need to be investigated further – how, in other words, in the midst of such a brief but far-reaching and multi-layered event as the Essex rebellion, Shakespeare's play found its place. Having suggested how the performance was later put to use by the authorities, we now need to go back to the reasons which brought the Chamberlain's Men to become involved in the first place. We also need to determine what these reasons might reveal of the minds and opinions of those who must have projected some of their hopes onto the 'play of Kyng Rychard'.

This brings us back to the Earl of Essex's supporters and particularly to Charles Percy. Charles Percy's artistic leanings, or indeed the fact that he knew Shakespeare's works, did not matter in the least to the authorities – but these elements matter to us, of course.

In a manuscript letter of 27 December (1600), which has gone almost unnoticed, Charles Percy writes from Dumbleton, Gloucestershire to a Mr Carlington in London. His letter (see Figure 3), which found its way into the Domestic State Papers possibly because it was seized 'upon the companions of Essex in his attempt upon London',[52] contains a direct reference to one of the plays of Shakespeare's Henriad, *Henry IV, Part 2*, as it happens:

> Mr Carlington: I am heere so pestred with contrie businesse
> that I shall not bee able as yet to come to London: If I stay
> heere long in this fashion at my return I think you ~~shall~~ will
> find mee so dull that I shall bee taken for Justice
> Silence or Justice shallow. wherefore I am to entreat
> you that you will take pittie of mee and as occurrences
> shall searue, to send mee such news from time to ~~hap~~ time
> as shall happen, ~~which thoutgh~~ the knowledge of the
> which, thoutgh [*sic*] perhaps thee will not exempt mee from
> the opinion of a iustice shallow at London, yet I will
> assure you, thee will make mee passe for a very sufficient
> gentleman in Glocestshire: If I doe not alwaies make you
> answere. I pray you do not therefore desist from your
> charitable office, the place being so fruitfull from whence
> you write and heere so barren that it will make my
> head ake for inuention, but if any thing happen heere
> that may bee unknown unto you in those parts you shall
> not faile but to heare of it. I pray you direct your letters
> to thee three cups in breedstreet [Bread Street?] where I haven
>   taken order
> for the sending of them down: And so in the mean while
> I will ever remain
>
> > your assured friend
> > Charles Percy
> Dumbleton in Glocestshire
> this 27. of December.
>
> > you need not to forbeare sending of
> > news hither in respect of their stalenes
> > for I will assure you, heere thee will
> > bee very new.[53]

114

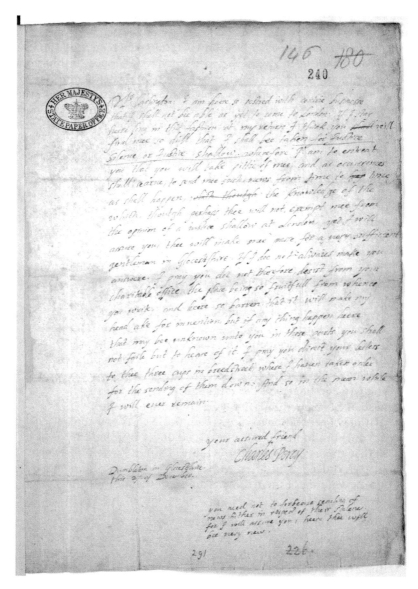

Figure 3   Charles Percy to Mr Carlington, 27 December (1600), PRO SP12/275/146

Charles Percy's frustration at being cut off from London life is plain in this letter to the extent that he compares himself to Shakespeare's country justices. One could perhaps detect a craving for more artistic (?) 'invention' and a little less cultural barrenness (cf. 'so barren'). Interestingly, this last term appears to be a direct echo of Shakespeare's *Henry IV, Part 2*. There is indeed a scene set seemingly in Gloucestershire in which Falstaff visits Justice Shallow's house and commends the judge's 'goodly dwelling'. Shallow, however, answers that it is unfortunately 'Barren, barren, barren' (5.3.6).[54] Charles Percy may also have remembered Falstaff's particularly successful satire of Shallow – the country justice who, according to the plump knight, was a running joke unto himself: 'I will devise matter enough out of this Shallow to keep Prince Harry in continual laughter the wearing out of six fashions' (5.1.69–72). He may also – even if this cannot be proved – have remembered Shakespeare's portrayal of his rebel ancestor, Henry Percy, better known as Hotspur, who was killed at the battle of Shrewsbury. In *Henry IV, Part 2* he is mourned by his widow and continues to cut a heroic picture: 'He was indeed the glass / Wherein the noble youth did dress themselves', says Kate Percy (2.3.21–2). There is much in the play which concerns rebellion, and there is also a passage (Act 3, scene 1),[55] which contains a long retrospective spoken by Henry IV on how Richard II lost his throne. All these elements might explain some of the reasons why Charles Percy approached the Chamberlain's Men asking for 'that play of Kyng Rychard', a work which could, in his eyes, and in the eyes of Essex's supporters, lend itself even more than *Henry IV* to politicized readings.[56]

Percy may perhaps have known Shakespeare personally, even if this will have to remain an unverifiable conjecture. After all, the estate most certainly alluded to in the letter – Dumbleton Hall – was in Gloucestershire, near the town of Campden and some 25 miles from Stratford-upon-Avon.[57] Another intriguing question, however, is how Charles Percy – who spent so much time on military campaigns in the Netherlands and Ireland – managed to get acquainted with Shakespeare's *Henry IV, Part 2* and more generally with the dramatist's work. Critics do not agree about the date of first performance of *Henry IV, Part 2*, some arguing for a 1596–97 performance (possibly December-January), others for a date in the spring or summer of 1598.[58] Both these scenarios allow Percy little time to see the play, as he appears to have been in the Netherlands and then in Ireland for most of 1598, while in March 1599 and May 1600 until October of that same year his private correspondence shows that he was abroad again, mostly fighting in Ireland.[59] He seems to have been in England in November 1600, more than three months before the Essex Rebellion.[60] The possibility that he saw Shakespeare's *Henry IV, Part 2* when on leave from military service should not be excluded, but it is more likely that he purchased or borrowed one of the two Quartos of the play which were both published in 1600, the year he returned from Ireland, a few months before the February 1601 rebellion.[61]

His correspondent's identity is equally uncertain. Not much can be gleaned from the official records concerning 'Mr Carlington'. What is certain is that Charles Percy assumed that Carlington had some degree of familiarity with the play and the humorous reference to Shakespeare's characters indicates that the two men seem to have known each other quite well. The Calendar of State Papers does have a reference to a 'Mr Carlington' in a letter dated 1574 with reference to Irish affairs, which happens to mention the first earl of Essex, Walter Devereux (Robert Devereux's father).[62] Another reference to Percy's mysterious correspondent is also found in a letter penned by Robert Cecil, which names a number of men who were arrested and questioned in connection with the Essex Rebellion. If this is the same man, one can surmise that Carlington had close connections to the Essex family, that he served the first earl and later became a follower of the second.[63]

The Chamberlain's Men's involvement

The men who, according to Augustine Phillips' testimony, approached the actors were 'Sr Charles Percy Sr Josclyne Percy and the L. Montegle with some thre more...'.[64] According to the deposition, these men spoke to 'some of the players' – perhaps only the principal actors in the company; they are indeed twice referred to again in the deposition as 'thys examinate [Phillips] and hys freindes'.[65] These may have been the rest of the players who, like Phillips, were 'sharers' in the company, i.e. Richard Burbage, John Heminges, Will Kemp, Thomas Pope and William Shakespeare.[66]

The actors thus agreed to perform for three men who were malcontents and had Catholic leanings. After his release from prison in 1602, Charles Percy wrote a letter to Cecil in which he called himself 'a poore gentilman distressed by the errour of his youth', and yet in April 1605 he was desirous to lead a force of English Catholics, which had been requested by the Spanish ambassador to serve the Archduke in the wars of Flanders.[67] Among these soldiers were men who, a few months later, would become involved in the Gunpowder Plot. Percy's elder brother fortunately dissuaded him from going; the ninth earl would later write to Robert Cecil explaining that he had 'already suffered enough for other men's Faults'.[68]

Perhaps Sir Charles managed to negotiate the play as a personal favour if indeed he knew some of the actors. This, however, is mere speculation. What is more certain is that, despite their claims of innocence and their apparent surprise at the choice of the play ('holdyng that play of Kyng Rychard to be so old & so long out of use'), it is difficult to believe that the actors were unaware that Richard II's reign would be a sensitive subject in the tense political climate of 1601, or that they failed to recognize these men as belonging to the banished Earl of Essex's entourage. The men's insistence on that play and no other, added to their will to give them 'xls. more then their ordynary for yt',[69] surely led them to conclude that there was more to it than just admiration for the work, even from a man like Charles Percy. What they probably did not know was that their performance would serve as a prelude to the rebellion.

The actors' concern about having 'small or no cumpney at yt' is interesting on two counts. Indeed, this implies that the understanding was that the play should be performed *publicly* at the Globe and that, far from being a private performance, Shakespeare's *Richard II* was meant to be used, in the minds of Essex's followers, as some kind of *political* statement.[70] As Peter Thomson wrote, 'The agreement to stage the play on Saturday, 7 February was an open statement by a company of players that they supported the maligned Earl of Essex. When, on Sunday, 8 February, Essex's discontent broke out into rebellion, such support was no longer easily distinguishable from treason'.[71]

Phillips, however, officially cleared his company of any hint of partisanship by declaring that he and his fellows never believed in the first place that such a project would be able to draw crowds. We do not know whether the performance was successful, what we do know is that the Essex rebellion itself certainly did not draw the crowds the earl's supporters had hoped for. This concern about insufficient profits – whether fabricated or not by the players – was also credible in the eyes of the authorities. Indeed, the phrase 'thys examinate and hys freindes' referred no doubt to the aforementioned six company sharers who were 'not only 'sharers' in the company's fortune but 'housekeepers' in their playhouse, entitled to a share in the owner's traditional half of the gallery takings'.[72] The players, defended by Phillips – who, according to Thomas Whitfield Baldwin, was in charge at the time of posting the bills and of scheduling the plays[73] – were thus protected by a *commercial* argument (they played for the money), even if their original intent may have been to lend their support to men known to belong to the banished Earl of Essex's entourage.[74]

On 24 February 1601 – the eve of the earl's execution – the Lord Chamberlain's Men acted before the Queen at Whitehall (we do not know which play, 'presumably not *Richard II*').[75] This may have been a coincidence – but perhaps it was the Queen's somewhat gruesome way of reaffirming her supremacy.[76]

The players got off lightly in the end, perhaps thanks to William Lambard, as W. Nicholas Knight has suggested,[77] or perhaps because they had been forced to change their allegiances and come to an understanding with the authorities. This is what the tone of the allusions in Ben Jonson's *Poetaster* seems to indicate. Interestingly, this play was first performed in 1601 under the title of *The Arraignment* – a name which may have oddly reminded audiences of the then recent Essex trial.[78] In *Poetaster* the adult players Histrio and Aesop inform to the government against the characters of Ovid and Horace (who may perhaps stand for Jonson). Tucca even promises Aesop (who is linked in the play to 'your *Globes*, and your *Triumphs*', which suggests the Chamberlain's men) 'a *monopoly* of playing confirm'd to thee and thy couey, vnder the Empirours broad Seale, for his seruice'.[79] Yet Jonson saw to it that Aesop's reward in the end was to be whipped. E. K. Chambers, less sceptical than usual, wondered: 'Can the Aesop episode be a reminiscence of the part played by Augustine Phillips in the Essex innovation?'[80] Or yet another intriguing question was Jonson – who had converted to Catholicism in the late 1590s – denouncing the players' collusion with the authorities and the withdrawal of their allegiance to Essex's group of malcontents?[81] There is indeed another scene in Jonson's *Poetaster* which seems almost to parallel Augustine Phillips' interrogation by the authorities. For those who knew of Phillips' deposition, this scene (Act 4, scene 4) had no doubt a particular flavour as Lupus interrogates the actor Histrio, who reveals that 'they directed a letter to me, and my fellow-sharers . . . to hire some of our properties; as a scepter, and a crowne . . . '. Lupus quickly comes to the conclusion that this can mean only treason: 'This is a coniuration; a conspiracy, this . . . . Plaier, I thanke thee. The Emperour shall take knowledge of thy good seruice . . . . A *crowne*, and a *scepter*? this is good: rebellion, now?'[82]

Whatever the truth behind these intriguing parallels, it cannot be doubted that the authorities knew they would get some mileage out of this performance – and that the actors themselves were ultimately small fry. Charles Percy and his friends had no doubt resorted to theatre because they could see the potential for sedition in drama (and probably in Shakespeare's *Richard II*), but the Elizabethan authorities *also* saw the potential behind this performance and they soon realized they could easily turn the tables on the conspirators using the malcontents' own arms. If Essex's supporters had sought – somewhat awkwardly – to historicize and politicize theatre, the judges and the most influential members of the Queen's Privy Council would also contribute to the dramatization and fictionalizing of history.

The dramatization and fictionalizing of history

Ironically, it appears that nothing happened on 7 February, from the point of view of Her Majesty's Privy Council: 7 February was left blank in the manuscript of the Acts of the Privy Council. The next day, history caught up with the Privy Councillors: 'Sondaie forenoone. At the Courte at Whitehall, the viij[th] of Februarie, 1600 .... This daye there were divers letters wrytten and signed by divers of their Lordships whereof there were no copyes kept, beinge dispatched in haste for the services followinge . . . '.[83]

History would soon be written, however, and it would be written along the lines of a plot with which the Elizabethans were familiar, as we shall see. Suffice it to say that the ambivalence and instability of drama were notions the authorities could easily exploit – and which, at the same time, they had already used not so long before as damning arguments in their prosecution of John Hayward for his *History of Henry IV*.

Both Hayward's work and what we think was the performance of Shakespeare's *Richard II* were in fact engulfed and sometimes amalgamated in the proceedings of Essex's trial for treason after the 1601 rebellion. It is noteworthy that the elements in Hayward's work which were found most devious – apart from the dedication to Essex – were the *History*'s many invented speeches. In the manner that Elizabethan writers of prose fiction often mixed different genres such as poetry or theatre, Hayward let his quill wander in the realm of fiction in his strikingly vivid accounts of historical characters. The Archbishop of Canterbury's speech (addressed to Bolingbroke as an encouragement) could, for instance, have easily elicited suspicion:

> our auncestors liued in the highest pitch and perfection of libertie, but we of servilitie, being in the nature, not of subiectes, but of abiectes, and flat slaues; not to one intractable Prince onely, but

to many proude & disdainefull fauorites; . . . And therefore we are now compelled to shake off our shoulders this importable yoke, and submit our selues to the soueraigntie of some more moderate and worthy person . . . .[84]

Written in direct speech, this passage is entirely Hayward's invention, or rather it is his dramatized interpretation of events, as the historian was interested in the exploration of human motivation behind great events. The dramatization of history was something the authorities regarded with some distrust, especially in the work of a historian. Yet this was what many authors of historical plays and tragedies – like Marlowe, Shakespeare, Jonson and many others – had also been engaged in. Neither was Hayward alone among historians in using this method, as F. J. Levy explains: 'Some historians . . . were moving in the same direction: they were coming to see the past in dramatic terms'.[85] By 1630, when Hayward's *Life and raigne of King Edward VI* (which also made use of invented speeches) was published posthumously, such practices had become less controversial. In the preface to the reader the publisher even cited Hayward's *History of Henry IV* as an example of the author's talents: 'This history is left vs from the pen of a worthy Author, of whom we haue another essay in Henry *the fourth*'.[86]

Almost contemporary to the publication of Hayward's *History* was John Chamberlain's letter of 1 March 1600 to Dudley Carleton, in which he mentioned the controversial epistle dedicated to Essex, only to wonder at the exact nature of the offence: 'I have got you a transcript of it that you may pick out the offence if you can, for my part I find no such buggeswords, but that everything is as it is taken'.[87] Sedition was clearly in the eye of the beholder – in this case in the authorities'. A few months later, as the political climate had become extremely tense as a result of the earl's failed *coup*, sedition was in the eyes of everyone, and the political and literary status of works such as Hayward's *History of Henry IV* – or indeed of Shakespeare's play about the reign of Richard II – had changed considerably.[88]

It was only well after these events that Ben Jonson sought to vindicate the rights of playwrights like himself and of antiquarians like Hayward to dramatize history. In *Sejanus* – a play performed in 1603 in which Shakespeare is known to have acted – the character of Cremutius Cordus may have been inspired by John Hayward. Cordus is an historian who is tried for treason by a prosecutor who is equally bent on establishing the topical and seditious character of his writings: 'Which I will proue from thine owne writings, here, / The Annal's thou hast publish'd; where thou bit'st / The present age, and with a vipers tooth...'.[89] Camden also would later exonerate Hayward as one historian to the other: 'an unfortunate thing for the author, who was punished . . . for his vntimely setting forth thereof...'.[90]

Like Shakespeare in *Richard II*, Hayward had dramatized parliamentary procedures, inventing whole speeches which he put in the mouths of historical figures.[91] He in fact relied far more on Holinshed for these scenes than Shakespeare did. Hayward in his dramatization of the parliament scenes wished to offer a full picture of what opposed viewpoints existed, and thus penned a number of speeches aimed at disclosing Bolingbroke's motivations and the opposition's constitutional misgivings.[92] The problem with such an approach was that, in times of crisis, it could be easily misconstrued, especially when parliament was depicted without the necessary precautions. Indeed, the Elizabethan state had an image of itself and of its parliament which differed widely from modern views on the subject. It still pictured itself largely as consentient and as a result 'there were powerful resistances to the emergence of the house of commons as a platform for adversary politics; and Parliament was conceived primarily as a unifying institution'.[93]

During Essex's trial, the earl was charged with wanting to call a parliament (Shakespeare's play and Hayward's work had dwelled on the process in their descriptions of Henry Bolingbroke's rise to power).[94] The earl was thus cast in the role of the ungrateful and impudent destroyer of Elizabethan harmony. The authorities suggested furthermore that the calling of a parliament was merely the first step in the earl's ascent. After accusing Essex 'of surprizing the Queene, and assembling a Parliament, hee [Edward Coke, the Queen's Attorney-General] ended his speech with this sharpe Conclusion: *It were to be wished that this* Robert *might be the last of this name Earle of* Essex, *who affected to be* Robert *the first of that name King of* England'.[95]

As one of the epigraphs to this chapter suggests, Robert Devereux had already a sense in May 1600 that his person was in danger of being fictionalized and dramatized – the image he had worked so hard to perfect and project was about to escape him: 'The prating tavern haunter speaks of me what he lists; the frantic libeller writes of me what he lists; they print me and make me speak to the world, and shortly they will play me upon the stage'.[96] As he and the Earl of Southampton entered Westminster Hall to be tried, in the very place where Richard II had been deposed before a parliament summoned by Henry Bolingbroke, Essex's history had begun to be written by other men than himself, by men – incidentally – who, like one of his prosecutors, Thomas Sackville, Lord

Buckhurst, co-author of the historical tragedy of *Gorboduc*, well knew what intimate links existed between history and drama.[97]

Ironically, the royal recipient of Essex's letter of May 1600 also feared the collusion of history and drama. Despite Essex's execution, the Queen did not get away unscathed and, like her correspondent, it was her turn to admit in 1601 that even she could not escape the political and cultural mechanisms which transformed history into theatre and set her fate upon a stage. On 4 August 1601, as she perused some of the historical archives of the Tower of London, presented to her by her Antiquarian, William Lambard, documents pertaining to Richard II's distant reign are said to have carried for her an immediate contemporary resonance: 'so her Majestie fell upon the reign of King Richard II. saying, "I am Richard II. know ye not that?"', adding 'He that will forget God, will also forget his benefactors; this tragedy was played 40[tie] times in open streets and houses'.[98] The play was certainly not old or stale for Elizabeth, who seemed haunted by it. The Queen also confided that she wished to find a truthful representation of Richard II; she again turned to Lambard: 'Then returning to Richard II. she demanded, "Whether I had seen any true picture, or lively representation of his countenance and person?"' That the Queen seemingly had a craving for historical truth was hardly surprising – she was perhaps curious to see through the mist of fictions and fantasies created in the course of the Essex rising and of the subsequent trial. The mist was thick, however, and it would not disperse easily.

The discovery of a 'popish plot'?

Shakespeare's fellow actors had been confronted by a group of men who were predominantly Catholic and who had projected some of their hopes onto what was probably the playwright's own *Richard II*. As the actors gave their consent, little could they foresee that their acceptance would mean that the Saturday afternoon performance at the Globe would become an episode in a larger story of ambition and betrayal. However minor, their part consisted in establishing that the rebels had well and truly premeditated their actions and had wished to air their intentions through a play performed in a public theatre.

Even if the evidence was piecemeal and the scenario often improvised, the plot was a well-weathered one – the 'popish plot' story was familiar to everyone and the opposition (primarily the great Roman Catholic 'Other') had been fictionalized and demonized countless times in the course of Elizabeth's reign, and, as we shall see, the practice continued and proved yet again useful. In the way that both the victims and the prosecutors of witchcraft trials sometimes found themselves collaborating to construct a stereotypical narrative of sacrilege and sorcery, both Essex and the authorities competed to establish their version of the 'popish plot' as the closest to historical truth.[99] However, despite the earl's efforts, his version was inevitably the less convincing.

Essex's entourage was made up of men of different beliefs, but of course, as the crisis worsened, the predominance of the Catholic element was something that could no longer go unnoticed and that eventually came to be used during the trial. Among the arguments brought forward in support of the charge of treason against the earl, one finds various accusations of conniving with the Pope and the King of Spain. One allegation – which had been used in the 1600 treason trial against the earl – was also that there had been contacts between the Jesuit Robert Parsons and Essex himself: 'It appears that he [William Alabaster] heard Wright confess writing to Father Parsons of his conference with the Earl of Essex, as stated in the examination above, that he Alabaster, tried to persuade Essex in favour of the Infanta's title'.[100]

That Essex actually negotiated with Parsons is doubtful. In his 1598 *Apology*, a work supposedly printed without the Earl's permission, Devereux actually denounced the intrigues of the Jesuits and used Parsons' claim that the Infanta held the best title to succeed to the Crown of England as an argument to justify war against Spain.[101] What remains certain is that the earl abided by a code of arms and honour which entitled him – he thought – to a right of intervention in high politics. It was, however, this code of honour which was to make him tragically unsuited to the demands of the Elizabethan state. Essex, for instance, 'could not submit to the unconditional quality implicit in a religious obedience'.[102] During his captivity, his chaplain is supposed to have told him: 'all your show of religion was hypocrisy ... you are in your heart either an atheist or papist, which doth plainly appear, in that all your instruments, followers, and favourers, were of this quality...'.[103] During his trial, the earl was also accused of the same ills by Attorney-General Coke: 'for you will appear to be of all religions: one while a papist an other while a Puritan, and that but to gaine unto yourself all sorts of people'.[104] In Elizabethan terms, this meant a straightforward condemnation of any independent role played by the nobility. If one did not conform, one had to be either 'an atheist or papist'. Lack of conformity lead implicitly to treason. To believe in God was to believe in the omnipotence of the Protestant Queen.

But of course Essex had turned that argument round on its head. When in 1598, the earl had been humiliated in public after receiving a cuff on the ear by the Queen, he had declared in a letter after the incident: 'Cannot Princes erre? Can they not wrong their Subiects? . . . They which beleeue not the infinite omnipotency of almighty God, may acknowledge an infinite power of royall Maiestie'.[105] In other words, to be loyal to an unjust sovereign was to be an atheist. A few years later, George Chapman, who had dedicated his translation of Homer to the heroic Essex, was to place almost the same words in the mouth of the actor playing the earl's equally ill-fated French counterpart, the Duke of Byron: 'and who will stir / To tell authority that it doth err?'[106]

Yet the argument of religion had also served the earl well. As Camden notes, 'And whereas religion is the greatest winner of mens affections, hee endeavoured to allure vnto him the Puritans and their Ministers, whom the Queene approued not, and withall the Papists; by pittying their afflicted estate'.[107] In the months preceding the insurrection, Essex had also warned King James against a so-called 'Spanish plot'. In letters to the King of Scotland he warned the Stuart sovereign against the power of Ralegh, Cobham, Burghley and Carew. All of these men commanded strategic parts of the country which were, Essex argued, 'most opportune for letting in of the *Spaniards*'. The earl tried to convince James 'That these men were well affected to the *Spaniard*, and were all at Secretary *Cecyls* becke'.[108] Essex also tried to persuade the King of Scotland to send an ambassador to England to declare his title to the succession.[109] The earl, and other Privy Councillors, for that matter, had long practised manipulations of this nature, the technique even had a name: 'projection'.[110]

Essex, too, was constructing his stereotypical 'popish plot' – but in selecting the elements for his story he made some mistakes. As a desperate ploy during his trial, the earl alleged that Robert Cecil had once said '*That the* Infantaes *title to the Crowne (after her Maiesty) was as good as any other*'.[111] Essex then refused to cite his source, but said that the Earl of Southampton had heard this reported also. Cecil pressed Southampton to reveal the person who had made such allegations. The earl complied and named William Knollys, who was called in to testify and cleared Cecil by saying that 'M. Secretary told him, that one *Doleman* had mainteined in a booke (not long since printed) that the *Infanta* of *Spaine* had a good title to the Crowne of *England*, which was all, as M. Comptroller said, that euer he heard M. Secretary speake of that matter'.[112] Southampton had got Elizabeth's Secretary of State out of a tight corner by revealing the name of the informant – Cecil had himself just begun a secret correspondence with King James and any mention of his being involved in the succession struggle could have compromised him and made him liable for treason. Later, Cecil probably did not forget what Southampton had done for him when it came to deciding on Henry Wriothesley's fate.[113] The episode sheds indirect light on the ideological warfare that had been raging since the mid-1590s. Cecil, like Essex, had been negotiating with the more moderate of the English Catholics (the Appellants). In doing so, he was running the same risk as Essex: he could be destabilized at any moment, accused of plotting with the Catholics, or worse still, with the supporters of the Infanta, the hispanophile Jesuits.[114]

These, however, were precisely the accusations which were wielded against Essex by William Barlowe (who had been appointed by the Queen to attend on the earl while under sentence of death) in the sermon he delivered at Paul's Cross on the Sunday immediately after the uprising, which reads, in the printed version published in 1601, like a slightly self-embarrassed piece of propaganda destined to vindicate the so-called Elizabethan settlement. Barlowe was in fact preaching by royal command and following precise instructions from Cecil, who – it appears – had turned the tables on Essex.[115] Robert Cecil's version of the 'popish plot' was unquestionably gaining the upper hand. Indeed, Barlowe recreated for his audience the whole genesis of the imaginary plot. Robert Parsons' *Conference about the Next Succession* was (Barlowe told his audience) the book responsible for Essex's downfall because the Jesuit persuaded the Earl he could have a direct hand in the succession and dispose of power as he wished:

> Parsons, who, as it is thought, vnder the name of one Doleman, makes the crowne of England a tennis ball, and tosseth it from Papist to Puritan, and from Puritan to Protestant, but the fault or vantage, viz. the whole sway of disposing it, when it is voide... hee ascribeth to the late Earles power of placing it where it should please him, and to him therefore he dedicates his booke, in my conscience I am perswaded, a principal, if not the originall poyson of the late Earles hart: wherein also he spendeth much labour, and filleth many leaues in proouing by stories of scripture, that it is lawfull for the subiect to rise agaynst his soueraigne...[116]

Barlowe's sermon was not devoid of ambiguity either – and this was possibly where the 'popish plot' story reached its limits. Even though the sermon loads Essex and establishes his guilt, it seeks to calm the minds of those for whom Essex remained a popular figure: 'Now for the late Earle: dead he is, and his soule, no doubt, with the saints in heauen...'.[117] This extraordinary statement anticipates the hagiographic literature that was to proliferate in ensuing years, when the earl was sung in ballads which proclaimed he was 'in heauen among the blest' and in which he himself declared (from the grave): 'I neuer loved Papistrye'.[118] Essex was also, in the eyes of some, a strong Protestant figure and his detractors were thus forced to tread carefully.[119]

For the authorities it had to be made clear that the severity of the sentence had been justified by the gravity of the threats. The earl's popularity and charisma was great none the less and it was therefore difficult to reconcile the denunciation of the Essex Rebellion as a 'popish plot' with the preservation of the earl's heroic aura. The earl had to appear as a misguided victim of evil counsellors, which of course was an ironical reversal of the reasons why Essex claimed he rebelled in the first place. Evidently, Barlowe, despite his efforts, could produce only a poor compromise. No doubt because he had been well briefed by Cecil, he was, however, reasonably successful when it came to adding the necessary local colour and political spice to the 'popish plot' story: 'Then looke to the commanders, two of the principall, stiffe and open Papists, and the fourth, by report, affected that way...'. England would indeed have been reduced to slavery by the agents of the counter-reformation: 'And such a slauery and misery, assure your selues, had ours been for Prince and religion, if we had stoode to the courtesie of armed Papistes and their reformation'.[120] All of this concurs with the spirit of Cecil's private notes about the insurrection in which – citing also randomly as examples Watt Tyler, Absalom, Jack Cade and Richard II – he compares the arguments used by Essex to justify the uprising to those of the partisans of the dukes of Anjou and Guise on the eve of the Saint Bartholomew Day Massacre in Paris: 'The night before the massacre in France the Papists gave forth that the Hugenits [Huguenots] went about to murder and root out the famely and faction of Guise'.[121] As this conscious reference to one of the bloodiest episodes in France's wars of religion seems to point out, Cecil had chosen a distinctly sectarian and Manichaean leading thread for his own very personal account of the events.

Setting aside for one moment the wild story of collusion with Spain or Rome concocted by the authorities, it appears that Essex's will to embrace oppositional social forces had in fact been mistaken for mere opportunism. His belief that it was the nobleman's duty to mend the wrongs of government led him straight to disaster. Had the political system been different the earl would no doubt have fared better for

'Essex's disposition attuned him to the problem of multi-culturality, as manifested during the 1590s in the conflicting claims of rival religions, and of honour, law and providentialist obedience, which heralded the breakdown of the Tudor Conformist synthesis'.[122] In the mid-1590s a Catholic petition had been addressed to Essex, asking the earl to support the authors' 'humble suite of tolleracion or Relaxacion', while tolerationist writers also dedicated works to him.[123] The earl's work was even continued after his death: Edward Sandys, for instance, whose views in the House of Commons were anti-Spanish, was to write a tolerationist treatise on religion in Europe, and such ventures obtained the active support of Henry Wotton, Essex's former secretary, who had been appointed Ambassador to Venice.[124]

* * *

The Chamberlain's Men had thus agreed to perform a play which, especially in the context of February 1601, they no doubt knew to be politically charged. Shakespeare's *Richard II* seems to have lent itself well to politicization, and this was not, incidentally, the last attempt to appropriate the play to promote specific agendas.[125] The actors most likely also knew that the men who had approached them were in their vast majority Catholics, and while this is far from proving that the players had Catholic leanings, it does tend to suggest that the actors may have lent a sympathetic ear to their demands and perhaps to their dreams of political change. They could not foresee that their performance would backfire on the Earl of Essex and his supporters and that their work would be used as evidence that Essex was preparing a *coup*. They were also unaware that this action was meant to rock not only the ship of state but also to throw official religion overboard. The earl's supporters had resorted to theatre in an attempt to influence politics, and now the authorities were using drama in their quest for *catharsis*. The *theatrum mundi* metaphor had become such a commonplace that it was anyone's to grab, including Francis Bacon who wrote mercilessly (about Gelly Meyrick, Essex's right-hand man) that 'So earnest hee was to satisfie his eyes with the sight of that Tragedie, which hee thought soone after his Lord should bring from the Stage to the State, but that GOD turned it vpon their owne heads'.[126] The Catholic writer and publicist Richard Verstegan, in a poem printed in 1601 entitled 'Visions of the worlds Instabillitie' – which may well have reflected some of the events of February of that same year – depicts a world which resembles a vast stage where men play their tragedies. Interestingly, the imagery is also close to the commonplace metaphors used by Shakespeare's gardeners in Act 3, scene 4 of *Richard II*: 'Superfluous branches / We lop away, that bearing boughs may live'.[127] Verstegan's poem too is about a 'princely garden' where the sprigs which grow too fast have to be trimmed, and sometimes left to perish:

> A spatious *Theatre* first mee thought I saw,
> All hang'd with black to act some tragedie,
> Which did mee vnto much attention draw . . .
> I saw a Holly sprig brought from a hyrst,
> And in a princely garden set it was,
> VVhere of all trees it stroue to bee the first,
> In stately height whereto it grew a pace:
> Talle Cedar trees it ouertopped far,
> And all with coral berries ouerspred,
> It seem'd the roses beauty for to mar,
> And to deface it with a skarlet red:
> Whereat the Gardner when hee it suspected,
> Or might perhaps misweene this trees intent,
> For all first fauour now grew il affected,
> And all the boughes a way did race and rent:
> Thus stood disgrac'd the stock so braue before,
> VVhich now of grief grew dead and sprong no more.[128]

Yet, as time passed and as a new sovereign ascended the English throne, such visions of *vanitas* gradually faded. The Chamberlain's Men had only been a little premature in their support for Essex, whose reputation began to be slowly restored under the rule of the Stuart monarch. Robert Pricket in *Honors Fame*, a work published in 1604 and dedicated to the earl of Southampton, argued that Essex had been the victim of a misunderstanding between the Queen and himself. The author even dismissed the trial and its fictitious plot altogether: 'When much was said but nothing duly proved' and 'Molehills were to mountaines raisde, / Each little fault was much dispraisde'.[129] For Pricket, the earl had fallen the victim to factious intrigues: 'Herein lay hid the secret ill, / She thought to chide, they sought to kill'.[130] One does not have far indeed to look to find the culprit, even if he is never explicitly named: 'And he that drest his fathers dish, / Lord, let his end be worse then his'.[131] In Samuel Daniel's *Philotas*, performed in 1604, it is also Robert Cecil, the Queen's Secretary of State (Craterus in Daniel's play) who is made to bear the bulk of the responsibility as Craterus' words in the play sound like direct echoes of Cecil's accusations during the Essex trial: 'You foster malcontents, you entertaine / All humors, you all factions must embrace'.[132] Daniel, none the less, had addressed these consensual and atoning lines to the new king in an effort to allay the tensions caused by the succession crisis in the last years of the Queen's reign:

> Burie that question in th'eternall graue
> Of darknesse, neuer to be seene againe:
> Suffice we haue thee whom we ought to haue[133]

With the benefit of hindsight, William Camden mused also: 'Thus in twelue houres was this commotion suppressed; which some called a feare, others an error...and to this day but few there are, which haue thought it a capitall crime'.[134] Despite these conciliatory lines, the fact remained that the authorities had not buried the tensions – both political *and religious* – which the earl's failed *coup* and his ensuing trial had brought to the fore in no uncertain terms. Shakespeare and the Chamberlain's Men had been caught in the turmoil and had been used both *with* and *without* their consent. Their performance had served as a small but significant episode in an overall story of politics and religious factionalism – two themes to which Shakespeare would later return, just over a decade later, with *King Henry VIII*.

6
Revisiting the Reformation: Shakespeare and Fletcher's *King Henry VIII*

> 'we are to iudge honourablie of our rulers,
> and to speake nothing but good
> of the princes of the people . . .'[1]

As the Duke of Buckingham is about to be executed with Henry VIII's consent, his sudden death wish is somewhat unsettling. The duke would like Time to create a 'monument' in honour of the monarch when he dies: 'And when old Time shall lead him to his end, / Goodness and he fill up one monument' (2.1.93–4).[2] Was William Shakespeare and John Fletcher's *King Henry VIII, or All Is True*, written in homage to that 'monumental' sovereign, Henry VIII? This, as we shall argue, is merely a rhetorical question. Shakespeare and Fletcher's play seems more to belie its title doubly: *Henry VIII* is certainly not a biographical work, nor is it simply a play about the religious truths brought about by the Reformation.

One senses, in fact, that *King Henry VIII, or All Is True* expresses one of the play's paradoxes in its title. *All Is True*'s outward claim to depict the whole truth may have to be read on several levels. In fact, as we shall see, both political and religious 'truths' will be under scrutiny in the course of the drama. It also seems that Shakespeare's association with the Protestant dramatist John Fletcher may not be as surprising as it appears at first sight from both an artistic and an ideological point of view. To a large extent, the two dramatists shared the same 'unease' about political and religious issues. Fletcher's work is, interestingly, one which 'looks to multiple allegiances, multiple generic inputs, and multiple authorships, aiming to delineate the negotiation of conflicting loyalties apparent in [his] plays'.[3] Despite the fact that he was born in a Protestant milieu with which he kept close links in later life, his 'local loyalties appear to have transcended nominal religious affiliations'.[4] Like Shakespeare, Fletcher seems to have been engaged in an insatiable quest for meaning, in the political and the religious domains, as his collaboration on *All is True* amply testifies.[5] Yet Shakespeare and Fletcher's play about Henry VIII was also born out of a specific artistic context, which informed their writing. It is to the study of this context that we must now turn.

Staging the Reformation: the artistic context of Henry VIII

Most critics agree that *King Henry VIII* was written around 1612–13, the earliest plausible date suggested being 1610.[6] Interestingly, in this first decade of the seventeenth century the theatre seemed to want to confront its audiences with the issues of the English Reformation. The Lord Admiral's Men, who were acting at the Fortune Theatre, produced two plays on the life of Cardinal Wolsey. Philip Henslowe paid Chettle in June and July 1601 for *The Life of Cardinal Wolsey* and in November 1601 Chettle, Drayton and Munday received payment for *The Rising of Cardinal Wolsey*, a sequel that was probably an attempt to build on the success of the first play. In the autumn of 1602 Henslowe had another commercial success with *Lady Jane*, a Tudor play on Jane Grey to which there was also a sequel.[7] None of these three plays has survived, unfortunately, but in 1607 Michael Drayton did write a narrative poem entitled *The Legend of Great Cromwell*, which was published in 1610 (it was included in the edition of *A Mirror for Magistrates* published that year) and reprinted in 1619.

Drayton's *Legend of Great Cromwell* drew on Foxe's *Book of Martyrs* and on an anonymous play, *Thomas, Lord Cromwell* which appeared in print in 1602 and was republished in 1613. *Thomas, Lord Cromwell* had been acted by Shakespeare's company, the Chamberlain's Men. The choice of Cromwell by the Chamberlain's Men appears natural enough in the light of the players' support for the Essex faction.[8] Cromwell had been Earl of Essex and Robert Devereux's grandfather, Thomas Wriothesley, had actively supported him as kinsman and servant.[9] *Thomas, Lord Cromwell* might have been an attempt on the part of the Chamberlain's Men to compete with the two Wolsey plays performed by their rivals, the Admiral's Men. Historically, the then Lord Admiral's uncle, the Duke of Norfolk, had in fact opposed Wolsey *and* Cromwell. Thus, in the midst of the very tense political struggle which characterized the last few years of Elizabeth's reign, both companies had been 'competing to show their parties' ancestors in the most favourable light, the Admiral's

Men by blackening Wolsey and exalting Norfolk, the Chamberlain's by showing the Howard's enemies in a more agreeable way'.[10]

Thomas, Lord Cromwell admits openly to bypassing Wolsey's life: 'Pardon if we omit all *Wolsayes* life, / Because our play dependes on *Cromwelles* death'.[11] It shows how Gardiner, with the assistance of Norfolk, managed to bring about Cromwell's downfall, as the Lord Chancellor is declared a traitor and condemned to death in a manner that might have reminded audiences of the very recent execution of another Earl of Essex – Robert Devereux – the year before the play appeared in print. At the very end of the play, as the King's reprieve arrives too late and Cromwell has fallen victim to court factionalism, Gardiner is made to confess his errors and to voice his regrets: 'My conscience now telles me this deede was ill: / Would Christ that *Cromwell* were aliue againe'.[12]

Again, court factionalism is denounced in no uncertain terms in Michael Drayton's Jacobean narrative poem, *The Historie of the Life and Death of the Lord Cromvvell, sometimes Earle of* Essex *, and Lord Chancellor of* England (written 1607). In one of the dedications to Drayton placed before the poem itself, the politician and poet Christopher Brooke sets the tone:

> Here shall you finde Factions (which are the rent,
> And disuniting of a league combin'd)
> Make hauock in a ciuill gouerment;
> The grace of Kings vnconstant as the winde.[13]

This was the same Brooke who would later publish *The Ghost of Richard III*, a denunciation of tyranny.[14] Drayton's poem is not just a vindication of a Protestant Cromwell. In passing and through Cromwell's fate it also underlines the flaws of the Reformation. The upstarts who profited from the sale of the clergy's lands are denounced: 'time doth tell, in some things they did erre'. Catholicism is not rejected wholeheartedly as the Reformation 'Not altogether free was from defect'.[15] Furthermore, Henry VIII is not left unscathed; his tyranny is denounced openly in the poem: 'For in his hie distemprature of blood / Who was so great whose life he did regard?'[16] The sovereign cuts a whimsical and gruesome figure; he certainly would have been hard put to advance the cause of 'true religion': 'What late was truth conuerted heresie'. Cromwell appears unequivocally as Henry's sacrificial victim: 'Himselfe to cleere and satisfie the sin, / Leaues me but late his instrument therein'.[17] Yet

Drayton's *Cromwell* is also a warning to those statesmen who would be tempted to flatter kings and thus be 'soothers to their tyrannies'.[18]

The tone of Samuel Rowley's *When You See Me, You Know Me* (first performed probably in 1604 and printed in 1605 and 1613) is much lighter. Yet despite the irony of Shakespeare and Fletcher's Prologue which is aimed directly at Rowley's play, the work is more than just 'a merry, bawdy play' with 'a fellow / In a long motley coat guarded with yellow' (*Henry VIII*, Prologue, 14; 15–16). Henry is still the hot-tempered sovereign of the 'Bluff-King-Harry' tradition.[19] But again, far from being the 'Great Reformer', he comes across as decidedly *unreformed*, especially in his repeated oaths throughout the play – 'Mother a god', 'Gods holy mother' – which stamp him as a Roman Catholic still. The impetus for reform is given by the King's fool, Will Summers, and by his son, the young Edward, Prince of Wales.[20] There is little doubt that high-lighting the Prince of Wales in this way was designed as a thinly disguised reference to Prince Henry, James I's heir, the hope of all Protestants.[21]

'Conscience' and 'truth'

Shakespeare and Fletcher, however, had sought to distance themselves from Rowley's rather trite propaganda piece. Shakespeare for one had been involved in another collaborative work, *Sir Thomas More*, a play written by several hands at roughly the same time as *Richard III* (1592–93).[22] Yet *More*, if Vittorio Gabrieli and Giorgio Melchiori are right, may have been revised and perhaps performed in the early 1600s.[23] More is a character who in some ways resembles Cromwell in his tragic fate, and, as John W. Velz has noted, '*Thomas Lord Cromwell* is perhaps the firmest link between *More* and *H8*'.[24]

More – like Cromwell and like the Duke of Buckingham in *Henry VIII* – appears as a figure of obedience and respect for authority (especially in the speech attributed to Shakespeare):

> For to the king God hath his office lent
> Of dread, of justice, power and command,
> Hath bid him rule, and willed you to obey;
> And to add ampler majesty to this,
> He hath not only lent the king His figure,
> His throne and sword, but given him His own name,
> Calls him god on earth. . . .

> (2.3.106–12)

But of course More really simply points out that the King's authority is derived from God – which magnifies the sovereign's legitimacy but also sets limits on it, as God is above all earthly rulers.

None the less much of the play skirts around religious issues – until the end when More is asked to ratify a set of articles. What these articles are is never specified. They may have been related to the Henrician Oath of Supremacy and to the Act of Succession. More is immediately suspicious of the casualness with which these papers have been presented to him to sign and appeals to his conscience. The play is suddenly halted:

> Subscribe to these articles? Stay, let us pause:
> Our conscience first shall parley with our laws.
>
> (4.1.73–4)

The latent tension between religious conscience and the ways of the political world is at its height at this point in the play. Previously, the Earl of Surrey – the poet Henry Howard – had introduced More to Erasmus in terms which implied that religion and politics could be reconciled: 'Now you shall view the honourablest scholar, / The most religious politician, / The worthiest counsellor that tends our state' (3.1.139–41).

Yet as More leaves the stage to be executed, Surrey the poet stays to speak the final words of the play. They are full of ambiguity:

> SURREY A very learned worthy gentleman
> Seals error with his blood. Come, we'll to court.
> Let's sadly hence to perfect unknown fates,
> Whilst he tends progress to the state of states.
>
> (5.4.119–22)

There has certainly been an 'error', but the question of who should bear the blame for it is left open. Surrey, who speaks here of 'unknown fates', was beheaded in 1547 by Henry VIII on a charge of treason. Such irony was perhaps intended by the authors of a play whose manuscript bears the marks of Edmund Tilney's pen. The Master of the Revels called for substantial revisions and there is reason to believe that the play, originally written in the early 1590s, was 'laid aside after Tilney had objected to it, and taken up again soon after Elizabeth's death, in 1603, when political objections would no longer be felt'.[25] The political resonances of what had happened during the reign of the Queen's father were still too strong to be staged.

Be that as it may, representing Thomas More on stage in 1613 was apparently still a delicate venture for Shakespeare and Fletcher. If *Sir Thomas More* is echoed in *Henry VIII*, it is mainly in broad terms: 'what Shakespeare seems to have remembered from *More* twenty years later was theme, character, and situation'.[26] *More* was a play which found a way to speak of divided allegiance, but which managed to remain on a moral terrain, always eschewing face to face confrontations with the burning religious issues of the age.[27] *More* looks towards *Henry VIII* in the sense that it strives to find a 'safe' medium to broach religious issues – that medium being 'conscience'.

'Conscience', that is, *freedom* of conscience, is indeed the thematic link between *Sir Thomas More* and Shakespeare and Fletcher's *Henry VIII*. Buckingham's speech before his execution shows how – *verbally* at least – a subject's conscience can challenge the official notions of justice and faith. 'Conscience' is precisely the word which enables the individual to regard himself or herself as 'faithful', even though he or she may be officially outlawed:

> I have this day received a traitor's judgement,
> And by that name must die; yet heaven bear witness,
> And if I have a conscience, let it sink me,
> Even as the axe falls, if I be not faithful.
> The law I bear no malice for my death –
> 'T has done upon the premises but justice –
> But those that sought it I could wish more Christians.

> (2.1.58–64)

Such openness on the part of an individual in the world of the play is rare. In *Henry VIII* censorship and surveillance dominate, to the extent that Henry's England resembles a totalitarian state: 'We are too open here to argue this. / Let's think in private more', says an anonymous Gentleman in Act 2 (2.1.167–8).

In such a context, the loaded religious vocabulary of the Reformation is handled with care by the characters and often defused: 'each of the words is detached from its ostensibly higher meaning, and degraded to the level of the material'.[28] Thus, 'conscience' is a word which undergoes many an ironic change in the play. It is soon obvious that the term is in fact divested of much of its religious and political meaning.[29] It is thus turned into a euphemism to describe Henry's whims or indeed his sexual appetite: 'his conscience / Has crept too near another lady', says Shakespeare's Duke of Suffolk (2.2.16–17). The King himself uses the term ambiguously: 'But conscience, conscience – / O, 'tis *a tender place*, and I must leave her' (2.2.141–2).[30] Anne Bullen's lady-in-waiting uses terms which are sexually explicit to describe Henry's so-called gifts that 'the capacity / Of your soft cheverel conscience would receive, / If you might please to stretch it' (2.3.31–3). Henry also finds it difficult to steer a course on his sea of troubles. The metaphors evoking his pangs of conscience suggest disorder: 'Thus hulling in / The wild sea of my conscience . . . ' (2.4.196–7).[31]

If freedom of conscience is denied, or even simply mooted, then 'truth' must surely be relative and uncertain. Despite its obvious Reformation context the play makes no claim to establish what 'truth' is or should be. Nevertheless, almost paradoxically, as most critics have found, the play is 'obsessed with truth and the varieties of truth and testimony'.[32] The circulation of news in the play is frequently self-contradictory and endlessly changing. There is certainly no sense that England is going from darkness to enlightenment as the Henrician Reformation progresses: 'But that slander, sir, / Is found a truth now, for it grows again / Fresher then e'er it was . . . ' (2.1.152–4). This impression is reinforced by our growing awareness that facts are validated by rumour only: ''Tis most true: / These news are everywhere – every tongue speaks 'em, / And every true heart weeps for 't' (2.2.36–8).[33] What we have noted in the case of conscience applies equally to truth. Despite the state's will to control thought and impose its truth, truth is not a unitary, let alone unifying concept in the play, as each character appears to have his or her own truth. Cardinal Wolsey's response to his accusers, 'When the King knows my truth' (3.2.301), is a case in point.

Furthermore, the sovereign most closely associated with the English Reformation is made to recognize – before Archbishop Cranmer and Jacobean audiences – that truth does not always win the day. Providence does not necessarily guarantee the victory of reformed truth:

> and not ever
> The justice and the truth o' th' question carries
> The due o' th' verdict with it . . .
>
> (5.1.129–31)

It is the king's duty – will suggest Henry later – to see that truth *does* win the day – a statement which may have had a particular ring for a sovereign like James I.

Women in Henry VIII – Catholic versus Protestant?

Katherine and Mary, Anne and Elizabeth – the role played by these four women in *Henry VIII* is seldom mentioned. It does seem, however, that the play reads history with the benefit of hindsight, reconstructing a version of events which is deliberately oriented. Mary is hardly cited in the play, and her mother is sidestepped, while Anne is shown to be on the rise, in so much as she will give birth to Elizabeth. Yet, in many ways, Elizabeth remains a pawn – an instrument in the hands of the dramatists used to foreshadow the prophetic arrival of James I on the throne of England.

Thus, *outwardly*, everything is set for the victory of the Protestant Elizabeth (and of her Stuart successor) and for the downfall of the Catholic Katherine and of her daughter Mary. None the less, as we shall argue, such teleological interpretations are complicated by a number of ambiguities and by Katherine and Anne's ambivalent dramatic presence.

If Mary disappears in the course of the play, her mother cuts too strong a scenic figure to be totally obliterated by the image of the new Queen. While terms like 'conscience' or 'truth' seem to fluctuate in their meaning, Katherine is the one picture of stability, integrity and religiosity in the play. This does not mean that the Queen is totally devoid of ambivalence, as we shall see. Yet it does make us realize that Katherine probably left a lasting impression on the minds of a Jacobean audience. Most of the scenes in which she appears provide us with a stunning mixture of emotional tension and spirituality – enough no doubt to inspire or unsettle according to the spectator's personal beliefs and sensitivity.

Her most obvious association is with Catholicism. Critics, such as Glynne Wickham, have noted this: 'Shakespeare rewards her with a dream which bears close resemblance to pictures of the Assumption of the Virgin Mary as depicted by such mannerist painters as Corregio, Guido Reni, and Murillo'.[34] The choice of Katherine's place of trial also has historical and theatrical resonances: 'The most convenient place that I can think of / For such receipt of learning is Blackfriars,' says Henry (2.2.136–7). Blackfriars was originally a Dominican friary before the dissolution of the monasteries and was therefore easily associated with Roman Catholic culture. Blackfriars was where the famous Henrician divorce hearing took place and in more recent times it had become the indoor theatre occupied by Shakespeare's company, the King's Men, where early performances of *Henry VIII* may have been staged.[35] These associations were deemed sufficient by Wickham to propound the idea that, almost a century later, theatre was symbolically vindicating the rights of the Catholic Katherine: 'Shakespeare is repealing in Blackfriars that very banishment which an English Court had imposed upon her in Blackfriars'.[36]

It is true that there are moments in the play when Shakespeare and Fletcher clearly mark Katherine as Catholic. Her gradual feeling of estrangement from the English sovereign is conveyed by a plea which, to the ears of Jacobean audiences, associated her with the world of European Catholicism: 'spare me till I may / Be by my friends in Spain advised, whose counsel / I will implore' (2.4.52–3). Before exiting dramatically in the midst of the divorce hearings, Katherine announces that she intends to appeal to the Pope.[37] Yet Shakespeare and Fletcher are still careful, it seems, to make her appear loyal to England. As Wolsey addresses her in Latin, the Queen insists she be spoken to in English, which would alienate her from England and make her sound foreign: 'A strange tongue makes my cause more strange, suspicious. / Pray speak in English' (3.1.45–6). Katherine is pictured here as a faithful *English* Catholic.

Despite his frustration, Henry has to recognize before the audience that Katherine is 'saint-like' (2.4.135), while other Catholic characters like Wolsey or Gardiner are cast in a dubious light. The Queen is a Catholic with a conscience – a term which is not used lightly in her case. In front of Wolsey and Campeius, the papal legate, she declares:

> There's nothing I have done yet, o' my conscience,
> Deserves a corner. Would all other women
> Could speak this with as free a soul as I do.

> (3.1.30–2)

The scene of Katherine's dream vision (4.2.82.1-94) during which '*six Personages, clad in white robes*' conduct a symbolic coronation of the former Queen (before the actual coronation of Anne a few scenes later) has also been said to harbour Catholic undertones.[38] Indeed, these 'personages' are seen to '*hold a spare garland over her head, at which the other four make reverend curtsies*'. Thus, for Ruth Vanita:

> The play draws on Mariolatric imagery, the most powerful imagery available in Christian culture for the celebration of the human and the divine as woman, to accomplish this link. The three great pageants toward the close of the play, constructed like paintings in their silence, irresistibly recall three scenes which would be familiar to

the audience from Church iconography: the Coronation or mystical marriage of Mary, the Assumption, and the Presentation of the Virgin.[39]

Interestingly, Katherine's 'apotheosis' is a scene in which Patience, one of her ladies-in-waiting is present. Historically the character's name is an invention: there is no record of anyone in the Queen's entourage of that name. There is good reason to believe that the character – whose name is heard on stage – was intended to work as a kind of allegorical extension of a quality (Patience) which the dramatists repeatedly associate with Katherine in the play.[40] Thus, in the scene of her 'apotheosis' Katherine is assisted by Patience, literally and metaphorically.

Let us not forget, however, that in the scene of her 'Apotheosis' Katherine is also assisted by Griffith whose unbiased account of Wolsey's life and death (4.2.11-68) greatly impresses her to the extent that finally she too wishes to shun all truths of a sectarian nature:

> After my death I wish no other herald,
> No other speaker of my living actions,
> To keep mine honour from corruption
> But such an honest chronicler as Griffith.
> Whom I most hated living, thou hast made me,
> With thy religious truth and modesty,
> Now in his ashes honour. Peace be with him.

> (4.2.69–75)

This speech is a warning about the over-interpretation of Katherine as a straightforward Catholic martyr. Even if the image she casts in the play is undoubtedly Catholic, other sources for her deathbed vision seem to qualify and complicate the picture. Gordon McMullan cites three possible sources for this scene. Marguerite of Angoulême, Duchess of Alençon and Queen of Navarre was said to have had a similar dream and 'Marguerite was a reforming Catholic, a staunch defender of early French reformers – the young queen Elizabeth had translated one of her early works as a gift for her Protestant stepmother, Queen Katherine Parr . . . '.[41] Holinshed also reports that Anne Bullen had a dream vision just before her death.[42] Finally, in Thomas Heywood's *If You Know Not Me, You Know Nobody* (first published 1605), Elizabeth has a dream in which she is also defended by angels after being threatened by friars; she wakes up with a Bible in her hand.[43]

These suggested sources cannot of course dispel our sense of Katherine's 'Catholicity', but they do qualify our interpretation of her faith. If Shakespeare and Fletcher *did* make her dream the dreams of Protestant women this may not be for sectarian reasons, but perhaps to draw attention to what unites these women in their faith and hopes beyond the shades of their religious differences. This is certainly the case for Katherine and Anne:

> Rather than differentiating between them, the play seems perversely and deliberately to blur the differences between Katherine and Anne, and thus to make the transition from Roman Catholicism to Protestantism, as both symbolized in and provoked by Henry's divorce and remarriage, a much more problematic and unresolved process than might at first appear.[44]

Despite Wolsey's sectarian categorization of Anne as a 'spleeny Lutheran' (3.2.99), the two women are not so different. As early as Act 2, Katherine's divorce and Anne's future treason and beheading seemed strangely and poetically foreshadowed in Buckingham's last words: 'the long divorce of steel falls on me' (2.1.76). As has already been suggested, there is no real sense of a religious progression from a Catholic to a Protestant era. Katherine's image lingers on in ways which no doubt made Jacobean audiences uncomfortable. As Kim H. Noling notes, 'Even though Anne is in the political ascendant, of the two queens it is Katherine whom the audience sees and hears last'.[45]

Anne also strangely resembles Katherine, as she too is surrounded by Marian imagery. Indeed, the scene in which the Lord Chamberlain comes to inform her that the King has made her Marchioness of Pembroke could be construed as a kind of secular Annunciation with the Lord Chamberlain acting as the Angel Gabriel. 'You bear a gentle mind, and heavenly blessings / Follow such creatures', says the Lord Chamberlain to Anne (2.3.57–8). Anne, the so-called Virgin, responds on the same biblical lines echoing, with the word 'handmaid', a term used in Luke 1:38 and 48, a passage prescribed for 25 March (Lady Day or Annunciation) in the Elizabethan Book of Common Prayer:[46]

> I do not know
> What kind of my obedience I should tender.
> More than my all is nothing; nor my prayers
> Are not words duly hallowed, nor my wishes
> More worth than empty vanities; yet prayers and wishes

Are all I can return. Beseech your lordship,
Vouchsafe to speak my thanks and my obedience,
As from a blushing handmaid, to his highness,
Whose health and royalty I pray for.

(2.3.65–73)

After the Annunciation the play also stages a sort of Nativity scene, when the Old Lady brings the King news of Elizabeth's birth. Like a kind of (paradoxical) angel herself the Old Lady formally announces to Henry:[47]

Now good angels
Fly o'er thy royal head and shade thy person
Under their blessed wings.

(5.1.159–61)

It is not the least of paradoxes in a play that never ceases to confront us indirectly with confessional issues that the Protestant Anne is made to play the role of the Virgin Mary – she is indeed the chosen vessel. In this way, Anne's sectarian categorization as a 'Lutheran' is as invalid as Katherine's so-called Roman Catholicism. The very complexity of the two queens' symbolic fabrics redefines assumptions about the Reformation and the movement of history. Thus, reversing the perspective, the dramatists show us how the Protestant Anne can be seen as a Marian figure, but still be considered as an expendable genitor by the Catholic Gardiner:

The fruit she goes with
I pray for heartily, that it may find
Good time, and live. But, for the stock, Sir Thomas,
I wish it grubbed up now.

(5.1.20–3)

Shakespeare, Fletcher and the Reformation(s)

One of the interpretative keys to *Henry VIII* lies perhaps in its Prologue:

For, gentle hearers, know
To rank our chosen truth with such a show
As fool and fight is, beside forfeiting

> Our own brains and the opinion that we bring
> To make that only true we now intend,
> Will leave us never an understanding friend.
>
> (Prologue, 17–22)

Shakespeare and Fletcher's *Henry VIII* is not a crudely demonstrative, didactic play (cf. 'such a show'), it is a work whose deep concern is the nature of truth itself – in this way, what truths the play conveys ('our chosen truth') is as much the main topic of the piece as the reign of Henry VIII.

As we have already suggested, the discourse of truth is closely connected with the issues of the Reformation. For a chronicler like Raphael Holinshed, the Reformation happened when the King finally opened his eyes to what was truly going on around him especially among his prelates: 'But now, when God had illuminated the eies of the king, and that their subtile dooings were once espied; then men began charitablie to desire a reformation: and so at this parlement men began to show their grudges'.[48]

In the play there is nothing that closely resembles such godly illuminations as far as Henry is concerned. Evidently, the dramatists had fewer qualms about staging Henry VIII than Holinshed, who was writing during the reign of Henry's daughter, Elizabeth. Holinshed was clearly embarrassed when, in the course of his chronicle, he had to mention Henry's book *against* Luther, for which the Pope famously gave him the title of 'Defender of the Faith'. The chronicler was forced to mention Henry's confessional inconsistencies with hindsight. Holinshed openly admits to censoring his own text, so as to preserve the King's reputation:

> Of which booke published by the king, I will not (for reuerence of his roiallie) though I durst, report what I haue read: bicause we are to iudge honourablie of our rulers, and to speake nothing but good of the princes of the people. Onelie this breefe clause or fragment I will adde (least I might seeme to tell a tale of the man in the moone) that king Henrie in his said booke is reported to rage against the diuell and antichrist to cast out his fome against Luther . . . I suppresse the rest for shame, and returne to our historie.[49]

Shakespeare and Fletcher do not preserve the King's reputation – it seems that Henry's role in the field of religious reform is in fact questioned.

The issues of the Henrician Reformation emerge in the play, but they appear in a fragmented, disconnected way. When the word first appears, it has all the insubstantial characteristics of a passing fad: 'The reformation of our travelled gallants / That fill the court with quarrels, talk and tailors' (1.3.19–20). Indeed, from the perspective of 1612–13, the Reformation could be construed as something that had been and might come again, as fashions do: 'Thus Reformation is equated with passing fashion, and a model of history is implied which is a far cry from the linear hopes of reformers. Suddenly, Reformation ceases to be the goal of history, becoming instead at best a temporary reorientation awaiting a further turn of the wheel'.[50]

When the issues appear more directly, they are often rooted in personal feuds. Thus, Wolsey's animosity towards Anne Bullen and Cranmer is explained by the Cardinal's fear of seeing his ambitions thwarted by people who wish to gain favour with the King:

> Yet I know her for
> A spleeny Lutheran, and not wholesome to
> Our cause, that she should lie i'th'bosom of
> Our hard-ruled King. Again, there is sprung up
> An heretic, an arch-one, Cranmer, one
> Hath crawled into the favour of the King
> And is his oracle.

> (3.2.98–104)

The terms 'Lutheran' and 'heretic' are just bywords to describe the threat of up-and-coming new influences around the King. It is also noteworthy that – in the scene of the council meeting, during which Cranmer is directly accused by the Lord Chancellor and Archbishop Gardiner – the words 'reformed' and 'reformation' are used by Cranmer's Catholic opponents:

> CHANCELLOR[51] . . . you that best should teach us
> Have misdemeaned yourself, and not a little,
> Toward the King first, then his laws, in filling
> The whole realm, by your teaching and your chaplains' –
> For so we are informed – with new opinions,
> Diverse and dangerous, which are heresies
> And, not reformed, may prove pernicious.

> GARDINER Which reformation must be sudden too,
> My noble lords, for those that tame wild horses
> Pace 'em not in their hands to make 'em gentle,
> But stop their mouths with stubborn bits and spur 'em
> Till they obey the manage. If we suffer,
> Out of our easiness and childish pity
> To one man's honour, this contagious sickness,
> Farewell, all physic. And what follows then?
> Commotions, uproars, with a general taint
> Of the whole state, as of late days our neighbours,
> The upper Germany, can dearly witness,
> Yet freshly pitied in our memories.
>
> (5.2.47–65)

This passage does not make clear who is reforming what – its irony blurs the audience's perspective on the changes which are supposed to be taking place. When Henry intervenes to defend Cranmer it is surprising to see how lightly the King speaks of what has happened. The religious debates are set aside and Henry seems to treat the whole episode as a misunderstanding between people who should be friends:

> Well, well, my lords, respect him.
> Take him, and use him well: he's worthy of it.
> . . .
> Make me no more ado, but all embrace him.
> Be friends, for shame, my lords! . . .
>
> (5.2.187–8, 192–3)

We are gradually made aware of the futility of the Henrician Reformation, especially when the King dispels all ideological debates at the snap of his fingers with 'Come, lords, we trifle the time away' and, speaking of his newborn child, 'I long / To have this young one made a Christian' (5.2.212–13).[52] History has to move on in other words, but Henry's restlessness renders the whole movement of history almost insignificant. The meaningful outcome of these events is postponed *sine die*, as it were. As Gordon McMullan writes,

> The restless displacement of queens in Henry's life and reign, each change both conclusive and inconclusive, embodies the long-term process of Reformation: England moves from reign to reign in the

hope of religious resolution just as Henry moves from queen to queen in the hope of a son and heir.[53]

Indeed, Shakespeare depicts a restless and frustrated King Henry who – while the papal legates seem bent on coming to no conclusion – is made to complain: 'I may perceive / These cardinals trifle with me. I abhor / This dilatory sloth and tricks of Rome' (2.4.232–4). In the ensuing scenes Wolsey is condemned for trying to delay the divorce proceedings and for denying the ecclesiastical supremacy of Henry VIII (3.2.337–43). The King, who had seemed oblivious to Wolsey's so-called machinations in the first half of the play, is shown to be more determined and even becomes an all-seeing monarch nearer to the close.

In Act 5, when Cranmer is examined by the Council, the King and his physician appear, to quote Shakespeare and Fletcher, '*at a window above*' to observe the scene (5.2.18.1). The King, eavesdropping on his wrangling subjects, gives them his very personal definition of royal supremacy, one that is not devoid of totalitarian intentions: 'Is this the honour they do to one another? / 'Tis well there's one above 'em yet' (5.2.25–6). It is not so much that 'God had illuminated the eies of the king', to quote Holinshed again; it is rather that the long arm of tyranny is extending itself.[54]

Wolsey vs. Cranmer?

Given that the play tackles – directly or indirectly – the issues of the Henrician Reformation, the apparent opposition between the Catholic Wolsey and the Protestant Cranmer may have to be investigated more closely.

It is true that *Henry VIII* has *some* of the characteristics of a propaganda play like Rowley's *When You See Me, You Know Me*. Cardinal Wolsey is quickly demonized by characters like Buckingham: 'This holy fox, / Or wolf, or both – for he is equally ravenous / As he is subtle, and as prone to mischief / As able to perform't . . .' (1.1.158–61). Buckingham's son-in-law, the Earl of Surrey, completes the picture with a striking appellation: 'Thou scarlet sin' (3.2.255). Wolsey's robes become an iconic and synecdochic symbol of mischief: 'Your long coat' (3.2.276), 'a piece of scarlet' (3.2.280). Sectarian attacks usually demonize by depersonalizing their victims. Yet Shakespeare and Fletcher never allow this process to reach completion, as Wolsey's intense and complex personality comes gradually to the fore in the course of the play.

If Wolsey appears as the arch-villain at the beginning of the play it is because of his privileged political position – a niche which he has carved out for himself. Thus, behind the Lord Chamberlain's references to witchcraft, there is in filigree a jealous critique of the lowborn Cardinal's political sway: 'never attempt / Anything on him, for he hath a witchcraft / Over the King in's tongue' (3.2.17–19).

Such sectarian criticism partly conceals the fact that Henry makes a scapegoat of Wolsey. Indeed, Wolsey is used by Henry to reinforce his supremacy, in the wake of Buckingham's execution. It is only when Wolsey is too slow in answering Henry's demands that the Cardinal is accused of asserting papal jurisdiction in England, and thus of denying the ecclesiastical (*and political*) supremacy of the sovereign (3.2.337–41).

When Wolsey's downfall begins, his ensuing repentance seems genuine and somewhat unsettling. Holinshed has Wolsey declare that all the things he did were 'not regarding my seruice to God, but onelie to satisfie his [Henry's] pleasure'.[55] In Shakespeare and Fletcher's play it is also the King's pleasure that led him astray. Wolsey's repentance has in fact the features of a veiled accusation directed against his sovereign:

> Had I but served my God with half the zeal
> I served my King, he would not in mine age
> Have left me naked to mine enemies.
>
> (3.2.455–7)

Wolsey's downfall did not effect a religious reformation in the kingdom, it merely gave more powers to the sovereign. Holinshed sees Wolsey's disgrace as speeding things up for Henry especially as far as Henry's law of supremacy was concerned: 'In this submission the cleargie called the king supreame head of the church of England, which thing they neuer confessed before, wherevpon manie things followed after, as you shall heare'.[56]

Far from being the mere object of sectarian demonization Wolsey emerges from his disgrace as somewhat reformed: 'Vain pomp and glory of this world, I hate ye! / I feel my heart new opened. O, how wretched / Is that poor man that hangs on princes' favours!' (3.2.365–7). Indeed, the Cardinal has learned that one can never expect too much in terms of favours from a sovereign like Henry. It may well be that Wolsey is the only character in the play – apart from Katherine of Aragon – to have effected a kind of reformation, or at least to have reached some sort of spirituality. The Cardinal's claim that the King cured him has an ironical ring, however, as what we know of Henry in the play tends to demonstrate that he was an involuntary agent of change:

> I know myself now, and I feel within me
> A peace above all earthly dignities,
> A still and quiet conscience. The King has cured me . . .
>
> (3.2.378–80)

Cranmer follows in Wolsey's footsteps in the sense that he too is demonized. Wolsey, who knows the ropes, feels threatened by the Archbishop's capacity to attract favour, and this again translates into sectarian terms: 'An heretic, an arch-one, Cranmer, one / Hath crawled into the favour of the King' (3.2.102–3). Yet this artificial polarization is quickly dispelled. Cranmer resembles Wolsey – he is equally tied to his sovereign's whims for better or for worse: 'Thy truth and thy integrity is rooted / In us, thy friend . . . ' says Henry to Cranmer (5.1.114–15). The dramatists even have Henry swear Catholic oaths in defence of the Protestant Archbishop, which slightly undermines the symbolic value of his choice of Cranmer in the history of Protestantism: 'He's honest, on mine honour. God's blest mother, / I swear he is true-hearted, and a soul / None better in my kingdom' (5.1.153–5); 'By holy Mary, Butts, there's knavery!' (5.2.32).

With Cranmer's symbolic godfathering of Elizabeth ('You must be godfather and answer for her', says Henry (5.2.196)), in the last scene of the play (5.4) one can almost believe in an overall Protestant narrative, which begins with a slippage of function between father and godfather:

> the final tableau shows a king whose intemperance is a failure of manliness and therefore of political efficacy and who must be replaced by a Protestant martyr as a symbolic father-figure for England. The iconography thus decentres the King, removing him from full paternity and leaving the circumstances of Elizabeth's birth (and consequently her legitimacy) as shrouded as is her death in Cranmer's prophecy.[57]

One is indeed caught by the power of Cranmer's opening gambit: 'Let me speak, sir, / For heaven now bids me; and the words I utter / Let none think flattery, for they'll find 'em truth' (5.4.14–16). As we shall see, however, the contents of this prophecy (which has no chronicle source) are far from straightforward. There is also one further complication, often overlooked by critics – the controversial nature of prophecies in the play. This is precisely what casts a dubious light on Cranmer's *finale*.

Indeed, Henry's reign is plagued by prophecies, such as the story that causes Buckingham's fall because its contents were considered a potential threat to the King:

> SURVEYOR   He was brought to this
> By a vain prophecy of Nicholas Hopkins.
> KING What was that Hopkins?
> SURVEYOR   Sir, a Chartreux friar,
> His confessor, who fed him every minute
> With words of sovereignty.
>
>   (1.2.146–50)

Prophecies are uncertain, and they may be fabricated, but what is clear is that they are not always without effect, and can work on the imagination: 'I told my lord the Duke, by th' devil's illusions / The monk might be deceived, and that 'twas dangerous / For him to ruminate on this so far until / It forged him some design . . . ' (1.2.178–81). This prophecy is also commented on by the anonymous gentlemen who reflect on the events of the play as a kind of chorus (2.1.21–3).

As Alistair Fox has demonstrated, prophecies under the reign of Henry VIII were often a means of subversion, especially for ordinary folk who had otherwise little hold on the course of historical events.[58] They could be a means of protest against change, and in this way they were regarded as dangerous by the authorities who wished to impose their official version of events, and their view of where history was going. Interestingly, the same year Elizabeth was born (1533) Holinshed mentions in his *Chronicles* the trial of Elizabeth Barton who was brought before the Star Chamber and charged with high treason for spreading seditious rumours based on prophecies, which were deemed dangerous by the government. She also had accomplices among the Catholic clergy:

> the forenamed Elizabeth Barton and other hir complices were attainted of treason, for sundrie practised deuises and tales by them aduanced, put in vse, and told, sounding to the vtter reproch, perill, and destruction of the kings person, his honour, fame and dignitie: for they had of a diuelish intent put in the heads of manie of the kings subiects, that to the said Elizabeth Barton was giuen knowledge

by reuelation from God and his saints, that if the king proceeded to the diuorse, and maried another, he should not be king of this realme one moneth after, and in the reputation of God not one daie nor houre.[59]

In many ways, Cranmer's speech has all the traits of an official prophecy (one that unites the Tudor and Stuart lines) spoken to consolidate an audience's belief in the strength of a Protestant state. But at the same time it is a complex piece of theatre written with hindsight and with knowledge of the present. The liberties it takes with time are as seductive as they are also politically dire. One of the implications of Cranmer's prophecy is that James should model himself on Elizabeth, an affirmation which certainly irritated the Stuart sovereign. James was criticized obliquely by poets who sang the praises of his predecessors:

> She shall be –
> But few now living can behold that goodness –
> A pattern to all princes living with her
> And all that shall succeed.

> (5.4.20–3)

The true feat of Cranmer's prophecy is that it announces another miraculous birth. 'Yet a virgin' (5.4.60), Elizabeth will manage to 'engender' her successor, King James: 'Her ashes new create another heir' (5.4.41). Yet the prophecy explicitly sets a high standard for James. The legacy is a difficult one for the Stuart king, who – supposedly – 'from the sacred ashes of her honour / Shall star-like rise as great in fame as she was / And so stand fixed' (5.4.45–7).

There are other unsettling elements in Cranmer's prophecy – as we gradually become aware that it does not fit into the so-called Protestant discourse of millenarian hope. The prophecy can be read more as a social comment, and in this way it resembles more 'popular' forms of prophecies, which, as we have said, are a response to specific social needs and tensions. As a result, such prophecies tend to be subversive. Archbishop Cranmer's prophecy does indeed convey a surprisingly egalitarian message which contests the alleged natural superiority of those who are noble by birth and not by deed:

God shall be truly known, and those about her
From her shall read the perfect ways of honour
And by those claim their greatness, not by blood.

(5.4.36–8)

As the play is about to close, Cranmer's prophecy about the reign of Elizabeth I and that of James I cannot dispel the impression that Henry VIII's reformist intentions remain futile, or at the very least inconclusive. It was probably obvious to any member of Shakespeare and Fletcher's audience that England had still not received the 'thousand thousand blessings' (5.4.19) promised by Archbishop Cranmer, and that it was far from such proleptic statements as, 'God shall be truly known' (5.4.36) and 'Our children's children / Shall see this and bless heaven' (5.4.54–5).[60]

* * *

''Tis ten to one this play can never please / All that are here', says the Epilogue (1–2) of Shakespeare and Fletcher's *Henry VIII*. How could it please everyone, as the dramatists had underlined the contradictions of English history behind its apparent continuity and progress.[61] The Reformation was a topic which, at all events, seemed to dissatisfy all parties, judging, for instance, by what John Harington had to say about it:

> And I conclude that which all honest men I think will assent with me, that the beginning of Reformation that King Henrie the viiith made was not so sincere, but that it was myxed with private and politique respectes, of gayne, of revenge, of fancie; and finally that even in Protestants opinions it was not worthie the name of a Reformation; and I am sure the Papistes counte it a confusion, a destruction, and a deformation.[62]

Shakespeare, who had denounced the unsavoury collusion between religion and high politics in a play like *Richard III*, who had had a hand in the writing of *Thomas More* – a work which vindicated the 'conscience' of an individual against reason of state – had dared to confront the complexities of the Henrician schism once again with *Henry VIII*. If the religious creeds of his patrons had been diverse during his theatrical career, Shakespeare, it seems, never veered in his view that religious reformations are not 'once and for all events'. Nor was he tempted to impose meaning upon history. There is no teleology, nor is there any revealed truth, even in a play like *All is True (Henry VIII)*. Shakespeare and Fletcher acknowledge the Henrician schism mostly through its political consequences. Their anachronisms show, none the less, that there is no clear cultural demarcation line between the world of the late Middle Ages and the so-called age of reform. Something has happened which has altered the world, but the full meaning of these events is denied. If the dramatists turn history into story they refrain from turning it into fable.

Conclusion

'Shackspeers Plaies are printed in the best Crowne paper, far better than most Bibles', complained William Prynne.[1] The paranoid and monomaniac author of *Histrio-mastix, The Players Scourge* (1633) – a mammoth and delirious sum of anti-theatrical arguments – obviously took great pleasure in propounding the false idea of a radical incompatibility between theatre (Shakespeare's plays in particular) and the religious culture of early modern England. The different chapters of this book show, on the contrary, that Shakespeare had an unfailing interest in religious questions. Indeed, religion in his English history plays is not just a byword for politics, nor does a secularist vein necessarily run through all Shakespeare's work, as the dramatist's approach to confessional issues betrays his genuine concern for matters of religion.

From an historical point of view, the probable implication of Shakespeare's own company – the Chamberlain's Men – in the Essex rebellion with the staging of a spurious version of *Richard II* is indicative of the fact that the playwright may have wanted to side with the religious malcontents. Yet the episode has larger ideological consequences. No doubt it also demonstrated to the players how matters mixing religion and politics could easily become inflated almost beyond recognition, when a well-tried sectarian scenario was applied to events in an attempt to shape their interpretation.

Early modern England remained extremely volatile. For those who were ideologically committed and who happened to be on the wrong side of the fence, this was a world which could appear frustrating and deeply unjust. The Catholic Cardinal William Allen had spoken of 'this great miserie, and mutation of state and Religion in this our realme of England'. He reproached the English 'for tollerating the wicked

Jesabell' and castigated Elizabeth, who, in his eyes, was nothing but a 'pretensed Queene', 'an incestuous bastard', who even 'abused her bodie'.[2] For men of Allen's ilk there was little room for compromise and half measures. Elizabethan polemics produced cartloads of stereotypical images, of clear-cut and conveniently demonized adversaries who could be dismissed at will. Yet, paradoxically, the pamphlet war did nothing to clarify issues – it only made the interpretative crisis greater, as it quickly became obvious to many and especially to playwrights like Shakespeare, that polemical images were reversible. With a high degree of lucidity, one of the great decision-makers of Elizabethan and Jacobean England, Secretary of State Robert Cecil, remarked in 1605 that 'whosoever shall behold the papistes with puritane spectacles, or the puritan with papistical, shal see no other certeynte, that the multiplication of false images.'[3] Such so-called interpretative strategies fostered antagonisms, widened confessional rifts and only worsened the century-long fracture between Catholics and Protestants. As has been pointed out in the course of this book, the risk for us, as we look back on Elizabethan England, is to embrace these skewed visions by taking at face value the writings of those who never ceased wearing their distorting spectacles. The danger would be to accept 'as value-free social reportage what were deeply ideological, polemically structured acts of interpretation, textual interventions produced from within . . . ' to further specific agendas.[4]

Shakespeare's history plays have a different story to tell. The way in which the playwright focuses on religious debates in these plays indicates his awareness that religious controversies are largely fabricated by the more committed agents of history. What is also equally apparent in the series of plays we have studied is the enduring presence of a set of questions which the self-styled proponents of religious truth can never answer satisfactorily. How, for instance, does one come to terms with religious change? Does history have a meaning? Are our lives conditioned by providence? Can we shape our destiny? How does one deal with the dead? How does one reconcile religious conscience with the necessities of everyday life and of politics at large? How far should faith influence our lives? What is religious truth? These are some of the many recurring questions which we have identified in the course of this book.

Shakespeare stages characters who are groping for meaning, looking in different, sometimes opposite directions and picking up diverse material to construct tentative answers. The sense of flux and instability which is a characteristic of his history plays is also the hallmark of a period caught in religious and ideological turmoil. Despite the rigidity of religious polemics, reference points kept changing and religious labels were sometimes applied in ways which made Shakespeare's contemporaries uneasy. John Harington regretted that 'these odious tearmes of traytors used to Papists by those that have bene Papistes and served Papistes themselves, hath both encreased their number and their malice'.[5] Another contemporary, Edward Sandys, condemned the lies produced by religious propaganda which, according to the author of *A Relation of the State of Religion* (1605), had blurred Christian truth:

> And verily in this kinde, both the Protestants and Papistes seeme generally in the greatest part of their stories, to be both to blame, though both not equally, having by their passionate reports much wronged the truth, abused this present age, and preiudiced posteritie: insomuch, that the onely remedie now seeming to remaine, is to read indifferently the stories on both parts, to count them as advocates and to play the Iudge betweene them.[6]

Sandys's Jacobean irenic dream of objectivity was not necessarily one that Shakespeare shared entirely or indeed advocated unambiguously in his work.[7] Holinshed, one of the playwright's main sources for his histories, pleaded for 'libertie of conscience' and the settlement of religious disagreement 'rather... with the word than with the sword'.[8] It cannot be said that Shakespeare clearly promoted compromise solutions in the field of religion. It seems rather that these were not the terms in which he envisaged or even approached such questions. He is clearly toying with the old and the new in his plays and this ability to associate recent and more traditional forms is an artistic feature of his work, but it is also a capacity which Shakespeare had in common with many of his fellow Elizabethans.

As an artist, Shakespeare could read beyond the antagonistic models created by religious propaganda and so could a substantial number of his contemporaries. This is something which we, as modern interpreters of Shakespeare, also need to do, as we tend to overlook the fact that early modern English men and women could find ways to accommodate religious difference without necessarily negating it altogether. In our attempts to interpret Shakespeare's plays we should not therefore underestimate 'the ability of the culture to absorb new beliefs while retaining old ones, to forge hybrid forms, to accommodate contradictions and ambiguities'.[9] As Christopher Marsh explains, "Sixteenth-century people... often seem to have been adept at living with contradictions. This does not appear to have been an 'either/or' society, though attempts were under way to turn it into one".[10]

This is not to say that there were never any points of disjuncture or that these disruptions never influenced a dramatist with such an acute ear as Shakespeare. In this book our point has been that the play-wright's histories self-consciously harbour the old and the new, that they engage with many of the religious issues of their time, but – more fundamentally – that they not only have the power to pose pressing questions but also to allow potential contradictions to remain. This is a logic which is largely alien to us, but it is one which was able to 'absorb the new without necessarily abandoning the old, and without necessarily resolving the resultant contradictions'.[11] This was not, for all that, a culture of consensus; nor is Shakespeare's dramatic work an exercise in fence-sitting. There is always a real sense of unease in his plays – a paradoxical sense that if confrontational models ceased to exist altogether, indeterminacy would also be too much to bear. One Elizabethan writer condemned the tendency to 'conceive a mixt Religion, compounded of that which is best in both'. The Elizabethans' mongrel religion appeared to another writer as a confessional 'hodge podge of altogither'.[12] Fluidity created anxiety – a feeling which still affects us as interpreters of Shakespeare and which perhaps prevents us from accepting the full implications of Shakespeare's hybrid faith – a faith he shared with many of his fellow Elizabethans in an era traversed by cultural and religious instability.[13]

Notes

Introduction: Shakespeare's Hybrid Faith

1. E. Duffy, *The Stripping of the Altars, Traditional Religion in England c. 1400–c. 1580* (New Haven, CT and London: Yale University Press, 1992), p. 3. For an overview of how these debates began, see J. Candido, ed., *King John, Shakespeare: The Critical Tradition* (London and Atlantic Highlands, NJ: Athlone Press, 1996), pp. 14–15; and, more recently, T. Kozuka, 'Shakespeare in Purgatory: a Study of the Catholicising Movement in Shakespeare Biography' (unpublished PhD thesis, University of Warwick, 2003). K. Jackson and A. F. Marotti sketch the broader philosophical context in their seminal article: 'The Turn to Religion in Early Modern English Studies', *Criticism*, 46 (2004) 167–90.

2. As Arthur Marotti writes, 'Any discussion of religion and Shakespeare is an overdetermined one, related, as it is, to the emotionally invested ideological or confessional appropriations of that author as well as to the underlying schemes of cultural and literary history that have been constructed to contain his writings and those of other early moderns' (A. F. Marotti, 'Shakespeare and Catholicism', in *Theatre and Religion, Lancastrian Shakespeare*, ed. R. Dutton, A. Findlay and R. Wilson (Manchester and New York: Manchester University Press, 2003), p. 218). For a similar nineteenth-century appraisal, see C. Knight Watson, 'Was Shakspeare [sic] a Roman Catholic?', *Edinburgh Review*, 123 (1866) 146).

3. Davies was Rector of Saperton, Gloucestershire, until 1708. His note on Shakespeare's religion, which he made some seventy years after the dramatist's death, cannot be dated more precisely. Davies' terse statement is sometimes taken almost at face value by scholars: see, for instance, D. N. Beauregard, 'New Light on Shakespeare's Catholicism: Prospero's Epilogue in *The Tempest*', *Renascence*, 49.3 (1997) 160–1; 172 *et passim*.

4. Chateaubriand and Carlyle, cited in H. Mutschmann and K. Wentersdorf, *Shakespeare and Catholicism* (New York: Sheed and Ward, 1952), p. vi.

5. He was shortly followed by the Frenchman A.-F. Rio, who published his *Shakespeare catholique* (Paris: Bray et Retaux) in 1864. Both Rio's and Simpson's books were reviewed (unfavourably) in 1866 in the *Edinburgh Review* (C. Knight Watson, 'Was Shakespeare a Roman Catholic?', *The Edinburgh Review*, 123 (1866) 146–85).

6. See H. S. Bowden, *The Religion of Shakespeare, Chiefly from the Writings of the Late Mr. Richard Simpson* (London: Burns & Oats, 1899); W. S. Lilly, 'What was Shakespeare's Religion?', in his *Studies in Religion and Literature* (London: Chapman and Hall, 1904), pp. 1–30; and Richard Wilson's recent homage to Simpson in his introduction to *Theatre and Religion, Lancastrian Shakespeare*, pp. 1–39.

7. R. Simpson, 'Was Shakespeare a Catholic?', *The Rambler, A Catholic Journal and Review*, New Series, vol. 2, part 7 (1854) 35. Simpson expounded his theory

more fully in a series of articles published in 1858 (R. Simpson, 'What was the Religion of Shakespeare? [part 1], *The Rambler, A Catholic Journal and Review*, new series, vol. 9 (1858) 168–87; 'What was the Religion of Shakespeare? [part 2], *The Rambler, A Catholic Journal and Review*, new series, vol. 9 (1858) 232–319; 'What was the Religion of Shakespeare? [part 3], *The Rambler, A Catholic Journal and Review*, new series, vol. 9 (1858) 302–87). His conclusion to the last of these essays makes him appear somewhat of a proselyte. Confident that Shakespeare chose to die a Catholic, he writes: 'Shall this lesson be lost upon the people of England that almost worship him? Are you, dear Protestant reader, a wiser man than Shakespeare?' (p. 319).

8. Peter Milward seems to have followed in a similar vein of criticism (without the implicit social prejudices of these two authors), especially in his recent work, *The Catholicism of Shakespeare's Plays* (Southampton: Saint Austin Press, 1997) in which he claims that the dramatist's Catholicism is 'a precious key, even the only key, to unlock the hidden heart of Shakespeare and to sound the hitherto unsounded depths of his mystery' (p. 141). Many of his earlier works, however, especially his books on Elizabethan and Jacobean religious polemics, are important contributions to the field of the history of ideas (*Religious Controversies of the Elizabethan Age: a Survey of Printed Sources* (Lincoln, NB and London: University of Nebraska Press, 1977); *Religious Controversies of the Jacobean Age: a Survey of Printed Sources* (London: Scolar Press, 1978)).

9. Mutschmann and Wentersdorf, *Shakespeare and Catholicism*, p. 35.

10. E. A. J. Honigmann, *Shakespeare: the 'Lost Years'* (Manchester and New York: Manchester University Press, 1998 [1985]), pp. 114; 125 *et passim*.

11. For a nuanced critique of some of Honigmann's views, see R. Bearman, '"Was William Shakespeare William Shakeshafte?' Revisited", *Shakespeare Quarterly*, 53.1 (2002) 83–94. See also Honigmann's response: 'The Shakespeare/Shakeshafte Question, Continued', *Shakespeare Quarterly*, 54.1 (2003) 83–6.

12. Eric Sams, for instance, writes that 'there is no reason to dispute that Shakespeare was not only a cradle Catholic, but a death-bed one also', but hardly explains why one should be so certain (E. Sams, *The Real Shakespeare, Retrieving the Early Years, 1564–1594* (New Haven, CT and London: Yale University Press, 1995), p. 12).

13. G. Taylor, 'Forms of Opposition: Shakespeare and Middleton', *English Literary Renaissance*, 24.2 (1994) 296.

14. Cf. H. Hammerschmidt-Hummel's *Die verborgene Existenz des William Shakespeare: Dichter und Rebell im katholischen Untergrund* (Freiburg: Herder, 2001) and E. A. J. Honigmann's criticism of some of the book's premises in 'Catholic Shakespeare? A Response to Hildegard Hammerschmidt-Hummel', *Connotations*, 12.1 (2002/3) 52–60. See also R. Wilson, *Secret Shakespeare, Studies in Theatre, Religion and Resistance* (Manchester and New York: Manchester University Press, 2004). Clare Asquith follows in a similar vein but, unlike Wilson, singularly overstates her case in *Shadowplay: the Hidden Beliefs and Coded Politics of William Shakespeare* (New York: Public Affairs, 2005). Stephen Greenblatt's recent 'fictional' biography of Shakespeare is more cautious, particularly in its depiction of the young

Catholic Shakespeare: *Will in the World: How Shakespeare became Shakespeare* (London: Cape, 2004), esp. pp. 87–117.

15. As Park Honan writes prudently, 'We can only be tentative; an "alternative narrative" can give us no more than pictures from beyond the edges of Shakespeare's known experience' (P. Honan, *Shakespeare, A Life* (Oxford: Oxford University Press, 1998), p. 65).

16. In such cases, Michael Davies writes, 'we are left with nothing but a false syllogism, a snake with its tail in its own mouth' (M. Davies, 'On this Side Bardolatry: the Canonisation of the Catholic Shakespeare', *Cahiers Élisabéthains*, 58 (2000) 38).

17. 'I cannot prove that Shakespeare was a Catholic,' wrote Gary Taylor, adding characteristically, 'But then, if he were one, he would have had strong incentives to prevent *anyone* from being able to prove it' (Taylor, 'Forms of Opposition', p. 298). Michael Alexander was to write likewise that 'The possibility that William Shakespeare was a Roman Catholic is a question under active scholarly discussion. It is not likely ever to be proved either way . . .'. But Alexander begs his readers subsequently to suspend their disbelief in order for him to make his case for a Catholic Shakespeare (M. Alexander, 'Shakespeare's Catholicism? or "You would pluck out the heart of my mystery"', *Quadrant*, 42.12 (1998) 46). Similarly, Eamon Duffy has to admit that no proof has yet been conclusive, but his turn of phrase is significant: 'if we cannot quite be sure that Shakespeare was a Catholic, it becomes clearer and clearer that he must have struck alert contemporaries as a most unsatisfactory Protestant' (E. Duffy, 'Bare Ruined Choirs: Remembering Catholicism in Shakespeare's England', in *Theatre and Religion, Lancastrian Shakespeare*, p. 56). In an earlier article, Duffy had concluded similarly that: 'Whether or not Shakespeare can be claimed as a Catholic writer, he was certainly not a Protestant one' (*The Tablet*, 27 April 1996, p. 538). More recently, Richard Wilson, in the introduction to the proceedings of a 1999 conference devoted in part to Shakespeare's alleged Catholicism, has recognized that such a scenario remains a hypothesis: 'For though the startling idea that he was born and brought up not "in love" but *in hate* for Elizabeth and her empire remains only a hypothesis, there can be few theories with a greater potential for transforming the way we see and study Shakespeare'. It is equally striking to note that it is the potentially revolutionary aspects of this theory which are seemingly put forward rather than its degree of plausibility (Wilson, 'Introduction', in *Theatre and Religion, Lancastrian Shakespeare*, p. 32). In *Secret Shakespeare*, Wilson goes further and makes his argument more complex. He sketches a fascinating figure, that of a closet Catholic, a quietist Shakespeare in the fashion of the French philosopher Montaigne. Wilson cannot prove his point definitively, but the fact that it cannot be proved proves it for him: Shakespeare sought to cover up his crypto-Catholic identity and wrote his entire work 'out of silence', as Wilson puts it, concluding in the following fashion: 'We might infer this. But the fact that we could not prove it, unless we broke the taboo and desecrated the tomb, is the ultimate guarantee of Shakespeare's secrecy and so sets the seal upon his work, which likewise depends for cultural power on remaining forever questionable . . .' (Wilson, *Secret Shakespeare*, pp. 295, 297). For a conclusion similar in tone,

cf. I. Wilson's *Shakespeare: The Evidence, Unlocking the Mysteries of the Man and His Works* (London: Headline, 1993), pp. 411–12.

18. See, for examples of this polarization: A. F. Marotti, 'Alienating Catholics in Early Modern England: Recusant Women, Jesuits, and Ideological Fantasies', in *Catholicism and Anti-Catholicism in Early Modern English Texts*, ed. A. F. Marotti (Basingstoke: Macmillan, 1999), pp. 1–34.

19. As Claire McEachern perceptively points out, 'to identify a theology is a far cry from specifying the mixture of values, sentiments, emotions, convictions, and practices that constitute individual devotion. The authors most of interest to literary scholars in this regard are so not because their brand of religion is so apparent but because it is so complexly layered and multiply determined, evincing a slippage between official doctrine and personal belief that preoccupied the Tudor–Stuart authorities as well as modern scholars' (C. McEachern, 'Introduction', in *Religion and Culture in Renaissance England*, ed. C. McEachern and D. Shuger (Cambridge: Cambridge University Press, 1997), pp. 6–7).

20. Beatrice Batson has noted how much questions of methodology seemed to have plagued Christian readings of Shakespeare's plays (E. B. Batson, ed., *Selected Comedies and Late Romances of Shakespeare from a Christian Perspective* (Lewiston, Queenstown, Lampeter: Edwin Mellen Press, 2002), p. viii).

21. P. Collinson, 'William Shakespeare's Religious Inheritance and Environment', in his *Elizabethan Essays* (London and Rio Grande: Hambledon Press, 1994), p. 251.

22. See, for instance, H. Thurston, 'A Controverted Shakespeare Document', *The Dublin Review*, 173 (1923) 161–76; J. H. de Groot, *The Shakespeare's and 'The Old Faith'* (Fraser: Real-View-Books, 1995 [1946]), esp. pp. 3–110; J. G. McManaway, 'John Shakespeare's "Spiritual Testament"', *Shakespeare Quarterly*, 18.3 (1967) 197–205; D. L. Thomas and N. E. Evans, 'John Shakespeare in The Exchequer', *Shakespeare Quarterly*, 35.3 (1984) 315–18; F. W. Brownlow, 'John Shakespeare's Recusancy: New Light on an Old Document', *Shakespeare Quarterly*, 40.2 (1989) 186–91; and Wilson, *Secret Shakespeare*, pp. 50–2. The issue has again been debated recently with Robert Bearman's proposal that John Shakespeare's 'Catholic' testament may have been a forgery (see: ' "John Shakespeare's Spiritual Testament": A Reappraisal', *Shakespeare Survey*, 56 (2003) 184–203). Bearman, who resumes some of J. O. Halliwell-Phillips' points made about the document more than a century ago, is however unable to prove his case definitively (see J. O. Halliwell-Phillips, *Outlines of the Life of Shakespeare*, 2 vol. (London, 1898), vol. 2, pp. 399–404).

23. Collinson, 'William Shakespeare's Religious Inheritance and Environment', p. 250. Collinson adds: 'That John Shakespeare was a municipal officer when the guild chapel was Protestantised proves nothing. Indeed, the fact that the great doom painting was whitewashed over rather than destroyed suggests the kind of crypto-Catholic conduct of which Puritans often complained' (p. 250).

24. See Marotti, 'Shakespeare and Catholicism', in *Theatre and Religion, Lancastrian Shakespeare*, p. 221.

25. Collinson, 'William Shakespeare's Religious Inheritance and Environment', p. 219.

26. P. Collinson, 'Comment on Eamon Duffy's Neale Lecture and the Colloquium', in *England's Long Reformation 1500–1800*, ed. N. Tyacke (London: University College London Press, 1998), p. 72. The so-called settlement was in fact the result of intense political manoeuvring and left many important matters *unsettled*: 'When it initially proved impossible to obtain a passage of the necessary legislation through the House of Lords because of Catholic opposition, a religious debate was staged which was a charade, intended to provide a pretext for imprisoning some of the recalcitrant bishops and so massaging a parliamentary majority in favour of the settlement' (P. Collinson, 'The Mongrel Religion of Elizabethan England', in *Elizabeth, The Exhibition at the National Maritime Museum*, ed. Susan Doran (London: Chatto & Windus, 2003), p. 28).

27. P. Marshall, *Reformation England 1480–1642* (London: Arnold, 2003), pp. 118–19. MacCulloch concurs with this interpretation of the Queen's Protestantism: 'Protestantism indeed, but not in the uncompromising form prevailing in the Church of Edward VI' (D. MacCulloch, *The Later Reformation in England, 1547–1603*, 2nd edn. (Basingstoke: Palgrave, 2001 [1990]), pp. 25–6). On the failures of Elizabethan evangelism, particularly in the north of England, see C. Haigh, 'Puritan Evangelism in the reign of Elizabeth I', *The English Historical Review*, 72 (1977) 30–58, esp. 56.

28. B. L. MS Cotton Julius FVI f. 161; see also J. Guy, *Tudor England* (Oxford: Oxford University Press, 1988), pp. 259–60.

29. 'The Reformation was something which happened in the reigns of Elizabeth and James I' (P. Collinson, *The Birthpangs of Protestant England* (Basingstoke: Macmillan, 1988), p. ix).

30. Indeed, Peter Marshall remarks that: 'The Elizabethan Church settlement of 1559, or arguably the final promulgation of the Thirty-nine articles in 1571, marks the terminal date of the English Reformation considered as an officially directed restructuring of doctrine and worship. But in terms of restructuring the religious beliefs of the mass of the English people, these dates more closely resemble starters' flags than finishing posts' (Marshall, *Reformation England*, p. 233). Christopher Haigh has also pointed out that the success or failure of the Reformation was a question of whose perspective was adopted: 'By the minimal standards established by the crown and enforced by the bishops, Reformation had succeeded; by the standards evangelical ministers set themselves, it had failed' (C. Haigh, 'Success and Failure in the English Reformation', *Past and Present*, 173 (2001) 48–49).

31. J. J. Scarisbrick, *The Reformation and the English People* (Oxford: Oxford University Press, 1984), p. 1.

32. C. Haigh, *English Reformations, Religion, Politics, and Society under the Tudors* (Oxford: Clarendon Press, 1993), p. 280.

33. Haigh, *English Reformations*, p. 16. Haigh's critique of the Whig conception of historical change is equally pertinent: 'Change will seem easy if its opponents are left out of the story, or treated as silly old fogeys destined for defeat' (p. 16). Haigh, like Eamon Duffy, also rejects the traditional accounts of the causes of the Reformation, i.e. that 'The early Tudor monopolistic Church was weakened by spiritual decadence and mere conformism, and its leadership divided by ambition and faction, so it could not resist the challenge of heresy'. This version of events was – surprisingly enough – one which

had been fostered by the English Jesuits themselves: Father Robert Parsons had, through a 'form of "Catholic whiggery"', writes Haigh, put forward this partisan scenario in order 'to defend the novelty of his own order and the missionary method, and to discredit the conservative, hierarchically minded clergy who attacked the Jesuits and their ways' (C. Haigh, 'From Monopoly to Minority: Catholicism in Early Modern England', *Transactions of the Royal Historical Society*, 5th series, 31 (1981) 129; 130).

34. Haigh, *English Reformations*, p. 15. See D. Kuller Shuger, *Habits of Thought in the English Renaissance, Religion, Politics, and the Dominant Culture* (Berkeley, Los Angeles and Oxford: University of California Press, 1990), p. 9. Shuger sees the defining of what she calls 'sacred *loci*' as fundamental to the functioning of early modern society: 'What makes a society Christian is not just that its people are mostly Christians, nor that Christianity is the state religion, but that grace and peace and eternal righteousness . . . are at work in its midst, taming the powers of evil. The early modern attempts to identify where in a community this work takes place – to identify, that is, its sacral loci – are attempts to imagine the nature of Christian social order' (D. Kuller Shuger, *Political Theologies in Shakespeare's England, The Sacred and the State in* Measure for Measure (Basingstoke: Palgrave, 2001), p. 47.

35. Shuger, *Habits of Thought*, p. 225.

36. 'Most particularly, Collinson has transformed our understanding of 'Puritanism', a phenomenon we can no longer view as an 'opposition party', the symmetrical counterpart of Catholic recusancy, but rather as a set of attitudes and impulses making for 'further Reformation' which was situated close to the mainstream of contemporary Protestantism' (Marshall, *Reformation England*, p. 5).

37. MacCulloch, *The Later Reformation in England*, p. 55. Peter Marshall even argues that: 'Debates about what it meant to be a Protestant continued up to the Civil War, itself a kind of violent referendum on the sort of Protestant nation England ought to be and become' (Marshall, *Reformation England*, p. 166).

38. Marshall, *Reformation England*, p. 169. Indeed, Peter Lake notes that 'This rendered the national Church a very broad Church indeed; one which, given the laxity with which conformity was, in practice, enforced under Elizabeth, included everyone who was not a Protestant sectary or Separatist or an avowedly popish recusant' (P. Lake, 'Religious Identities in Shakespeare's England', in *A Companion to Shakespeare*, ed. D. S. Kastan (Oxford: Blackwell, 1999), p. 63).

39. See A. Walsham, *Church Papists: Catholicism, Conformity and Confessional Polemic in Early Modern England* (Woodbridge: Boydell and Brewer, 1993). Peter Lake points out that the label was an instrument to force people to take sides openly: 'Catholic *engagés* and evangelicals like Parsons and Campion were developing the concept of the Church Papist as a way to tighten the dominant definition of what being a Catholic in England meant and thus force as many Church Papists into overt recusancy as possible' (Lake, 'Religious Identities in Shakespeare's England', p. 71).

40. Collinson, 'The Mongrel Religion of Elizabethan England', in *Elizabeth, The Exhibition at the National Maritime Museum*, p. 31 *et passim*. This is where I disagree slightly with Arthur Marotti's view that Catholicism in

Elizabethan England was 'residual': 'the older, but residual, Catholic culture whose 'symbolic residue' was everywhere in Shakespeare's England' (Marotti, 'Shakespeare and Catholicism', p. 227). Indeed, Peter Marshall explains that: 'It is clear that by about 1580 a new and distinctive English (Roman) Catholic community was coming into existence, and that both 'survival' and "rebirth" played a part in the process' (Marshall, *Reformation England*, p. 178; see also on this point C. Haigh's 'The Continuity of Catholicism in the English Reformation', *Past and Present*, 93 (1981) 37–69, esp. 53, 62–3 and 69). Martin Ingram has also spoken usefully of 'popular religious cultures' in the sixteenth and seventeenth centuries, meaning by that that Protestantism was not a uniformly dominant culture. Indeed, as he explains, 'within that gravitational field there existed a *range* of *overlapping* and *interacting* religious cultures, not related in any clear-cut way to the divisions of the social hierarchy, and in complex interaction with official doctrines and precepts which were themselves by no means unitary or unchanging' (M. Ingram, 'From Reformation to Toleration: Popular Religious Cultures in England, 1540–1690', in *Popular Culture in England*, c. *1500–1850*, ed. Tim Harris (Basingstoke: Macmillan, 1995), pp. 118; 100).

41. M. C. Questier, *Conversion, Politics and Religion in England, 1580–1625* (Cambridge: Cambridge University Press, 1996), pp. 205–6. This notion of flux is complicated by the fact that conversion is not a once-for-all process, that it has to be worked at and maintained. This is a point argued by Nicholas Tyacke, who sees this as a long-term process (cf. the concept of a 'Long Reformation'): 'Moreover, it was not a question of a once-for-all conversion, let alone of simply waiting for those who had known a fully functioning Catholic Church to die off. Each new generation required to be nurtured afresh . . . ' (N. Tyacke, 'Introduction', in *England's Long Reformation 1500–1800*, ed. N. Tyacke (London: University College London Press, 1998), p. 22).

42. Lake, 'Religious Identities in Shakespeare's England', in *A Companion to Shakespeare*, p. 79. See also P. Lake, with M. Questier, *The Antichrist's Lewd Hat: Protestants, Papists and Players in Post-Reformation England* (New Haven, CT and London: Yale University Press, 2002), pp. 318–19 *et passim*.

43. I have compiled these statistics with the help of M. Spevack's *Harvard Concordance to Shakespeare* (Cambridge, MA: Harvard University Press, 1973). The play which contains the most allusions is . . . *Richard III*!

44. See, for instance, the following classic or recent studies: W. R. Elton, *King Lear and the Gods* (San Marino: Huntington Library, 1966); G. Wills, *Witches and Jesuits: Shakespeare's Macbeth* (New York: Oxford University Press, 1995); Shuger, *Political Theologies in Shakespeare's England*; S. Greenblatt, *Hamlet in Purgatory* (Princeton, NJ and Oxford: Princeton University Press, 2001). Maurice Hunt's *Shakespeare's Religious Allusiveness: Its Play and Tolerance* (Aldershot: Ashgate, 2004) has only one chapter devoted to the Second Henriad and Richard Wilson's *Secret Shakespeare* makes passing references to the histories. In recent years, only Donna B. Hamilton seems to have devoted a fair number of pages to Shakespeare's histories in her *Shakespeare and the Politics of Protestant England* (Lexington: University of Kentucky Press, 1992), with two important chapters on *King John* and *Henry VIII*.

45. See, for instance, T. Rist, *Shakespeare's Romances and the Politics of Counter-Reformation* (Lewiston: Edwin Mellen Press, 1999); V. B. Richmond,

Shakespeare, Catholicism, and Romance (New York: Continuum, 2000); and Batson, ed., *Selected Comedies and Late Romances of Shakespeare from a Christian Perspective.*

46. Many essays have been devoted to the religious aspects of this play – among the more recent are D. N. Beauregard's 'New Light on Shakespeare's Catholicism: Prospero's Epilogue in *The Tempest'*, *Renascence*, 49.3 (1997) 159–74; and Richard Wilson's chapter on the play in his *Secret Shakespeare*, pp. 206–29.

47. On religion as an ideological mask for *realpolitik*, and for a nuanced qualification of such views, see McEachern, 'Introduction', in *Religion and Culture in Renaissance England*, pp. 4–5. In his introduction to a recently published collection of essays, Ewan Fernie writes promisingly of 'Shakespearean spirituality as a distinctive, inalienable, and challenging dimension of the plays'. His point, however, is that 'a fresh consideration of spirituality might reinvigorate and strengthen politically progressive materialist criticism', or that 'spirituality holds out the hope of a more positive leap into a revolutionary alternative' – ideas which suggest unfortunately that religious and spiritual issues will be used again as instruments to further political agendas ('Introduction: Shakespeare, Spirituality and Contemporary Criticism', in *Spiritual Shakespeares*, ed. E. Fernie (Abingdon and New York: Routledge, 2005), pp. 3, 10).

48. For a survey and critique of New Historicist and Cultural Materialist thought applied to the study of Shakespeare's history plays, see my 'Power of Myths and Myths of Power: Shakespeare's History Plays and Modern Historiography', in *Shakespeare and History*, ed. H. Klein and R. Wymer, Shakespeare Yearbook 6 (Lewiston, Queenstown, Lampeter: Edwin Mellen Press, 1996), pp. 37–51. See also S. Mullaney, 'After the New Historicism', in *Alternative Shakespeares vol. 2*, ed. T. Hawkes (London and New York: Routledge, 1996), pp. 17–37; and D. S. Kastan, whose view is largely that 'New Historicism is neither new enough nor historical enough to serve' (*Shakespeare After Theory* (London and New York: Routledge, 1999), p. 29). Likewise Lionel Basney has judiciously observed that: 'Sceptical criticism, for explicable reasons, has concerned itself primarily to explain how institutions and social roles are emptied of conventional moral meanings, so that they become instruments of ideological control. This is clearly one truth about how culture functions, one we cannot ignore: there is no such thing as a completely sacralized culture. On the other hand, the subversive or emergent culture we are asked to see working its way up between the stones of the dominant culture may itself be shaped by moral demands or religious faith. There is no such thing, that is, as a completely secular or functional culture' (L. Basney, 'Is a Christian Perspective on Shakespeare Productive and/or Necessary?', in Batson, ed., *Shakespeare and the Christian Tradition*, p. 26; see also in the same volume, John D. Cox's article, 'Shakespeare: New Criticism, New Historicism, and the Christian Story', pp. 37–50).

49. S. Greenblatt, 'Shakespeare and the Exorcists', in his *Shakespearean Negotiations, The Circulation of Social Energy in Renaissance England* (Oxford: Clarendon Press, 1988), pp. 109; 119.

50. Greenblatt, 'Shakespeare and the Exorcists', p. 120.

51. For recent critiques of Greenblatt's secularizing argumentation and of his reading of *King Lear*, see P. Whitfield White, 'Theater and Religious Culture', in *A New History of Early English Drama*, ed. J. D. Cox and D. S. Kastan (New York: Columbia University Press, 1997), p. 148; J. Knapp, 'Jonson, Shakespeare, and the Religion of Players', *Shakespeare Survey*, 52 (2000) 60 *et passim*; G. Taylor, 'Divine [Sences]', *Shakespeare Survey* 52 (2000), pp. 21 and 29 esp.; J. D. Cox, *The Devil and the Sacred in English Drama, 1350–1642* (Cambridge: Cambridge University Press, 2000), pp. 151–65.

52. Indeed, as Deborah Shuger has observed, religion remains largely the 'great code' which enables individuals to read and interpret the real: 'Religion during this period supplies the primary language of analysis. It is the cultural matrix for explorations of virtually every topic: kingship, selfhood, rationality, language, marriage, ethics, and so forth. Such subjects are, again, not masked by religious discourse but articulated in it; they are considered *in relation* to God and the human soul. That is what it means to say that the English Renaissance was a religious culture, not simply a culture whose members generally were religious' (Shuger, *Habits of Thought in the English Renaissance*, p. 6).

53. See P. Whitfield White, *Theatre and Reformation, Protestantism, Patronage and Playing in Tudor England* (Cambridge: Cambridge University Press, 1993); B. Crockett, *The Play of Paradox, Stage and Sermon in Renaissance England* (Philadelphia: University of Pennsylvania Press, 1995); H. Diehl, *Staging Reform, Reforming the Stage: Protestantism and Popular Theater in Early Modern England* (Ithaca, NY: Cornell University Press, 1997). John Foxe, one of the early reformers – who was himself a playwright – had declared that 'players, printers, preachers' were 'set of God, as a triple bulwark against the triple crown of the Pope, to bring him down' (J. Foxe, *Acts and Monuments*, cited in E. K. Chambers' *The Elizabethan Stage*, 4 vols. (Oxford: Clarendon Press, 1923), vol. 1, p. 242, n.).

54. 'The first generation of English Protestants and perhaps the second too entertained little hostility towards plays. Nor, for that matter, were they opposed to other cultural forms such as popular music and pictures, at least not *per se*. They objected only to the use of these media to convey false doctrine . . . ' (Collinson, *The Birthpangs of Protestant England*, p. 102); see also P. Collinson, 'From Iconoclasm to Iconophobia: the Cultural Impact of the Second English Reformation', in *The Impact of the English Reformation, 1500–1640*, ed. P. Marshall (London: Arnold, 1997), p. 283 *et passim*.

55. Indeed, Peter Lake remarks that there was an inherent pessimism among many Protestants from the 1580s onwards: 'For all the triumphalism and flattery about the achievements of the Elizabethan regime and inevitable victory of the light of the Gospel over the Antichristian darkness of popery that suffused hot Protestant discourse, there was a persistent undertone of panic and pessimism running through much Protestant comment on the contemporary world' (Lake, 'Religious Identities in Shakespeare's England', in *A Companion to Shakespeare*, p. 68).

56. There may have been a trace of such polemics in John Speed's wild accusations of collusion between Shakespeare and the English Catholic activist Robert Parsons, S.J.: 'this Papist and his Poet', argued the historian, had in fact a lot in common; they were 'of like conscience for lies, the one ever

faining, and the other ever falsifying the truth' (J. Speed, *The Theatre of the Empire of Great Britain* (n. p., 1611), p. 637. S.T.C.: 23041).

57. This is something which did not escape William Prynne's monomaniac and paranoid attention. Prynne's *Hystrio-Mastix* (1633) constitutes an extreme example of anti-theatricalism: 'It is instructive to note that in a later generation that resolute Protestant William Prynne was so hostile to the theatre in any shape or form that he sympathized with Gardiner and others of his cloth for all their reactionary Catholicism, invoking not just patristic and Protestant opponents of plays but many papists and even the Prophet Mohammed to bolster his already over-burdened freight of authorities against the stage' (Collinson, *The Birthpangs of Protestant England*, p. 103). On Catholic reluctance to embrace theatre, see M. O'Connell, *The Idolatrous Eye, Iconoclasm and Theater in Early-Modern England* (Oxford: Oxford University Press, 2000), who points out Cardinal Borromeo's hostility to theatre (even religious drama) and underlines the 'curious symmetry' of Borromeo's assault on theatre 'with the contemporaneous anti-theatricalism of English Protestant writers and ecclesiastics', which shows that both Catholics and Protestants had come to 'a moment of anxiety and critical reflection on the question of theatricality that transcended specific differences in the historical conditions of the theaters' (p. 32). On Jesuit drama, see A. Shell, *Catholicism, Controversy and the English Literary Imagination, 1558–1660* (Cambridge: Cambridge University Press, 1999), pp. 173, 187, 194–5, 210–13. On anti-theatricalism, see J. Barish, *The Antitheatrical Prejudice* (Berkeley: University of California Press, 1981); Crockett, *The Play of Paradox*, pp. 5–7 *et passim*; and R. Targoff, 'The Performance of Prayer: Sincerity and Theatricality in Early Modern England', *Representations*, 60 (1997) 49–69.

58. In some ways there were resemblances between priests and theatre people: 'since, during the Renaissance, the majority of priests and playwrights both belonged to the same highly anomalous category of educated plebeians, one might expect certain affinities between their sociological perceptions, it being a curiosity not sufficiently remarked that the clerisy – the spokesmen for official ideology in the Christian West – were not, in general, drawn from its dominant classes' (D. K. Shuger, 'Subversive Fathers and Suffering Subjects: Shakespeare and Christianity', in *Religion, Literature, and Politics in Post-Reformation England, 1540–1688*, ed. D. B. Hamilton and R. Strier (Cambridge: Cambridge University Press, 1996), p. 47). See also J. Knapp, *Shakespeare's Tribe: Church, Nation, and Theater in Renaissance England* (Chicago and London: University of Chicago Press, 2002), pp. 7–9.

59. Knapp, *Shakespeare's Tribe*, p. 51.

60. As Debora Shuger writes, 'The issue which has been ignored is not whether Shakespeare teaches Christian doctrine – this *is* either a red-herring or twice-cooked cabbage – but how religious ideology, understood not as a uniquely privileged 'key' but as part of a cultural system, functions in these plays' (Shuger, 'Subversive Fathers and Suffering Subjects: Shakespeare and Christianity', p. 46).

61. On Elizabethan theatre's 'prospective' use of the retrospective mode, see J.-C. Mayer, 'Late Elizabethan Theatre and the Succession', in *The Struggle for the Succession in Late Elizabethan England, Politics, Polemics and Cultural*

Representations, ed. J-C. Mayer (Montpellier: Université Paul Valéry, 2004), pp. 371–93.

62. D. S. Kastan, *Shakespeare and the Shapes of Time* (London and Basingstoke: Macmillan, 1982), p. 55.

63. See, for instance, K. Poole, 'Saints Alive! Falstaff, Martin Marprelate, and the Staging of Puritanism', *Shakespeare Quarterly*, 46 (1995) 47–75; and her *Radical Religion from Shakespeare to Milton, Figures of Nonconformity in Early Modern England* (Cambridge: Cambridge University Press, 2000). M. Hunt, 'The Hybrid Reformations of Shakespeare's Second Henriad', in his *Shakespeare's Religious Allusiveness: Its Play and Tolerance* (Aldershot: Ashgate, 2004), pp. 19–46.

64. Indeed, George Santayana declared that Shakespeare 'is remarkable among the greater poets for being without a philosophy and without a religion' (G. Santayana, 'The Absence of Religion in Shakespeare', in *Interpretations of Poetry and Religion* (1900), ed. W. G. Holzberger and H. J. Saatkamp (Cambridge, MA: MIT Press, 1989), p. 100).

65. At all events, Shakespeare's Catholic audience members were part and parcel of the complex process which led to the production and construction of the cultural meaning of his plays: 'A text's meanings, as they emerge in history, are not produced solely by its author's intentions, which in various ways get disrupted and dispersed as the text is materialized and encountered; rather, its meanings are generated in the complex negotiation between the pressure it exerts, as both a formal and material structure, and the often perverse productivity of its readers or spectators (in the case of a play), who experience the text with unpredictable desires, expectations, and abilities' (Kastan, *Shakespeare After Theory*, p. 54).

66. An excellent example being Donna Hamilton's *Shakespeare and the Politics of Protestant England.*

67. Hunt, *Shakespeare's Religious Allusiveness*, p. ix.

1 Theatre, Witchcraft and the Crisis of Faith in *King Henry VI, Parts 1 and 2*

1. G. B., *A most wicked worke of a wretched witch (the like whereof none can record these manie yeeres in England. Wrought on the Person of one Richard Burt, Servant to Maister Edling of Woodhall in the Parrish of Pinner in the Countie of Myddlesex, a myle beyond Harrow. Latelie committed in March last, An. 1592 and newly recognised according to the truth* (London, 1592), p. 1. S.T.C.: 1030.5.

2. G. B., *A most wicked worke*, p. 6.

3. See S. Clark, *Thinking with Demons, The Idea of Witchcraft in Early Modern Europe* (Oxford: Oxford University Press, 1997), pp. 31, 64 *et passim*. As Clark remarks, however, such topics were not the sole hunting ground of Protestants – Catholic writers too were concerned by these moral and metaphysical questions. Christina Larner explains this logic of contrariety: 'The norms, practices, and values of a given society can never be perfectly fulfilled nor represent perfection. They cannot easily be defined by reference to some absolute good, because juxtaposition to such a good would show up the imperfections of existing human practices rather than justify them; instead

these norms are defended by contrasting them with absolute evil' (C. Larner, *Enemies of God, The Witch-hunt in Scotland* (Edinburgh: John Donald, 2000 [1983]), p. 134).

4. G. B., *A most wicked worke*, p. 3.

5. Another slightly earlier work – Henry Holland's *Treatise Against Witchcraft* (1590) – uses a similar logic of contrariety. Its author's opening premise is also that 'there are two spirituall kingdomes in this world, which have continual hatred & bloody wars, without hope of truce for ever. The Lord and king of the one, is our Lord Jesus, the tyrannical usurper of the other, is Sathan'. The author further rails against those he calls 'the Neuters of this worlde', those who would seek to remain aloof from these spiritual wars (H. Holland, *A Treatise Against Witchcraft* (Cambridge, 1590), sig. A2ʳ. S.T.C.: 13590).

6. For a full analysis of the links between the two works, see M. Gibson, *Reading Witchcraft, Stories of Early English Witches* (London and New York: Routledge, 1999), pp. 153–6.

7. Thomas Cooper, among many others, called 'Poperie the nurse of Witchcraft' (T. Cooper, *The Mystery of Witchcraft* (London, 1617), p. 120, cited in K. Tetzeli von Rosador, 'The Power of Magic: From *Endimion* to *The Tempest*', *Shakespeare Survey*, 43 (1991) 5).

8. See J. Lyly, *Endymion*, ed. D. Bevington, Revels Plays (Manchester and New York: Manchester University Press, 1996). Historians have remarked that witchcraft seems indeed to have been a major preoccupation in the 1580s and 1590s. The indictments for witchcraft in the Home Circuit Assizes reached an all-time high during those two decades (see J. Sharpe, *Instruments of Darkness, Witchcraft in Early Modern England* (Philadelphia: University of Pennsylvania Press, 1996), p. 109).

9. We shall adopt the dates of composition suggested by the Arden 3 editors of these plays – '1592, or earlier, depending on how far conjecture is allowed to influence judgement' for *Henry VI, Part 2* (cf. W. Shakespeare, *King Henry VI, Part 2*, ed. R. Knowles, Arden 3 (London: Thomson Learning, 2001 [1999]), p. 111. All references are to this edition), and 1592 for *Henry VI, Part 1* – *Part 1* being described by Philip Henslowe as a new play in March 1592 (cf. W. Shakespeare, *King Henry VI, Part 1*, ed. E. Burns, Arden 3 (London: Thomson Learning, 2000), p. 8. All references are to this edition). Our belief is that *Part 2* (which first appeared in print in 1594 under the title *The First Part of the Contention of the Two Famous Houses of York and Lancaster*) preceded the play known only under its First Folio title, *The first Part of Henry the Sixt*. For a full and lucid discussion of these matters, see: Shakespeare, *King Henry VI, Part 2*, ed. R. Knowles, p. 113.

10. 'The change in sources in 1590 is simply from reproduction of documents produced by the participants in witchcraft prosecutions, to narrative recreation of events. Early witchcraft pamphlets are unique amongst popular crime literature in their use of documentary proof. Other crime pamphlets seldom used documents, consistently preferring narrative both in Elizabethan and Jacobean times. But in witchcraft pamphlets this was unusual until 1590' (Gibson, *Reading Witchcraft*, p. 114).

11. 'Mere tattle and chat, even bogus and make-believe could serve this purpose as effectively as carefully corroborated evidence' (A. Walsham, *Providence in*

Early Modern England (Oxford and New York: Oxford University Press, 1999), p. 64).

12. It is estimated that between the 1560s and the suppression of the witchcraft statutes in 1736 over 100 tracts of this nature were published in England. These pamphlets served a purpose – they provided 'an alternative view of witchcraft which falls, as it were, between . . . theological abstractions . . . and the all too concrete concerns of a villager worrying about the bewitchment of his cattle' (Sharpe, *Instruments of Darkness*, p. 95).

13. Clark, *Thinking with Demons*, p. 537.

14. C. Marlowe, *The Tragedie of Doctor Faustus*, in *The Complete Works of Christopher Marlowe*, ed. F. Bowers, 2 vols. (Cambridge: Cambridge University Press, 1981), vol. 2, p. 163 ([1.1.] 69–74). The play is first mentioned by Philip Henslowe in 1594 and was only published in 1604 and 1616.

15. K. Dockray, *Henry VI, Margaret of Anjou and the War of the Roses: A Sourcebook* (Stroud: Sutton, 2000), p. xxiv. Henry VII petitioned the Pope to obtain Henry VI's canonization. Henry VI's alleged prophetic powers could be used also to strengthen the belief that Henry VII's reign was part of a divine plan (S. Anglo, *Images of Tudor Kingship* (London: Seaby, 1992), p. 66).

16. Ronald Knowles points out that: 'Though often considered the same as a pilgrim, strictly speaking the palmer permanently made pilgrimage to holy shrines, under vows of poverty, bearing a palm branch or leaf, and carrying a staff which indicated a visit to the Holy Land' (Shakespeare, *King Henry VI, Part 2*, ed. R. Knowles, p. 347 (n. to l. 97)).

17. Shakespeare, *King Henry VI, Part 2*, ed. R. Knowles, p. 201 (n. to l. 65).

18. See G. Bullough, ed., *Narrative and Dramatic Sources of Shakespeare*, 8 vols. (London: Routledge; New York: Columbia University Press, 1960), vol. 3, p. 90.

19. As Ronald Knowles remarks, 'If this is Providence, it is of a kind difficult to credit, except in the simple mind of this king' (R. Knowles, 'The Farce of History: Miracle, Combat, and Rebellion in *2 Henry VI*', *Yearbook of English Studies*, 21 (1991) 169).

20. As D. P. Walker explains, 'If the spirit of God, or a good angel, the messenger of God, dwells in a man and speaks through his mouth, the utterances claim supreme authority and may well add to, or alter, the original revelation. . . . And once the revelation has been petrified in canonical scriptures, such activities become still more obviously heretical' (D. P. Walker, *Unclean Spirits, Possession and Exorcism in France and England in the Late Sixteenth and Early Seventeenth Centuries* (London: Scolar Press, 1981), p. 17).

21. R. Hooker, *The Folger Library Edition of the Works of Richard Hooker*, vol. 1, pp. 127–8, cited in F. W. Brownlow, *Shakespeare, Harsnett, and the Devils of Denham* (Newark, London and Toronto: University of Delaware Press; Associated Ups, 1993), p. 51.

22. A contemporary of Scot – Henry Holland – wrote similarly that '*Myracles are ceased: Ergo:* All the miraculous works of witchcraft are ceased . . . ' (Holland, *A Treatise Against Witchcraft*, sig. E1^r).

23. R. Scot, *The Discoverie of Witchcraft* [1584], intro. H. R. Williamson (Arundel: Centaur Press, 1964), book 7, chapter 14, p. 138.

24. It should be noted in passing that Scot was not quite the enlightened thinker he is often thought to have been. Much of his argumentation was fiercely

anti-Catholic – he was certainly not a detached and tolerant observer of social phenomena (see also Sharpe, *Instruments of Darkness*, p. 54).

25. Scot, *The Discoverie of Witchcraft*, book 1, chapter 7, pp. 35–6.
26. G. Gifford, *A Discourse of the subtill Practises of Devilles by Witches and Sorcerers. By which men are and have bin greatly deluded: the antiquitie of them: their divers sorts and Names. With an Aunswer unto divers frivolous Reasons which some doe make to proove that the Devils did not make those Aperations in any bodily shape* (London, 1587), sig. H4^r. S.T.C. 11852.
27. G. Gifford, *A Dialogue Concerning Witches and Witchcraftes* (1593), intro. B. White (London: Shakespeare Association, 1931), sig. G2^r.
28. As Stuart Clark writes perceptively, 'Presumably Gifford hoped that Essex villagers would come to recognize this hidden agenda in every traditional witchcraft narrative. But for them to see familiar actions and events as so unlike what they seemed to be required reconceptualization on a major scale, and only constant clerical intervention could avoid the absurdity of them never knowing, in any particular instance, how to choose between the appearance of phenomena and their 'demonological' reality. As the dialogue closes, we are not sure that anyone who needs to be has in fact been convinced ... Nor, it seems, was Gifford sure' (Clark, *Thinking with Demons*, pp. 515–16). There are in fact many indications that 'the temptation to resort to counter-magic, even among the educated and godly, could be immense' (Sharpe, *Instruments of Darkness*, p. 157).
29. Scot, *The Discoverie of Witchcraft*, book 8, chapter 2, p. 144.
30. Scot, *The Discoverie of Witchcraft*, book 8, chapter 6, pp. 148–9.
31. Scot, *The Discoverie of Witchcraft*, book 8, chapter 6, p. 149.
32. Indeed, Geoffrey Bullough remarks that: 'Theatrical spirits had been popularized by *Dr Faustus* and *Friar Bacon and Friar Bungay*, but Shakespeare may have tried to parallel Joan of Arc's familiars in *1 Henry VI*. Later the oracles come true, and we remember them. The irony of prophecy was to play an ever-increasing part in the Lancaster-York sequence' (Bullough, ed., *Narrative and Dramatic Sources of Shakespeare*, vol. 3, p. 93).
33. Scot, *The Discoverie of Witchcraft*, book 12, chapter 2, p. 189. On the fulfilment of this prophecy, see also F. K. Barasch, 'Folk Magic in *Henry VI, Parts 1 and 2*: Two Scenes of Embedding', in *Henry VI: Critical Essays*, ed. T. A. Pendleton (New York and London: Routledge, 2001), p. 121.
34. K. Thomas, *Religion and the Decline of Magic, Studies in Popular Beliefs in Sixteenth- and Seventeenth-Century England* (Harmondsworth: Penguin, 1971), p. 155.
35. Walsham, *Providence in Early Modern England*, pp. 228–9.
36. Walsham, *Providence in Early Modern England*, pp. 229–30.
37. Walsham, *Providence in Early Modern England*, p. 280.
38. W. Shakespeare, *All's Well That Ends Well*, in *William Shakespeare, The Complete Works*, eds S. Wells and G. Taylor (Oxford: Clarendon Press, 1986), 2.3.1–6.
39. Walsham, *Providence in Early Modern England*, p. 241.
40. Larner, *Enemies of God*, p. 9.
41. K. M. Briggs, *Pale Hecate's Team, An Examination of the Beliefs on Witchcraft and Magic among Shakespeare's Contemporaries and His Immediate Successors* (London: Routledge, 1962), p. 59.

42. Shakespeare, *King Henry VI, Part 2*, ed. R. Knowles, p. 166. For the view that witchcraft and factional struggle often went hand in hand, see D. Willis, 'Shakespeare and the English Witch-Hunts: Enclosing the Maternal Body', in *Enclosure Acts, Sexuality, Property, and Culture in Early Modern England*, ed. R. Burt and J. M. Archer (Ithaca, NY and London: Cornell University Press, 1994), p. 99 *et passim*.

43. '. . . the said duchess may appear, more of malice than of any just cause thus to have been troubled' (J. Foxe, *Acts and Monuments*, cited in N. S. Levine, 'The Case of Eleanor Cobham: Authorizing History in *2 Henry VI*', *Shakespeare Studies*, 22 (1994) 110). Eleanor's story also seems to have been put to political/polemical uses, as several critics have remarked. M. R. Smith argues also that 'Shakespeare's final treatment of the Duke and Duchess of Gloucester . . . is not consistent with any coherent ideological description of historical events, Protestant or Catholic' (M. R. Smith, '*Henry VI, Part 2*, Commodifying and Recommodifying the Past in Late-Medieval and Early-Modern England', in *Henry VI: Critical Essays*, ed. Pendleton, p. 195).

44. Scot, *The Discoverie of Witchcraft*, book 13, chapter 14, pp. 259–60.

45. Scot, *The Discoverie of Witchcraft*, book 15, chapter 22, p. 361. The same writer further adds that witchcraft is 'incomprehensible to the wise, learned or faithfull; a probable matter to children, fooles, melancholike persons and papists' (book 16, chapter 2, p. 389).

46. Historically, these last three were in fact members of the Catholic clergy who also had close ties with Duke Humphrey: Roger Bolingbroke (or Bultingbroke) was a prominent Oxford priest, Thomas Southwell was canon of St Stephen's Chapel in the palace of Westminster and John Home (Shakespeare's 'Hume'), also known as Hunne, was canon of Hereford and St. Asaph and Eleanor's chaplain (see: R. A. Griffiths, 'The Trial of Eleanor Cobham: An Episode in the Fall of Duke Humphrey of Gloucester', *Bulletin of the John Rylands Library Manchester*, 51.2 (1969) 386–7).

47. See Brownlow, *Shakespeare, Harsnett, and the Devils of Denham*, pp. 111–23 *et passim*. We shall come back to Harsnett later to highlight what was most probably the hidden agenda behind his writing of the *Declaration*. Shakespeare continued to be interested in the dramatic potential of exorcism, judging by Pinch's very Catholic conjuring of spirits in *The Comedy of Errors* (*c*. 1594): 'I charge thee, Satan, housed within this man, / To yield possession to my holy prayers, / And to thy state of darkness hie thee straight: / I conjure thee by all the saints in heaven' (W. Shakespeare, *The Comedy of Errors*, ed. C. Whitworth (Oxford: Oxford University Press, 2002), 4.4.55–8).

48. *Anno xxiii. Reginæ Elizabethæ. At this present session of Parliament by prorogation holden at Westminster the xvi day of Januarie* (London, 1581), chapter 2, sig 1^{r-v}. S.T.C.: 9484. In 1578 a stir had been caused by the discovery in London of wax figures, one of them bearing the name 'Elizabeth'. This was 'taken to be evidence of a plot to kill the queen and two of her advisers by image magic' (Sharpe, *Instruments of Darkness*, p. 45).

49. Similar cases surfaced during Elizabeth's reign and they were almost systematically tied to accusations of high treason. For instance, in 1594 Jane Shelley was held in the Fleet Prison for having 'gone about to sorcerers, witches and charmers, to know the time of your majesty's death, and what shall become

of the state', wrote Richard Young to the Queen (cited in Sharpe, *Instruments of Darkness*, p. 46).

50. E. Hall, *The Union of the Two Noble and Illustre Famelies of Lancastre and Yorke* (1548), cited in *Narrative and Dramatic Sources of Shakespeare*, ed. G. Bullough, p. 102.

51. The same stage direction is used in the first quarto (1594) (see the facsimile edition in Shakespeare, *King Henry VI, Part 2*, ed. R. Knowles, p. 384). In fact, as James J. Paxson quite rightly points out, 'Joan's speech and the scene's interlinear directions give us the fullest material expression of devils on Shakespeare's stage; the scene is remarkable if only for the specificity of the directional rubrics, rubrics that prompt precise choreographic or kinesic effect of a sort rarely witnessed in Shakespeare even with his human characters' (J. J. Paxson, 'Shakespeare's Medieval Devils and Joan La Pucelle in *1 Henry VI*, Semiotics, Iconography, and Feminist Criticism', in *Henry VI: Critical Essays*, ed. Pendleton, pp. 130–1).

52. Hall, *The Union*, cited in *Narrative and Dramatic Sources of Shakespeare*, ed. G. Bullough, vol. 3, p. 61.

53. This was no doubt because, like Eleanor Cobham, her figure had become politicized (see R. F. Hardin, 'Chronicles and Mythmaking in Shakespeare's Joan of Arc', *Shakespeare Survey*, 42 (1990) 25–34; and, for a well-documented analysis of how the French and the English constructed their image of Joan of Arc, see R. Hillman, *Shakespeare, Marlowe and the Politics of France* (Basingstoke: Palgrave, 2002), pp. 112–70).

54. Stow, however, has no qualms about calling her 'a monstrous woman' (J. Stow, *The Annales of England, faithfully collected out of the most autenticall Authors, Records, and other Monuments of Antiquitie* (London, 1592), p. 597. S.T.C.: 23334.).

55. R. Holinshed, *Chronicles*, cited in *Narrative and Dramatic Sources of Shakespeare*, ed. G. Bullough, vol. 3, p. 77.

56. Scot, *The Discoverie of Witchcraft*, book 3, chapter 14, p. 72.

57. See especially the striking conjuration scene in Act V (5.2.23–28.1).

58. Walker, *Unclean Spirits*, pp. 4–5.

59. Walker, *Unclean Spirits*, p. 6.

60. On John Darrell, see Thomas Freeman's seminal article: 'Demons, Deviance and Defiance: John Darrell and the Politics of Exorcism in Late Elizabethan England', in *Conformity and Orthodoxy in the English Church, c. 1560–1660*, ed. P. Lake and M. Questier (Woodbridge: Boydell Press, 2000), pp. 34–63.

61. On this point, see Freeman, 'Demons, Deviance and Defiance', p. 37.

62. Freeman, 'Demons, Deviance and Defiance', p. 48.

63. Freeman, 'Demons, Deviance and Defiance', p. 58.

64. The hidden agenda behind Harsnett's *Declaration* may thus have been more complex than Stephen Greenblatt's view that 'Harsnett's response is to try to drive the Catholic church into the theater' (S. Greenblatt, *Shakespearean Negotiations, The Circulation of Social Energy in Renaissance England* (Oxford: Clarendon Press, 1988), p. 112).

65. See Lyly, *Endymion*, ed. David Bevington, p. 27. Further references to the play are to this edition.

66. [London]: Printed [by T. Scarlet] for William Wright, [1592?]. S.T.C. 10841.

67. See Larner, *Enemies of God*, p. 31.

68. Anonymous, *Newes from Scotland*, sig. B2^r.
69. Anonymous, *Newes from Scotland*, sig. B3^{r-v}.
70. Anonymous, *Newes from Scotland*, sig. C4^v.
71. See James VI, *Daemonologie, in Forme of a Dialogue, Divided into three Bookes* (Edinburgh, 1597), pp. 16–17. S.T.C.: 14364.
72. James VI, *Daemonologie*, pp. 54–5.
73. 'The reason for any evil at all in the creation was, as Augustine had explained, to grace it with antitheses "like a beautiful poem"' (Clark, *Thinking with Demons*, p. 95).
74. Clark, *Thinking with Demons*, p. 552.
75. One thinks indeed of a much later play, in which one of Shakespeare's kings – Leontes – makes this remarkable statement: 'If this be magic, let it be an art / Lawful as eating' (W. Shakespeare, *The Winter's Tale* [*c.* 1610], in *William Shakespeare, The Complete Works*, ed. S. Wells and G. Taylor, 5.3.110–11).
76. John Dryden, 'Prologue to the Tempest or the Enchanted Island', in *After 'The Tempest'*, sig. A4^r, lines 19–26, cited in B. H. Traister, *Heavenly Necromancers, The Magician in English Renaissance Drama* (Columbia: University of Missouri Press, 1984), p. 149.
77. Royal and 'magical magic' constantly competed with each other during the 1590s (see Tetzeli von Rosador, 'The Power of Magic: From *Endimion* to *The Tempest*', esp. pp. 4–5).
78. Clark, *Thinking with Demons*, p. 138.
79. Clark, *Thinking with Demons*, p. 135. Shakespeare would again explore this logic of contrariety in his Jacobean tragedy of *Macbeth* with its multiple inversions of contraries (on this last point, see Stuart Clark, 'Inversion, Misrule and the Meaning of Witchcraft', *Past and Present*, 87 (1980) 126).
80. Meta-drama never totally extinguished these concerns. Good examples of this are the stories which surfaced in the mid 1590s about an extra devil who appeared in a production of *Dr Faustus* at the Theatre and scared both the actors and the audience. The anonymous play *The Puritan Widdow* (1606) staged a fake conjuration of demons and demystified the conjuror's powers. Yet, interestingly, the fake conjurer has doubts about his false art, because he fears it might in fact succeed: 'But here lyes the fear on't, how < if > in this false conjuration, a true Devill should pop up indeed?' (3.5.125–7) (cited in J. D. Cox, *The Devil and the Sacred in English Drama, 1350–1642* (Cambridge: Cambridge University Press, 2000), p. 156). As John D. Cox points out astutely, 'If the best of intellectual opinion could not distinguish demonic from human illusion, then it is understandable that audiences in the theatre – and perhaps even actors themselves – might regard the illusions they witnessed (or performed) differently from the way a modern audience does' (pp. 152–3).

2   Acting the Insubstantial in *King Richard III*

1. All references to *Richard III* are taken from the following edition: W. Shakespeare, *The Tragedy of King Richard III*, ed. J. Jowett, Oxford World Classics (Oxford and New York: Oxford University Press, 2000).

2. Anthony Hammond has indeed remarked that 'the verb can be read in the passive voice, implying that Richard's role has been determined by providence' (W. Shakespeare, *King Richard III*, ed. A. Hammond, Arden 2 (London: Methuen, 1981), p. 127, n.).

3. M. Neill, '"*Exeunt with a Dead March*": Funeral Pageantry on the Shakespearean Stage', in *Pageantry in the Shakespearean Theater*, ed. D. M. Bergeron (Athens, GA: University of Georgia Press, 1985), p. 168. Shakespeare's *Titus Andronicus* opens on a funeral and is framed by two sets of interments, while *Julius Caesar* and Marlowe's *2 Tamburlaine* fall into two halves, each ending with a funeral (see M. Neill, *Issues of Death, Mortality and Identity in English Renaissance Tragedy* (Oxford: Clarendon Press, 1997), p. 291).

4. R. C. McCoy, *Alterations of State: Sacred Kingship in the English Reformation* (New York: Columbia University Press, 2002), p. 68.

5. 'As concerning mediators (the spokes men, by whome we might haue accesse vnto God the father, we haue none other but Jesus Christ, in whose name only al thinges ar obteined of the father. It is very foule and altogether Heathenish, that whiche we see done euery where in the Popes Churches, not only bicause thei wil haue an infinit nomber of meansmakers to speake for them, and that altogether without the authoritie of Gods word ...' (J. Jewel, *An Apologie, or aunswer in defence of the Church of England, concerninge the state of Religion used in the same* (London, 1562), f. 17^r (S.T.C.: 14590)).

6. Neill, *Issues of Death*, pp. 246–7.

7. Historically, it is ironical to note that even though Richard had Henry VI buried at Chertsey Abbey – a relatively discreet and insignificant place of burial – the dead king became an almost immediate object of popular veneration. In the end, an outbreak of Henrician miracles forced Richard to change his plans: 'the Chertsey miracles persisted to such an extent that, in 1484, Richard III had Henry's body removed to Windsor where it was interred with great ceremony. It was probably hoped that, by giving the ill-used corpse a decent burial in a place of honour, the burden of hatred and suspicion that had fallen on Richard's shoulders might be alleviated' (S. Anglo, *Images of Tudor Kingship* (London: Seaby, 1992), p. 62).

8. See Neill, *Issues of Death*, p. 265.

9. The play in fact opens on the ghost's two lines spoken in Latin, in which he claims that blood spilt has to be avenged promptly: '*Cresse cruor sanguinis, satietur sanguine cresse, / Quod spero scitio. O scitio, vendicta*'. The ghost's Latin no doubt reinforced its mystery, until the lines are finally glossed a little later in the scene. The Latin is a reminder that the play is influenced by Senecan tragedy, but it may also be a linguistic sign that the ghost is speaking the language of those who are in a Roman Catholic purgatory. Some kind of effect, at the very least, was intended on the part of the dramatist (see Anonymous, *The True Tragedie of Richard The Third* (1594), ed. W. W. Greg, Malone Society (Oxford: Oxford University Press, 1929), sig. A3^r).

10. Cited in *The Oxford Companion to Shakespeare*, ed. M. Dobson and S. Wells (Oxford: Oxford University Press, 2001), p. 130.

11. Quoted in F. E. Halliday, *A Shakespeare Companion* (Harmondsworth: Penguin, 1964), p. 369.

12. 'I knowe the Auncients have one or two examples of Tragicomedies, as *Plautus* hath *Amphitrio*. But if we marke them well, wee shall finde that they never or verie daintily matche horne Pipes and Funeralls' (P. Sidney, *The Defence of Poesie* (1595), in *The Defence of Poesie, Political Discourses, Correspondence, Translations*, ed. A. Feuillerat (Cambridge: Cambridge University Press, 1923), p. 40.

13. Neill, *Issues of Death*, p. 294. W. Shakespeare, *Hamlet*, in *William Shakespeare, The Complete Works*, ed. S. Wells and G. Taylor (Oxford: Clarendon Press, 1986), 1.2.12.

14. Acts 19: 19 (Geneva Bible, 1560 edition). See also Shakespeare, *The Tragedy of Richard III*, ed. Jowett, p. 160 (note). However, contrary to Saul, Richard does not convert on the road to Damascus, even if the many allusions to Paul in Richard's mouth give us the impression that he may have had the potential to convert, or at least change, especially when near the end of the play he appears tormented by his conscience: 'By the Apostle Paul, shadows tonight / Have struck more terror to the soul of Richard / Than can the substance of ten thousand soldiers / Armèd in proof and led by shallow Richmond' (5.4.195–8). On Richard's references to Saint Paul, see A. Fox, 'Richard III's Pauline Oath: Shakespeare's Response to Thomas More', *Moreana* 15 (1978), esp. pp. 14–15; and J. B. Harcourt, ' "Odde Old Ends, Stolne . . . ": King Richard and Saint Paul', *Shakespeare Studies*, 7 (1974) 98–9.

15. On the issues of exorcism and magic, see Chapter 1.

16. D. Cressy, *Birth, Marriage and Death: Ritual, Religion, and the Life-Cycle in Tudor and Stuart England* (Oxford: Oxford University Press, 1997), pp. 402–3.

17. In Act 3, for instance, Buckingham endeavours to persuade the Lord Cardinal to act as an intermediary and to encourage the Queen to hand over the heir to the throne to Richard, the Lord Protector. The Cardinal, however, is adamant that he will not go against the sacredness of sanctuary. Buckingham then retorts: 'You are too senseless-obstinate, my lord, / Too ceremonious and traditional' (3.1.44–5). 'Ceremonious' and 'traditional' are words which stem from anti-Catholic polemics and are clearly anachronisms (see Shakespeare, *The Tragedy of Richard III*, ed. Jowett, p. 234 (note)). Editors have likewise remarked that the mention of Richard's 'prayer book' was omitted in Q1 of *Richard III*. This might have been a compositor's error, but it is more likely that the line was cut. It could indeed have been taken as an anachronistic reference to the Elizabethan Book of Common Prayer: 'Two props of virtue for a Christian prince, / To stay him from the fall of vanity; / And see, a prayer book in his hand, / True ornaments to know a holy man. – ' (3.7.91–4).

18. W. Allen, *A Defense and Declaration of the Catholike Churchies Doctrine, touching Purgatory, and Prayers for the Soules Departed* (Antwerp, 1565), p. 118. S.T.C.: 371.

19. Allen, *A Defense*, f. 282^v. For an overview of the polemical backdrop to the John Jewel-William Allen dispute, see P. Marshall, *Beliefs and the Dead in Reformation England* (Oxford and New York: Oxford University Press, 2002), pp. 124–5.

20. Jewel, *An Apologie*, f. 66^v.

21. Eamon Duffy has also underlined the great dependence of the dead upon the living, as the dead 'were powerless to help themselves, and so were at the

mercy of their kindred who, as inheritors of their property, could use it in good works to secure the speedy release or could divert it to other uses, and so leave them in torment' (E. Duffy, *The Stripping of the Altars, Traditional Religion in England 1400–1580* (New Haven, CT and London: Yale University Press, 1992), p. 349).

22. Jewel, *An Apologie*, f. 16^v.
23. *Articles agreed on by the Bishoppes, and other learned menne in the Synode at London, in the yere of our Lorde Godde, M.D.LII. for the avoiding of controversie in opinions, and the establishment of a godlie concorde, in certeine matters of Religion* (London, 1553), sig. B3^v. S.T.C.: 10034. In the thirty-nine articles of 1563 (approved by Parliament in 1571), 'The doctrine of Scholeaucthoures' was changed to 'The Romishe doctrine' thus adding a substantial polemical edge to the denial of purgatory – the real enemy was then clearly identified (*Articles ecclesiastical* (London, 1571), p. 14. S.T.C.: 10036^a).
24. It was equally incompatible with the Calvinist doctrine of predestination expounded, for instance, by the Elizabethan William Perkins: 'God hath Predestinated some, other hath he rejected' (W. Perkins, *A golden chaine, or the description of theologie, containing the order of the causes of salvation and damnation according to Gods woord* (London, 1591), sig. S8^r *et passim*. S.T.C.: 19657).
25. Marshall, *Beliefs and the Dead*, pp. 63, 12.
26. Marshall, *Beliefs and the Dead*, p. 46.
27. G. Marc'hadour, 'Introduction to Thomas More's *Supplication of Souls*', in *The Yale Edition of the Complete Works of Thomas More*, 15 vol. (New Haven and London: Yale University Press, 1990) vol. 7, p. lxxvii. See also: J. Le Goff, *The Birth of Purgatory*, trans. A. Goldhammer (Chicago: University of Chicago Press, 1984), p. 13.
28. Shakespeare, *The Tragedy of Richard III*, ed. John Jowett, p. 45.
29. In the prologue to Kyd's *Spanish Tragedy* Andrea shares the stage with Revenge, a character who watches the play with Andrea and thus serves 'for Chorus in this Tragedie' (T. Kyd, *The Spanish Tragedie*, in *The Works of Thomas Kyd*, ed. F. S. Boas (Oxford: Clarendon Press, 1955 [1901]), 1.1.91, p. 7).
30. Despite their evil resemblances Richard and Margaret are opposed on one decisive count. If, for the ambitious Duke of Gloucester, the past is to be remembered, it must be to honour him only: 'Let me put in your minds, if yours forget, / What you have been ere now, and what you are; / Withal, what you have been, and what I am' (1.3.131–3).
31. As Jowett writes, 'the horrible otherworld is merely intimated in the language in which Richard's origins are described. Whereas the devious and clutching otherworld is a fact of the narrative in *The Spanish Tragedy*, in *Richard III* it is an impression: perhaps merely how characters imagine themselves, perhaps – even less – simply the figures of speech by which they express their anguish' (Shakespeare, *The Tragedy of Richard III*, ed. John Jowett, p. 25).
32. Geoffrey Bullough surmises that Shakespeare drew partly on Seneca to write *Richard III*. He 'went direct, either to the Latin, or to translations such as Jasper Heywood's *Troas* (1559), *Thyestes* (1560), and *Hercules Furens* (1561), and Thomas Newton's *Seneca His Tenne Tragedies* (1581)' (G. Bullough, *Narrative and Dramatic Sources of Shakespeare*, 8 vols. (London: Routledge; New York: Columbia University Press, 1960), vol. 3, p. 236. For a detailed

study of the classical sources of Clarence's dream, see H. F. Brooks, '*Richard III*: Antecedents of Clarence's Dream', *Shakespeare Survey*, 32 (1979) 145–50.

33. Kyd, *The Spanish Tragedie*, in *The Works of Thomas Kyd*, 1.1.35, p. 5.

34. Neill, *Issues of Death*, p. 256.

35. Shakespeare's (ambiguous) syncretism is again apparent here, whereas in *The Spanish Tragedy* Kyd seemed less prone to adapt Andrea's description of the netherworld to Elizabethan ghost lore (see F.W. Moorman, 'The Pre-Shakespearean Ghost', *Modern Language Review*, 1 (1906) 91).

36. Hugh M. Richmond also finds that 'in its episodic structure the play nominally follows the models of Dante's *Inferno*, or Chaucer's *Monk's Tale*, or the Dances of Death so popular around 1500 . . . ' (H. M. Richmond, '*Richard III* and the Reformation', *Journal of English and Germanic Philology*, 83 (1984) 514).

37. See G. Creigh and J. Belfield, eds, *The Cobler of Caunterburie and Tarlton's Newes out of Purgatorie* (Leiden: Brill, 1987), p. 117.

38. Anonymous, *Tarltons newes out of Purgatorie* (London, 1590), sig. B2^{r}. Thomas Nashe's sarcastic lines about so-called conjurers in *The Terrors of the Night* are also a revealing example of cultural bric-a-brac – even if in this instance the phenomenon is perceived negatively by Nashe: 'they begin to get them a Library of three or foure old rustie manuscript books, which they themselves nor anie els can read; and furnish their shops with a thousand *quid pro quos*, that would choake anie horse: besides, some wast trinkets in their chambers hung up, which maye make the world halfe in jealouzie they can conjure' (T. Nashe, *The Terrors of the night, Or, A Discourse of Apparitions* (London, 1594), sig. E1^{r}. S.T.C.: 18379).

39. Marshall, *Beliefs and the Dead*, p. 133.

40. 'Accounts of miraculous appearances of souls from purgatory continued to be recorded, to edify the faithful, and to confirm them in their recusancy' (Marshall, *Beliefs and the Dead*, pp. 242–3).

41. Marshall, *Beliefs and the Dead*, p. 234. Thomas More had wielded the emotional argument with great efficacy in his *Supplication of Souls*: 'For yf youre father / youre mother / youre chylde / youre brother / youre suster / youre husbande / youre wyfe / or a very straunger to / lay in youre syghte some where in fyre / and that your meanes myght helpe hym: what hart were so hard / what stomake were so stony / that could syt in reste at supper or slepe in reste a bedde / and let a man ly and burne?' (T. More, *The Supplication of Souls*, in *The Yale Edition of the Complete Works of Thomas More*, ed. G. Marc'hadour vol. 7, p. 218, ll. 18–23). More's *Supplication* was a response to Simon Fish's explosive *A Supplication of Beggars* which denounced purgatory as a financially profitable doctrine for the Roman Catholic Church. For a detailed overview of early Tudor polemics on the subject of purgatory, see Marshall, *Beliefs and the Dead*, pp. 47–53.

42. Marshall, *Beliefs and the Dead*, p. 244.

43. On Reginald Scot, see Chapter 1. K. Thomas, *Religion and the Decline of Magic, Studies in Popular Beliefs in Sixteenth- and Seventeenth-Century England* (Harmondsworth: Penguin, 1971), pp. 705–6.

44. See Marshall, *Beliefs and the Dead*, pp. 252–3.

45. L. Lavater, *Of Ghosts and Spirites Walking by Night* (1572), cited in F. W. Moorman, 'Shakespeare's Ghosts', *Modern Language Review*, 1 (1906) 199.

46. '. . . the vanishing of spirits was in any case less an empirical observation than a rhetorical and polemical trope in the campaign against Catholicism. In other contexts, Protestant writers were quite ready to affirm that popular belief in ghosts was far from moribund' (Marshall, *Beliefs and the Dead*, p. 246).

47. See J. Bath, ' "In the Divell's likenesse": interpretation and confusion in popular ghost belief', in *Early Modern Ghosts*, ed. J. Newton (Durham: Centre for Seventeenth-Century Studies, 2002), p. 76.

48. 'It would be wrong to associate the belief in ghosts with any particular denomination. It was to be found among almost all religious groups, and at virtually every social level' (Thomas, *Religion and the Decline of Magic*, p. 708).

49. S. Greenblatt, *Hamlet in Purgatory* (Princeton, NJ and Oxford: Princeton University Press, 2001), p. 151.

50. Greenblatt, *Hamlet in Purgatory*, p. 194.

51. Devilish apparitions were common in churchyards and cemeteries according to Thomas Nashe, as these places were strategic for the Devil: 'If anie aske why he is more conversant & busie in churchyards and places where men are buried, than in anie other places? It is to make us beleeve, that the bodies & soules of the departed rest entirely in his possession, and the peculiar power of death is resigned to his disposition' (*The Terrors of the night*, sig. B3^v. S.T.C.: 18379).

52. See *OED*, 'Shadow', sb., 7, 'spectral form, phantom' and 6 b, *obs.* 'applied to an actor in contrast with the reality represented'.

53. Stephen Greenblatt underlines the meaningful contrast between 'shadows' and 'substance': 'the contrast between shadow and substance marks his stubborn hold on what he takes to be the reality principle. Richard clings tenaciously to a distinction between images in his mind and the hard realities of the actual world, a distinction that enables him to rally his spirits in order to urge his men into battle . . . ' (Greenblatt, *Hamlet in Purgatory*, p. 216).

54. Anonymous, *The True Tragedie of Richard The Third*, sig. A3^r, ll. 7–10.

55. Katharine Goodland argues that '*Richard III* thus probes the relationship between funeral ritual and communal consciousness, registering a sense of loss for the medieval structure of communal mourning and remembrance that was dismantled by the Reformation' (K. Goodland, ' "Obsequious Laments": Mourning and Communal Memory in Shakespeare's *Richard III*', in *Shakespeare and the Culture of Christianity in Early Modern England*, ed. D. Taylor and D. Beauregard (New York: Fordham University Press, 2003), p. 45).

56. As Richard P. Wheeler points out regarding Old Queen Margaret, 'the very fact that Margaret's prophetic power is manifested in a curse obscures the clarity of the sacred perspective' (R. P. Wheeler, 'History, Character and Conscience in *Richard III*', *Shakespeare Criticism*, 31 (1998) 328).

57. Geneva Bible, 1560 edition.

58. Margaret's cursing may well align her with divine providence, but her invectives are disturbing at the very least. The Church Fathers had debated the fact that some curses could be considered as a form of prophecy. Pope Gregory

the Great had argued, however, that 'God is said to curse and yet man is forbidden to curse, because what man does from the malice of revenge, God does only in the exactness and perfection of justice' (cited in M. Steible, 'Jane Shore and the Politics of Cursing', *Studies in English Literature*, 43.1 (2003) 13).

59. Neill, *Issues of Death*, p. 247.
60. Neill, *Issues of Death*, p. 245.
61. Allen, *A Defense*, p. 163. On the performative complexities of prayer in *Richard III* see R. Targoff, ' "Dirty" Amens: Devotion, Applause, and Consent in *Richard III*', *Renaissance Drama*, 31 (2002) 64 *et passim*.
62. Both extracts quoted (in modernized spelling) in C. Devlin, *Hamlet's Divinity* (London: Rupert Hart-Davis, 1963), p. 46.
63. See Devlin, *Hamlet's Divinity*, p. 46. Indeed, the *OED* gives 'to punish, or exact punishment for (a crime, wrong, or sin)' for 'revenge', vb., 6.
64. *The seconde Tome of Homelyes* (London, 1563), sig. Mmm.i^v. S.T.C.: 13663.
65. *The seconde Tome of Homelyes*, sig. Mmm.ii^r.
66. *The seconde Tome of Homelyes*, sig. Mmm.ii^{r-v}.
67. T. Browne, *Religio Medici* [written *c.* 1635], cited in Neill, *Issues of Death*, p. 39.
68. T. More, *History of King Richard III*, in *Holinshed's Chronicles of England, Scotland, and Ireland*, 6 vols. (London, 1808), vol. 3, p. 403.
69. E. Hall, *The Union of the Two Noble Famelies of Lancastre and Yorke* (1548), in *Narrative and Dramatic Sources of Shakespeare*, vol. 3, p. 291.
70. Shakespeare may have been influenced by *A Mirror for Magistrates* where Richard says that he saw the ghosts of those he killed all around his tent crying out for revenge, or by the anonymous *True Tragedy of Richard III* (printed in 1594) where he is given the following words: 'Meethinkes their ghoasts comes gaping for revenge, / Whom I have slaine in reaching for a Crowne' (Anonymous, *The True Tragedie of Richard The Third*, sig. H1^v, ll. 1880–1). But in both of these works the ghosts do *not* appear on stage. See also: S. Wells, 'Staging Shakespeare's Ghosts', in *The Arts of Performance in Elizabethan and Early Stuart Drama, Essays for G. K. Hunter*, ed. M. Biggs, P. Edwards, I.-S. Ewbank, E. M. Waith (Edinburgh: Edinburgh University Press, 1991), p. 53.
71. Indeed, F. W. Moorman noted that Shakespeare here 'substitutes dramatic action for narrative' (Moorman, 'Shakespeare's Ghosts', p. 193). Furthermore, their position on stage could even have been central and the overall effect produced by their appearance quite striking (Wells, 'Staging Shakespeare's Ghosts', p. 55).
72. Stephen Greenblatt's analyses are extremely convincing as regards this scene: 'By bringing the ghosts onstage and having them address the two sleeping adversaries, Shakespeare suggests that the dead do not simply rot and disappear, nor do they survive only in the dreams and fears of living individuals: they are an ineradicable, embodied, objective power. They function as the memory of the murdered, a memory registered not only in Richard's troubled psyche . . . but also in the collective consciousness of the kingdom and in the mind of God' (Greenblatt, *Hamlet in Purgatory*, pp. 179–80).
73. See M. Garber, *Dream in Shakespeare: From Metaphor to Metamorphosis* (New Haven, CT: Yale University Press, 1974), p. 26.

74. E. Jones, *The Origins of Shakespeare* (Oxford: Clarendon Press, 1977), p. 226.
75. Critics have noted the resemblance between this episode and the story of the Dream of Constantine (see Jones, *The Origins of Shakespeare*, p. 230).
76. As Stanley Wells points out, the ghosts in *Richard III* are not merely a hallucination or a dream vision: 'The ghosts . . . escape disqualification under this clause on the grounds that for two men simultaneously to dream the same dream must be regarded as more than a coincidence' (Wells, 'Staging Shakespeare's ghosts,' p. 51).
77. The deceased in the early modern period were 'disorderly dead', as Peter Marshall explains: 'illegal immigrants across a border that was supposed to remain sealed and impermeable until the end of time' (Marshall, *Beliefs and the Dead*, p. 264).
78. Nashe, *The Terrors of the night, Or, A Discourse of Apparitions*, sig. C2^r.
79. J. Gee, *New Shreds of the Old Snare* (1624), cited in: Greenblatt, *Hamlet in Purgatory*, p. 256.
80. W. Tyndale, *An Answer to Sir Thomas More's Dialogue* (Cambridge: Parker Society, 1850), p. 143.
81. 'Wherefore reflecting upon our accusation of this doctrine, I saw it was unjust: and thus resolved by a powerfull demonstration (issuing from the premisses) that *Purgatory* is no *heresy*, nor *Antichristianisme* (as we pretend with greater violence, then reason) but a parcell of the true, ancient, Catholick, and Apostolick faith, as the *Papists* do confidently believe' (T. Higgons, *The First Motive of T.H. Maister of Arts, and Lately Minister, To Suspect the Integrity of his Religion*, 2 parts (London, 1609), part 2, pp. 58–9. S.T.C.: 13454). Higgons's tract attacked the three leading Protestant polemicists, Lawrence Humphrey, Richard Field and Thomas Morton, on the basis of the principal scriptural and patristic texts from which the existence of Purgatory could be established, that is, Matthew 12: 32 and the Dialogues of Pope Gregory the Great (a recusant edition of which appeared in 1608) (see M. Questier, *Conversion, Politics and Religion, 1580–1625* (Cambridge: Cambridge University Press, 1996), p. 86). Higgons' book was countered by other polemicists and the debate continued to rage. Higgons himself later changed his views again. In May and June 1626, John Donne preached twice against purgatory at Paul's Cross – thus the issue had certainly not become unimportant for Protestant reformers.
82. 'Despite what Protestant polemicists often asserted, there may have been no absolute necessary dependence of ghosts on purgatory' (Marshall, *Beliefs and the Dead*, p. 262). In 1561 the French exile and prebendary of St Paul John Veron had penned a lively dialogue – *The Huntyng of Purgatory to Death* – denouncing purgatory as an unscriptural imposition.
83. E. Mazzola, *The Pathology of the English Renaissance, Sacred Remains and Holy Ghosts* (Leiden, Boston, Köln: Brill, 1998), p. 61.
84. W. Shakespeare, *Henry V*, in *William Shakespeare, The Complete Works*, Prologue l. 10.
85. Here I am using Peter Marshall's argument about the meaning of ghost stories (see Marshall, 'Old Mother Leakey and the Golden Chain: Context and Meaning in an Early Stuart Haunting', in *Early Modern Ghosts*, p. 96).
86. The world of Shakespeare and his contemporaries was undergoing 'a far-reaching reconfiguration of the cultural and emotional nexus that bound

the living and the dead, of the idioms in which feelings, anxieties, and aspirations about the dead could be expressed' (Marshall, *Beliefs and the Dead*, p. 188).

3   Religious Conscience and the Struggle for the Succession in *Richard II*

1. In *The Life and Death of Jack Straw* (composed 1591–93 and first published in 1593), the King is portrayed as a boy who is oblivious to the fact that his (evil) counsellors and tax collectors are oppressing the common people. A work which was probably not available at booksellers', but to which Shakespeare may well have been indebted, was the anonymous *Thomas of Woodstock* – if Peter Corbin and Douglas Sedge are right in dating this incredibly daring portrayal of Richard II as a tyrant-king back to the 1591–95 period. The play was apparently never printed during Shakespeare's time; it survived only in manuscript (see Anonymous, *Thomas of Woodstock, or Richard the Second, Part One*, ed. P. Corbin and D. Sedge (Manchester: Manchester University Press, 2002), p. 4 *et passim*).
2. Most editors agree on 1595 as the probable date of composition for *Richard II* (W. Shakespeare, *Richard II*, ed. P. Ure, Arden Shakespeare (London and New York: Routledge, 1961), p. xxix; W. Shakespeare, *King Richard II*, ed. A. Gurr, New Cambridge Shakespeare (Cambridge: Cambridge University Press, 2003 [1984]), p. 1; W. Shakespeare, *King Richard II*, ed. C. R. Forker, Arden 3 (London: Thomson Learning, 2002), p. 111). All references to *Richard II* are taken from Charles Forker's Arden 3 edition.
3. For non-Shakespearean uses of the theme, see L. B. Campbell, *Shakespeare's Histories, Mirrors of Elizabethan Policy* (London: Methuen, 1964), p. 191 *et passim*.
4. See, for instance, *The Copy of a Letter Written by a Master of Art of Cambridge* (1584); *A Declaration of the True Causes of the Great Troubles* (1592); *An Advertisement Written to a Secretary of My Lord Treasurer's of England* (1592). These were all penned by Catholic controversialists (for a brief description of these works, see Shakespeare, *King Richard II*, ed. Forker, pp. 6–9).
5. On Sunday, 25 February 1593, Robert, Earl of Essex took the oath of supremacy and the oath of a privy councillor. In the early 1590s the Queen's Privy Council had become an ageing body and was in great need of new blood. At twenty-seven, Essex was then seen as definitely on the rise; he was recognized as one of the Queen's chief advisers in matters of state and particularly in the domain of foreign affairs. The antiquary and historian William Camden reminds us in passing of the associations between Bolingbroke – the defender of his murdered uncle, Woodstock – and Robert, Earl of Essex. In the eyes of some of the Catholics, recalls Camden in his history of the reign of Elizabeth I, Essex had antecedents for the crown and these Catholics 'cast their eyes upon the Earle of Essex . . . feigning a Title from *Thomas of Woodstock*, King *Edward* the third's sonne, from whom hee derived his Pedigree' (W. Camden, *The historie of the most renowned and victorious princesse Elizabeth* (London, 1630), book 4, p. 57. S.T.C.: 4500.5). In Book 2 of his *Civil Wars* Daniel highlights the noble virtues and 'glorious worth' of

Henry Bolingbroke even if, admits Daniel, his cause might not have been 'as lawfull'. This admission brings Daniel to wish that the deposition of Richard had not happened. Thus, instead of telling the sorrowful story of England's civil wars he could have sung the deeds of Robert, Earl of Essex, whose blood was so close to Bolingbroke's (S. Daniel, *The first fovvre bookes of the ciuile wars between the two houses of Lancaster and Yorke* (London, 1595), book 2, ff. 42^r – 43^r, S.T.C.: 6244). See also Richard McCoy's seminal study, *The Rites of Knighthood, The Literature and Politics of Elizabethan Chivalry* (Berkeley: University of California Press, 1989), p. 88 *et passim*. For a discussion of the part played in the Essex rebellion by Shakespeare's company – the Chamberlain's Men – see Chapter 5.

6. Peter Ure glosses helpfully thus: 'in banishing you we absolve you from your duty to us' (Shakespeare, *Richard II*, ed. Ure, p. 32).
7. J. Stow, *The Annales of England, faithfully collected out of the most autenticall Authors, Records, and other Monuments of Antiquitie* (London, 1592), p. 507. S.T.C.: 23334.
8. Shakespeare, *Richard II*, ed. Gurr, p. 5.
9. J. Knapp, *Shakespeare's Tribe: Church, Nation, and Theater in Renaissance England* (Chicago and London: University of Chicago Press, 2002), p. 85. Knapp also rightly points out that the motif is present in other plays of the period: Christopher Marlowe's *Edward II*, George Peele's *Edward I*, the Robin Hood plays of Anthony Munday and Henry Chettle. 'All these plays', argues Knapp, 'unfold what I call a counter-crusading plot: a narrative in which English characters turn against the Crusades and also turn them around, to search for a new Holy Land in the English isle' (p. 86).
10. William Cecil, Lord Burghley had sought to point the way by suggesting that Catholics would not be persecuted for their religion if they remained loyal to the Crown: 'none of these sort are for their contrary opinions in religion prosecuted or charged with any crymes or paines of treason, nor yet willingly searched in their consciences for their contrarie opinions, that savour not of treason' (W. Cecil, *The Execution of Justice in England* (London, 1583), sig. B1^v. S.T.C.: 4902).
11. See P. Holmes, *Resistance and Compromise, The Political Thought of the Elizabethan Catholics* (Cambridge: Cambridge University Press, 1982), p. 143. The book in question is W. Rainolds, *Calvino-Turcismus. Id est Calvinisticæ perfidiae, cum Mahumetana Collatio... Quatuor libris explicate... Authore G. Reginaldo* (Antwerp, 1597). A decade before Rainolds' book William Allen had sharply criticized the Queen for the same reasons: 'she hathe by messingers and letters, dealte with the cruel and dreadfull Tirante and enemie of our faithe the *Great Turke* himself, (againste whom our nobles kinges have in olde time so valiantly foughte, and vowed themselves to all perriles and peregrinations)...' (W. Allen, *An Admonition to the Nobility and People of England and Ireland concerninge the present warre* (n.p., 1588), p. 23. S.T.C.: 368). As Dennis Flynn also explains, 'the language of the crusade provided a conceptual framework for all the Catholic rebellions against Tudor reform, going back through the Northern Rising of 1569 to the Pilgrimage of Grace in the year after Sir Thomas More's execution. More himself, with Bishop John Fisher, Reginald Pole and the circle surrounding Catherine of Aragon, had fostered such a language by comparing heretic reformers to Turkish

infidels' (D. Flynn, *John Donne and the Ancient Catholic Nobility* (Bloomington and Indianapolis: Indiana University Press, 1995), pp. 145–6).

12. Daniel, *The First Fowre Bookes of the civile wars*, book 2, p. 43.
13. 'Gaunt's lines must be read ironically, although even some commentators seem not to be able to perceive the strange contradictions contained within them. The central point is that England is not an island and it is not protected from invasion in the way that Gaunt hopes it will be. The invasion is actually led by the banished Henry Bolingbroke, Duke of Hereford, Gaunt's own son, who deposes the king of the "scepter'd isle" . . . ' (A. Hadfield, *Shakespeare, Spenser and the Matter of Britain* (Basingstoke: Palgrave, 2003), p. 8).
14. The ultimate irony is, of course, that Bolingbroke falls short of his promise in *2 Henry IV*, dying on English soil in a room called 'Jerusalem': 'In that Jerusalem shall Harry die' (W. Shakespeare, *2 Henry IV*, in *The Complete Works*, eds S. Wells and G. Taylor (Oxford: Clarendon Press, 1986), 4.3.369).
15. These were: Q1 (1597), Q2 (1598), Q3 (1598).
16. This fuller text was reprinted in 1615 and – probably with the prompt-book with which it was collated – it provided the basis for the text reproduced in the 1623 folio of Shakespeare's works. A final quarto (Q6) – with a text derived from the second folio edition of Shakespeare's works (F2, 1632) appeared in 1634 (see M. Dobson and S. Wells, eds, *The Oxford Companion to Shakespeare's Works* (Oxford: Oxford University Press, 2001), p. 381; and Shakespeare, *King Richard II*, ed. Forker, p. 506).
17. See J. Clare, 'The Censorship of the Deposition Scene in *Richard II*', *The Review of English Studies*, 41 (1990) 90.
18. On *Richard II* and the Essex rebellion, see Chapter 5.
19. Shakespeare, *King Richard II*, ed. Gurr, pp. 9–10.
20. Shakespeare, *King Richard II*, ed. Gurr, p. 10. Charles R. Forker surmises that the scene 'was almost certainly present in the original copy but marked for deletion from the printed version for reasons of censorship' (Shakespeare, *King Richard II*, ed. Forker, pp. 515–16).
21. See Andrew Gurr's edition which reproduces the title page of the fourth quarto – the Malone copy (Shakespeare, *King Richard II*, p. 8).
22. S. Wells and G. Taylor, *A Textual Companion* (Oxford: Clarendon Press, 1987), p. 311.
23. See J.-C. Mayer, ed., *Breaking the Silence on the Succession, A Sourcebook of Manuscripts and Rare Elizabethan Texts* (c. *1587–1603*) (Montpellier: Université Paul Valéry, 2003), pp. 1–27.
24. This was the line which the Queen sought to maintain during her reign. This does not mean that such views were embraced unanimously, even at the highest levels of the state. Thomas Digges, who was employed by Elizabeth's own lord treasurer and administrator – William Cecil, Lord Burghley – devised in the mid-1580s an interregnum plan which, in the event of the Queen's sudden death, would give unprecedented powers to the Privy Council and to Parliament should the royal seat remain vacant for want of an heir apparent. The plan was proposed to the Queen by Burghley, but it was immediately rejected and – needless to say – it was never discussed in Parliament. The existence of such a plan proves nonetheless that senior Elizabethan political administrators could conceive (in exceptional circumstances and no doubt for a limited time) of the state being run *without*

a sovereign (see P. Collinson, 'The Monarchical Republic of Queen Elizabeth I', *Bulletin of the John Rylands University Library of Manchester*, 69.2 (1987) 418–19; 422 *et passim*).

25. Cf. Wells and Taylor, *Textual Companion*, p. 312. See also C. S. Clegg, ' "By the choise and inuitation of al the realme": *Richard II* and Elizabethan Press Censorship', *Shakespeare Quarterly*, 48.4 (1997) 443–4.

26. Charles R. Forker surmises that this may 'reflect a theatrical version different from the Folio's', or that it may have been a compositor's error (see Shakespeare, *King Richard II*, p. 392, n.). Yet the so-called error is found in *two* quarto editions, the 1608 and 1615 quartos of *Richard II*.

27. Jean Froissart reported that the Articles were read to Richard in the Tower, where he resigned and handed over the crown; then a parliament was called and Bolingbroke was elected (J. Froissart, *Of the Chronicles of Englande, fraunce, Spayne, etc.* (1525), vol. 2, chap. 313, sig. DDD2^v. S.T.C: 11397). Edward Hall also pointed out that 'The nobles and commons were well pleased that kyng Richard shoulde frankely and frely of his owne mere mocion [. . .] resigne his croune and depart from his regalitee' (E. Halle, *The Vnion of the two noble and illustrate famelies of Lancastre & Yorke* (1548), f. 9^r. S.T.C.: 12721). In book 3 of Samuel Daniel's *Civil Wars* Richard likewise resigned in the Tower and the news was later conveyed to Parliament.

28. Italics mine. (R. Holinshed, *Chronicles of England, Scotland and Ireland*, 6 vols. (London, 1807 [1586]), vol. 2, pp. 863–4).

29. Interestingly, one of Shakespeare's possible literary sources for *Richard II*, the anonymous *Thomas of Woodstock*, has Richard complain (well before the events leading to his deposition) about his peers' decision to summon a parliament without his consent. He is adamant that he will 'dismiss their sudden parliament / Till we be pleased to summon and direct it' (2.1.162–3). John of Gaunt, however, urges the King to 'confirm this parliament' (2.2.54) – to declare it legitimate – as it was the king's prerogative alone to summon and dissolve Parliament (Anonymous, *Thomas of Woodstock*, ed. Corbin and Sedge, pp. 84; 87).

30. R. Dutton, 'Shakespeare and Lancaster', *Shakespeare Quarterly*, 49 (1998) 18. Annabel Patterson has, for that matter, noticed Holinshed's particular interest in Parliament's role as an institution and, more specifically, in the circumstances leading to Richard II's deposition. She argues convincingly that the historian's interpretation of these events betrays his deep concern for questions of civil liberties: 'Holinshed, then, had identified the reign of Richard II as a point of definition of ancient constitutionalism' (A. Patterson, *Reading Holinshed's Chronicles* (Chicago and London: University of Chicago Press, 1994), p. 116). It is no mere coincidence either that John Milton, who in *The Tenure of Kings and Magistrates* (1648) had encouraged the Long Parliament to bring Charles I to justice, twice referred to Holinshed's account of Richard's deposition in his commonplace book (see Patterson, p. 116).

31. Italics mine. Stow, *The Annals of England*, p. 512.

32. Stow, *The Annals*, pp. 512–3.

33. For instance, according to the English Jesuit Robert Parsons there was a contract between the King and the commonwealth which implied that sovereigns were elected by the commonwealth: 'and his election & admission to the crowne, vvas orderly, and authorized by general consent of

parlament...' (R. Doleman (*vere* R. Parsons), *A Conference About the Next Succession to the Crowne of Ingland* ([Antwerp], 1594), part 2, p. 96. S.T.C.: 19398).

34. P. Collinson, 'John Stow and Nostalgic Antiquarianism', in *Imagining Early Modern London, Perceptions and Portrayals of the City from Stow to Strype, 1598 1720*, ed. J. F. Merritt (Cambridge: Cambridge University Press, 2001), p. 42 *et passim*; see also *DNB* article on Stow. As Annabel Patterson writes, 'it can be inferred that Stow was particularly interested in political protest and resistance' (Patterson, *Reading Holinshed's Chronicles*, p. 24).

35. *A Conference About the Next Succession to the Crowne of Ingland* ([Antwerp], 1594) S.T.C.: 19398. The work was printed in 1594 (under the pseudonym of R. Doleman); it began to appear in England in 1595, despite the government's efforts to stem its circulation (see P. Holmes, 'The Authorship and Early Reception of *A Conference About the Next Succession to the Crown of England*', *Historical Journal*, 23.2 (1980) 415–29).

36. The Jesuits supported the Infanta of Spain's remote title to the Crown of England (Isabella Clara Eugenia was Philip II's daughter) and sought to demonstrate that she was descended from John of Gaunt, Duke of Lancaster. This was one of several genealogical claims he made to promote the Infanta.

37. Doleman (*vere* Parsons), *A Conference*, part 2, p. 56.

38. As Ronald Corthell wrote, 'Noting the historiographical struggle for control over the story of Bolingbroke's takeover, Persons foregrounds historical writing as itself a form of political discourse' (R. Corthell, 'Robert Persons and the Writer's Mission', in *Catholicism and Anti-Catholicism in Early Modern English Texts*, ed. A. F. Marotti (Basingstoke: Macmillan, 1999), p. 46).

39. Doleman (*vere* Parsons), *Conference*, part 2, p. 63.

40. 'The other conditions also of good gouerment, are partly touched in the speach of the Archbishop, and much more expresly set downe in the king of England's oth, recorded by ancient wryters, for that he sweareth as both *Holinshead* and others do testifie, in ther inglish stories, in thes very words, to vvit. *That he wil during his life, beare reuerence & honor vnto almightie God, and to his Catholique church* ...' (Doleman (*vere* Parsons), *Conference*, part 1, p. 116).

41. Doleman (*vere* Parsons), *Conference*, part 2, p. 96.

42. Holmes, *Resistance and Compromise*, p. 152. To remedy this, he later played down the first part of the *Conference* (which dealt mostly with resistance theory) by summarizing it in a couple of pages in the 1596 Latin version of his discourse intended for the Pope. He also added a new chapter to the genealogical section of the book (part 2), to defend the sovereign rights of the Pope over Christian kings (cf. Holmes, 'The Authorship and Early Reception of *A Conference About the Next Succession to the Crown of England*', p. 424).

43. See: Nick Myers' introduction to the extracts of these two tracts in: *Breaking the Silence on the Succession*, ed. Mayer, pp. 107–10.

44. P. Wentworth, *A Pithie Exhortation to her Maiestie for Establishing her Svccessor to the Crowne, Wherevnto is added a Discovrse containing the Authors opinion of the true and lawful svccessor to her Maiestie* ([Edinburgh], 1598), p. iii (To the Reader). S.T.C.: 25245. Both works were finally printed in this single edition after Wentworth's death in 1597.

45. Wentworth, *A Pithie Exhortation*, p. 37.

46. Wentworth, *A Pithie Exhortation*, p. i (To the Reader).
47. Wentworth, *A Pithie Exhortation*, p. 80.
48. Wentworth, *A Discovrse*, p. 54.
49. Wentworth, *A Discovrse*, p. 53.
50. Clegg, ' "By the choise and inuitation of al the realme"', p. 433.
51. Andrew Gurr reminds us usefully that the scene required 'the presence of the throne, since Parliament was formally *rex in Parliamento*, the king, lords and commons together' (Shakespeare, *King Richard II*, ed. Gurr, p. 13, n.).
52. As the historian Nigel Saul remarks, 'the real Richard was never put on trial in Parliament' (N. Saul, *Richard II* (New Haven, CT and London: Yale University Press, 1997), p. 4). Only one source mentions the fact that someone asked for Richard to be heard in Parliament (to no avail of course): 'According to the *Traison et Mort*, Thomas Merks, the bishop of Carlisle, stood up at this point and declared that Richard should not be condemned unheard. No other source, however, mentions the bishop's intervention, and it seems that the story should be regarded as a fiction' (Saul, p. 422).
53. Cf. M. McKisack, *The Fourteenth Century 1307–1399* (Oxford: Clarendon Press, 1959), p. 494. Erasures of this kind were part of a strategy designed to stem the re-emergence of pro-Ricardian discourses and political fantasies which such writings could foster. In other words, as Paul Strohm argues, Lancastrian propaganda was determined 'to curb imagining – or to substitute for unruly imagining a more officially approved and structured imagination, stabilized and externally available in sponsored descriptions and official enactments' (P. Strohm, *England's Empty Throne, Usurpation and the Language of Legitimation, 1399–1422* (New Haven, CT and London: Yale University Press, 1998), p. 29). Historically also, Richard's deposition was ratified not by Parliament as such, but by an *ad hoc* gathering of prelates, lords and commons who had originally been assembled to meet as parliament. There was an obvious advantage in this, as 'Awkward questions as to the effect of the cession of the Crown on the validity of the parliamentary writs, or of the capacity of Parliament to judge the king, might thereby be evaded' (McKisack, p. 494).
54. This last possibility has been explored by theatre directors – often with extremely successful results. It was the case of Steven Pimlott's May 2000 Royal Shakespeare Company's production of *Richard II* at the 'Other Place' in Stratford-upon-Avon (reviewed in *Cahiers Élisabéthains*, 58 (2000) 80–2).
55. The audience has a very special role in *Richard II*, as Phyllis Rackin has also remarked: 'there is an extra role in the play not listed in the *dramatis personae*, a carefully calculated role complete with motivations, actions, errors, and discoveries, a role designed to be filled by the members of the audience' (P. Rackin, 'The Role of the Audience in Shakespeare's *Richard II*', *Shakespeare Quarterly*, 36.3 (1985) 263).
56. 'Like the crucifixion scenes in medieval drama where Christ spoke from the cross to accuse the audience crowded around the pageant wagon, Richard's deposition scene is presented not simply as a re-enactment of a past event but as immediate present action that engages its audience as participants' (Rackin, 'The Role of the Audience in Shakespeare's *Richard II*', pp. 270–1).

57. See A. Dillon, *The Construction of Martyrdom in the English Catholic Community* (Aldershot: Ashgate, 2002).

58. Shakespeare, *King Richard II*, ed. Gurr, p. 149, n.

4 'So mak'st thou faith an enemy to faith': Religion, Propaganda and Dreams of National Unity in *King John*

1. W. Shakespeare, *The Life and Death of King John*, ed. C. McEachern (Harmondsworth: Penguin, 2000), p. xxxi. Robert Smallwood has also remarked that: 'The story of King John . . . is told in a vacuum; the reign is caught from the past in a pinpoint of illumination, vividly but temporarily engaging our attention. At the close its implications must overleap the intervening years, or recede into the mists of history' (R. L. Smallwood, 'Introduction to *The New Penguin Shakespeare: King John*', repr. in *King John and Henry VIII: Critical Essays*, ed. F. A. Shirley (New York and London: Penugin, 1988), p. 176).

2. V. Mason Vaughan, 'Between Tetralogies: *King John* as transition', *Shakespeare Quarterly*, 35 (1984) 408.

3. We shall tackle the thorny issue of the dating of the play later on in this chapter in the section on Shakespeare and George Peele.

4. All references to the play are to A. R. Braunmuller's edition: W. Shakespeare, *The Life and Death of King John*, ed. A. R. Braunmuller (Oxford and New York: Oxford University Press, 1989).

5. W. Tyndale, *The obedience of a Christen man and how Christean rulers ought to governe where in also thou marke diligently thou shalt fynde eyes to perceave the conveyaunce of all jugglers* (London, 1528), ff. 157^{r-v}. S.T.C.: 2446.

6. Tyndale, *The obedience of a Christen man*, f. 158^r.

7. J. Bale, *King Johan* (1538–60), in *Narrative and Dramatic Sources of Shakespeare, vol. 4: Later English History Plays: King John, Henry IV, Henry V, Henry VIII*, ed. G. Bullough (London: Routledge; New York: Columbia University Press, 1962), p. 61.

8. Bale, *King Johan* (1538–60), in *Narrative and Dramatic Sources of Shakespeare*, p. 64.

9. Bale, *King Johan*, p. 70.

10. M. O'Connell, *The Idolatrous Eye, Iconoclasm and Theatre in Early-Modern England* (Oxford: Oxford University Press, 2000), p. 93.

11. For an illuminating analysis of Bale's iconoclasm in *Kyng Johan*, see P. Whitfield White, *Theatre and Reformation, Protestantism, Patronage and Playing in Tudor England* (Cambridge: Cambridge University Press, 1993), pp. 34–41 *et passim*.

12. See J. H. Morey, 'The Death of King John in Shakespeare and Bale', *Shakespeare Quarterly*, 45.3 (1994) 327–31; and A. J. Piesse, 'King John: Changing Perspectives', in *The Cambridge Companion to Shakespeare's History Plays*, ed. M. Hattaway (Cambridge: Cambridge University Press, 2002), p. 126.

13. R. Holinshed, *Chronicles* (1587 edn.), in *Narrative and Dramatic Sources of Shakespeare, vol. 4: Later English History Plays: King John, Henry IV, Henry V, Henry VIII*, ed. Bullough, p. 37.

14. Holinshed, *Chronicles* (1587 edn.), in *Narrative and Dramatic Sources of Shakespeare*, p. 48.
15. Holinshed, *Chronicles*, p. 49.
16. G. Hamel, '*King John* and *The Troublesome Raigne*, A Reexamination', in *King John, New Perspectives*, ed. D. T. Curren-Aquino (Newark: University of Delaware Press, 1989), p. 41.
17. W. Shakespeare, *King John*, ed. L. A. Beaurline (Cambridge: Cambridge University Press, 1990), p. 1. In his edition of *The Troublesome Raigne* J. W. Sider had declared previously that 'the evidence is not really conclusive either way' (J. W. Sider, *The Troublesome Raigne of John, King of England* (New York and London: Garland, 1979), p. xxiii).
18. W. Shakespeare, *King John*, ed. E. A. J. Honigmann, Arden Shakespeare (London and New York: Routledge, 1954 (repr. 1991)), p. lviii *et passim*. Honigmann has reiterated this thesis in a recent article: 'Shakespeare's self-repetitions and *King John*', *Shakespeare Survey*, 53 (2000) 175–83.
19. Shakespeare, *King John*, ed. Beaurline, p. 106.
20. Bullough, ed., *Narrative and Dramatic Sources of Shakespeare*, p. 2.
21. Smallwood, 'Introduction to *The New Penguin Shakespeare: King John*', p. 177.
22. As Brian Vickers writes, 'whoever wishes to dislodge *King John* from its position in 1595–96 is going to have to do the same with *Richard II*, for many scholars have commented on the close links between these two history plays' (B. Vickers, '*The Troublesome Raigne*, George Peele, and the date of *King John*', in *Words that Count*, ed. B. Boyd (Newark: University of Delaware Press, 2004), p. 105.
23. Shakespeare, *The Life and Death of King John*, ed. Braunmuller, p. 15.
24. Shakespeare, *King John*, ed. Beaurline, p. 1.
25. B. Boyd, '*King John* and *The Troublesome Raigne*: Sources, Structure, Sequence', *Philological Quarterly*, 74 (1995) 45.
26. Vickers, '*The Troublesome Raigne*, George Peele, and the date of *King John*', in *Words that Count*, ed. B. Boyd (Newark: University of Delaware Press, 2004), pp. 78–116. I wish to express my gratitude to Professor Vickers who very kindly let me read a copy of his article before publication. This section of my essay is much indebted to his work.
27. See Vickers, '*The Troublesome Raigne*, George Peele, and the date of *King John*', pp. 78–9.
28. 'Peele had nothing to learn from Shakespeare because he was incapable of learning from him. His dramatic structure, his characterization (or lack of it), his language – a curious mixture of the matter-of-fact (using little imagery) with vapid mythological allusions, pseudo-Marlovian exoticism, and Senecan rant – all these elements were fixed by the time he began writing for the public theatre' (Vickers, '*The Troublesome Raigne*, George Peele, and the date of *King John*'), p. 111.
29. Vickers, '*The Troublesome Raigne*, George Peele, and the date of *King John*', p. 111.
30. Anonymous, *The Troublesome Raigne of King John* (1591), in: *Narrative and Dramatic Sources of Shakespeare, vol. 4*, p. 75.
31. We shall henceforth assume that Peele is the author of *The Troublesome Raigne*.

32. Interestingly, Donna B. Hamilton suggests that the author of *The Trouble-some Raigne* may have been a defender of the Protestant conformist platform. Peele's theatrical anti-Catholicism may also have covered other allegiances: 'the association of *The Troublesome Raigne* with Thomas Orwin may support a revised reading of that play. Orwin, the printer of the anti-Martin Marprelate tracts, reprinted *The Troublesome Raigne* in 1591, the year of the Cartwright trial, and the year in which he also printed two other plays – *Campaspe* and *Sapho and Phao* by the courtly stylist John Lyly, author of some of the anti-Martinist tracts (D. B. Hamilton, *Shakespeare and the Politics of Protestant England* (New York and London: Harvester Wheatsheaf, 1992), p. 32).

33. Anonymous, *The Troublesome Raigne of King John*, p. 98.

34. *Tamburlaine, Part 1*, 2.6.32–3 and 4.1.56. A. R. Braunmuller has noted these resemblances (Shakespeare, *The Life and Death of King John*, p. 188, note to lines 340–3).

35. E. A. J. Honigmann, *Shakespeare: The Lost Years* (Manchester: Manchester University Press, 1998 [1985]), p. 119.

36. Peter Lake has very usefully analysed the way this type of anti-Catholic papal discourse functioned: 'the catholic threat was never merely political in the narrow invasion-, plot- and sedition-centred sense of the term. It was ideological, and thus for English protestants, at least, in constituting and constructing this sphere, in mobilising and associating all these different senses of the public together, the notion of "popery" was crucial. Popery in its foreignness and otherness threatened and hence, of course, helped to constitute the autonomy of a protestant England' (P. Lake, with M. Questier, *The Antichrist's Lewd Hat: Protestants, Papists and Players in Post-Reformation England* (New Haven, CT and London: Yale University Press, 2002), pp. 261–2).

37. Anonymous, *The Troublesome Raigne of King John*, p. 127.

38. Anonymous, *The Troublesome Raigne of King John*, p. 140.

39. D. F. Ash, 'Anglo-French relations in *King John*', *Études Anglaises*, 3 (1939) 357.

40. England, of course, is not an island – the idea is thus an ideological fantasy.

41. See, for instance, G. Peele, *The Battle of Alcazar* (pr. 1594), ed. W. W. Greg (Oxford: Oxford University Press, 1963 [1907]), sig. D1^r (2.3.743-8).

42. See G. Peele, *Edward I*, in *The Dramatic and Poetical Works of Robert Greene and George Peele*, ed. A. Dyce (London: Routledge, 1861), p. 373.

43. S. Doran, *Elizabeth I and Foreign Policy 1558–1603* (London and New York: Routledge, 2000), p. 55.

44. R. Cotton, *An Armor of Proofe, brought from the Tower of David, to fight against Spannyardes, and all enimies of the trueth* (London, 1596), sig. B4^r. S.T.C.: 5865.

45. T. Nun, *A Comfort against the Spaniard* (London, 1596), sig. A3^r. S.T.C.: 18748.

46. C. Gibbon, *A Watch-worde for Warre. Not so new as necessary: Published by reason of the disperced rumors amongst us, and the suspected comming of the Spanyard against us. Wherein we may learne how to prepare our selves to repell the Enemie, and to behave our selves all the tyme of that trouble* (Printed by John Legat, Printer to the Universitie of Cambridge, 1596), 'To the Reader', sig. A3^r. S.T.C.: 11492.

47. D. C. Wixson, ' "Calm words folded up in smoke": propaganda and spectator response in Shakespeare's *King John*', *Shakespeare Studies*, 14 (1981) 115.

A. R. Braunmuller's more recent analyses concur with Wixson's views and with our own, underlining the intimate interconnections between the play and its context(s) (see Shakespeare, *The Life and Death of King John*, pp. 38–9).
48. V. Mason Carr, *The Drama as Propaganda: a Study of* The troublesome raigne of King John (Salzburg: Institut für Englische Sprache, 1974), p. 118. Mason Carr also argued that 'without religious overtones, John is not a hero' (p. 79).
49. C. Cibber, *Papal Tyranny*, cited in E. M. Waith, 'King John and the Drama of History', *Shakespeare Quarterly*, 29.2 (1978) 193.
50. H. S. Bowden, *The Religion of Shakespeare. Chiefly from the Writings of the Late Mr. Richard Simpson, M.A.* (London, 1899), cited in *King John*, ed. J. Candido, Shakespeare: The Critical Tradition (London and Atlantic Highlands, NJ: Athlone Press, 1996), p. 303. Bowden also sought to persuade his readers that Shakespeare 'thought that the appeal to an international tribunal in the person of the Pope was not without its advantages' (Bowden, p. 306), a statement which cannot be supported by a close reading of the play. Richard Simpson, who influenced Bowden, had found that 'the political tendency of the old play is entirely suppressed' (R. Simpson, 'The Politics of Shakespeare's Historical Plays', cited in *King John*, ed. Candido, p. 207). In a less controversial account of the play, John Henry de Groot also found that Shakespeare had considerably toned down the anti-Catholicism of his source, *The Troublesome Raigne* (see J. H. de Groot, *The Shakespeares and 'The Old Faith'* (Fraser: Real-View-Books, 1995 [1946]), pp. 180–224).
51. The folio is currently preserved by the Folger Shakespeare Library. See: R. M. Frye, *Shakespeare and Christian Doctrine* (Princeton, NJ: Princeton University Press, 1963), pp. 282–8 *et passim*.
52. See the useful thread of papers published by the journal *Connotations*: R. Battenhouse, 'Religion in *King John*: Shakespeare's View', *Connotations*, 1.2. (1991) 140–9; R. Battenhouse, 'On *King John*: An Answer to Billington and Hobson', *Connotations*, 2.2 (1992) 172–81; C. Z. Hobson, 'A Comment on Roy Battenhouse, "Religion in *King John*: Shakespeare's view"', *Connotations*, 2.1 (1992) 69–75.
53. Honigmann, *Shakespeare: The Lost Years*, pp. 121, 122.
54. 'God is spoken for by voices which not only contradict each other but repeatedly belie themselves' (S. Buckhardt, *Shakespearean Meanings* (Princeton, NJ: Princeton University Press, 1968), p. 138).
55. As Jean E. Howard and Phyllis Rackin convincingly argue, 'In *King John* Shakespeare goes as far as he will ever go in making women, women's skeptical voices, and women's truth central to the history he staged, leaving his sources behind and venturing into the realm of the unwritten and the conjectural, and into the inaccessible domain (the no man's land) where the secrets of paternity are kept' (*Engendering a Nation, A Feminist Account of Shakespeare's English Histories* (London and New York: Routledge, 1997), p. 133). On the place of women in the unstable world of the play, see also: C. Levin, ' "I Trust I May Not Trust Thee": Women's Visions of the World in Shakespeare's *King John*', in *Ambiguous Realities Women in the Middle Ages and Renaissance*, ed. C. Levin and J. Watson (Detroit: Wayne State University Press, 1987), pp. 219–34.
56. S. Greenblatt, *Shakespearean Negotiations, The Circulation of Social Energy in Renaissance England* (Oxford: Clarendon Press, 1988), p. 128.

57. Pandulph will later manage to alienate Philip, however. The French king will later rebel against Rome in King John fashion, cf. his 'Am I Rome's slave?' (5.2.97). It is thus difficult to believe, with Burton Raffel, in 'the infinitely superior virtues of the Pope and of his representative' (B. Raffel, 'Shakespeare and the Catholic question', *Religion and Literature*, 30.1 (1998) 45).

58. Douglas C. Wixson also argues that: 'Debate is . . . the central feature of the play's structure; indeed, dialogue in *King John* is constructed on the basis of a dialectical occurring between opposing points of view. Each character has a platform to defend with wit, epithet, logic, or threat. The "platforms" constitute the audience's mental engagement in the play. In contrast to the pamphlet writers, Shakespeare makes no attempt to influence his audience' (' "Calm words folded up in smoke": propaganda and spectator response in Shakespeare's *King John*', p. 118).

59. Shakespeare, *The Life and Death of King John*, ed. Braunmuller, p. 41.

60. 'The church–state issues that dominated English politics during the last two decades of Queen Elizabeth's reign were the controversies within the English church over matters of liturgy and church polity. During that period, the primary language within which these controversies were conducted was anti-catholic rhetoric . . . '. (Hamilton, *Shakespeare and the Politics of Protestant England*, p. 30).

61. '*King John*, then, is a history play with a twist, one written in a different vein from the others, one more indeterminate and open than fixed and closed' (D. T. Curren-Aquino, 'Introduction: *King John* Resurgent', in *King John, New Perspectives*, ed. Curren-Aquino, p. 23).

62. Buckhardt, *Shakespearean Meanings*, p. 134.

63. V. Mason Vaughan, '*King John*, A Study in Subversion and Containment', in *King John, New Perspectives*, ed. Curren-Aquino, p. 74; D. Kehler, ' "So Jest with Heaven": Deity in *King John*', in *King John, New Perspectives*, p. 110; M. M. Reese, 'From *The Cease of Majesty*', repr. in *King John and Henry VIII: Critical Essays*, ed. Shirley, p. 171; see also: L. S. Champion, 'The "Un-end" of *King John*, Shakespeare's Demystification of Closure', in *King John, New Perspectives*, p. 173 *et passim*; E. M. W. Tillyard, 'From *Shakespeare's History Plays*', repr. in *King John and Henry VIII: Critical Essays*, p. 90 *et passim*; and more recently, P. Womack, 'Imagining Communities: Theatres and the English Nation in the Sixteenth Century', in *Culture and History 1350–1600* (Detroit: Wayne State University Press, 1992), esp. p. 138.

64. The parallels have been italicized. The text is cited in: L. B. Campbell, *Shakespeare's Histories: Mirrors of Elizabethan Policy* (San Marino: Huntington Library, 1968), p. 126; also in P. Pugliatti, *Shakespeare the Historian* (Basingstoke and London: Macmillan, 1996), p. 77.

65. A. Munday, *A Watch-woord to Englande To beware of traytours and tretcherous practises, which have beene the overthrowe of many famous Kingdomes and common weales, Written by a faithfull affected freend to his Country: who desireth God long to blesse it from Traytours, and their secret conspiracyes* (London, 1584), f. 40^v. S.T.C.: 18282. Munday's apparent loyalty to the government was not devoid of ambiguities however. See D. B. Hamilton's excellent *Anthony Munday and the Catholics, 1560–1633* (Aldershot: Ashgate, 2005).

66. Gibbon, *A Watch-worde for Warre*, sig. B2^v; sig. G4^r.

67. Gibbon, *A Watch-worde for Warre*, sig. G4^v.

68. See: Pugliatti, *Shakespeare the Historian*, p. 91.
69. Robert Davenport's seventeenth-century play on King John's reign is even harder hitting politically for Fitzwater allows himself to ask such forbidden questions as: 'To ease my groaning Country, is that Rebellion?' (*King John and Matilda, A Tragedy. As it was Acted with great Applause by her Majesties Servants at the Cock-pit in Drury Lane* (London, 1655 [composed 1628–34]) in *The Works of Robert Davenport*, ed. A. H. Bullen, Old English Plays New Series, vol. 3 (New York and London: Blom, 1964 [1882–89]), Act 5, scene 3, p. 81).
70. The exaggeration stems no doubt from Adrien Bonjour's influential essay on *King John* in which he finds a structural coherence to the play: the fall of John and the ensuing rise of the Bastard form, according to Bonjour, the play's dual movement ('The Road to Swinstead Abbey: A Study of the Sense and Structure of *King John*', repr. in *King John and Henry VIII: Critical Essays*, p. 120; see also pp. 122–3 *et passim*). L. A. Beaurline has also pointed out that the Bastard's importance has been over-emphasized: 'If anything saves England, it is Fortune and the awakened consciences of several characters' (Shakespeare, *King John*, p. 42). Recent criticism on the play shows that Bonjour's theory dies hard (see, for instance: A. J. Piesse, 'King John: Changing Perspectives', in *The Cambridge Companion to Shakespeare's History Plays*, ed. M. Hattaway (Cambridge: Cambridge University Press, 2002), p. 138).
71. King John chooses to moralize his dying moments and sees himself as damned (5.7.46–8) – here we are far from the Reformation hero, a part he was playing at the beginning of the play. The Bastard arrives to tell the King that the battle is not won and that he has lost the best part of his troops – this is the moment (5.7.59–64), furthermore, when Shakespeare has the King die, while all hope is lost.
72. On the merging of artistic and political themes at this point in the play, see D. S. Kastan, ' "To Set a Form upon that Indigest": Shakespeare's Fictions of History', *Comparative Drama*, 17.1 (1983) 15.
73. H. Garnet to the General, *ARSJ Fondo Gesuitico* 651, ff. 143–6 (London, 16 April 1596). (Original in Latin; trans. L. Hicks, London Jesuit Archives). A few lines later, the Jesuit was to continue to voice his incomprehension: 'It was the Religious who first brought religion into this kingdom; and it stood firm so long as the Religious continued their work. Why then should anyone be indignant if they labour to restore it to these same people?'
74. V. Mason Vaughan, 'King John', in *A Companion to Shakespeare's Works: The Histories*, ed. J. Howard and R. Dutton (Oxford: Blackwell, 2003), p. 379.
75. J. Knapp, *Shakespeare's Tribe: Church, Nation, and Theater in Renaissance England* (Chicago and London: University of Chicago Press, 2002), p. 175.
76. Knapp, *Shakespeare's Tribe*, p. 111.

5   The Discovery of a 'Popish Plot'? The Chamberlain's Men and the 1601 Essex Rising

1. PRO SP12/274/133, Earl of Essex to the Queen, 12 May 1600, printed in *Calendar of State Papers, Domestic series, of the reign of Elizabeth, preserved in the State Paper Department of Her Majesty's Public Record Office*, ed. M. A. E. Green (London, 1869), p. 435 (hereafter *CSP Dom.*).

2. 'A Skeltonian satirical ballad on some principal personages of Elizabeths Court', PRO SP12/278/23 (extract). This ballad is dated January 1601 in *CSP Dom.*, but internal evidence, such as the mention of a 'proclamation', suggests that it was composed *after* the Essex Rebellion.

3. The earl 'received sixty-six dedications between 1590 and 1600. Throughout the decade he received between five and seven dedications per year, ranging from chivalric treatises, through humanistic translations and musical compilations, to works of religious devotion and controversy' (A. Fox, 'The Complaint of Poetry for the Death of Liberality: the Decline of Literary Patronage in the 1590s', in *The Reign of Elizabeth I, Court and Culture in the Last Decade*, ed. J. Guy (Cambridge: Cambridge University Press, 1995), p. 231; see also appendix, pp. 245–8).

4. Quoted in R. C. McCoy, *The Rites of Knighthood, The Literature and Politics of Elizabethan Chivalry* (Berkeley, Los Angeles, London: University of California University, 1989), p. 96.

5. J. R. Dasent, ed., *Acts of the Privy Council of England* (London, His Majesty's Stationery Office, 1905), vol. 30 (1599–1600), p. 619 (hereafter *APC*).

6. M. James, 'At a Crossroads of the Political Culture: the Essex Revolt, 1601', in *Society, Politics and Culture: Studies in Early Modern England* (Cambridge: Cambridge University Press, 1986), p. 435.

7. *L'Isle and Dudley MSS*, 2:322, cited in L. Barroll, 'Shakespeare, Noble Patrons, and the Pleasures of "Common" Playing', in *Shakespeare and Theatrical Patronage in Early Modern England*, ed. P. Whitfield White and S. R. Westfall (Cambridge and New York: Cambridge University Press, 2002), p. 112.

8. *L'Isle and Dudley MSS*, vol. 2, p. 401, cited in Barroll, p. 112. Essex had actually left his command in Ireland and asked for an immediate interview with the Queen on the day of his return (28 September 1599). He was received by Elizabeth and subsequently placed under house arrest.

9. Attorney-General Edward Coke's private papers reveal also that he had certain doubts about Hayward's guilt (J. Hayward, *The First and Second Parts of the Life and Raigne of King Henrie IIII*, ed. J. J. Manning, Camden Society 4th series, vol. 42 (London: Royal Historical Society, 1991), p. 34). See also below.

10. Italics mine. PRO SP12/275/33 (undated in the original; dated *c.* 24 July 1600 in *CSP Dom.*), printed in E. K. Chambers, *William Shakespeare, A Study of Facts and Problems*, 2 vols. (Oxford: Clarendon Press 1930), vol. 2, p. 323.

11. B. Worden, 'Which Play was Performed at the Globe Theatre on 7 February 1601?', *London Review of Books*, 10 July 2003, pp. 22–3.

12. Frank Kermode, in a series of letters published in the *London Review of Books* has cast serious doubts on Worden's interpretation (see *LRB*, 6 November 2003 in particular).

13. 'The examination of Augustyn Phillypps servant unto the Lord Chamberlyne and one of hys players taken the xviii[th] of Februarii 1600 upon hys oth' (PRO, SP12/278/85). Phillips was examined by John Popham, Lord Chief Justice, Edmund Anderson, Chief Justice of Common Pleas, and Edward Fenner, Judge of the Queen's Bench. This document is one of the three depositions which mention the play – the others are Gelly Meyrick's and William Constable's (all three are printed in Chambers, *William Shakespeare*, vol. 2, pp. 324–5). See also below.

14. Phillips described the play in the following fashion: 'the play of the deposyng and kyllyng of Kyng Rychard the second' (PRO, SP12/278/85).

15. Samuel Schoenbaum with characteristic circumspection uses this phrase (' "Richard II" and the Realities of Power', *Shakespeare Survey*, 28 (1975) 7). The two most recent editors of Shakespeare's *Richard II* seem to concur also in the view that it was indeed Shakespeare's play that was performed in the afternoon of 7 February: Andrew Gurr remarks that 'there is no certain evidence that the performance was of Shakespeare's play, but since it was a play 'of King Henry the Fourth, and of the killing of Richard the second', it seems the most likely of the possible candidates and was certainly in the company's repertoire' (W. Shakespeare, *King Richard II*, New Cambridge Shakespeare, updated edn. (Cambridge: Cambridge University Press, 2003 [1984]), p. 7), while Charles R. Forker writes that the play is 'generally considered to have been Shakespeare's tragedy' (W. Shakespeare, *King Richard II*, ed. C. R. Forker, Arden 3 (London: Thomson Learning, 2002), p. 10). In an important article, Leeds Barroll also considers the play to be Shakespeare's *Richard II* ('A New History for Shakespeare and His Time', *Shakespeare Quarterly*, 39.4 (1988) 441–64).

16. Chambers, *William Shakespeare*, vol. 2, p. 323.

17. This is all we can surmise as 'The absences – perhaps caused by great responsibilities in the conspiracy – suggest again the complex limitations of the texts in hand. Absent from the group named by the deponents as involved in *Richard II* were the Earl of Essex and Sir Charles Danvers (both executed); the earl closest to Essex, Southampton (not executed but sentenced to the Tower for life); and two other peers close to Essex and Southampton: the Earl of Rutland and the Earl of Bedford. Both were spared but paid huge fines' (Barroll, 'A New History for Shakespeare and His Time', p. 445).

18. James, 'At a Crossroads of the Political Culture', p. 436.

19. James, p. 428.

20. *DNB*, vol. 5, p. 245. Lee is wrong though in assuming that Christopher Blount was Charles Blount's (the Lord Mountjoy) younger brother. Christopher Blount was only a very distant cousin of Mountjoy's. He was in fact the son of Thomas Blount of Kidderminster Manor. He had received a Catholic education in Douai at the English College from 1562 to 1577 and later joined the entourage of the Protestant Earl of Leicester. It was only in 1598 that he was to return to the Catholic faith: 'He was reconciled with the Church in Ireland by the Jesuit Fr. Fitzsimon in 1598; and thereafter he actively practiced his religion, to the extent of actively trying to convert others' (C. Devlin, *Hamlet's Divinity and Other Essays* (London: Rupert Hart-Davies, 1963), p. 127).

21. *APC*, vol. 31 (1600–1), p. 159.

22. See *APC*, vol. 31 (1600–1), pp. 160, 355–6, 484.

23. *APC*, vol. 31 (1600–1), pp. 160, 228, 355–6, 484.

24. *APC*, vol. 31 (1600–1), pp. 160, 228, 353.

25. *DNB*, vol. 12, p. 34.

26. *APC*, vol. 31 (1600–1), p. 159.

27. British Library, Harleian MS. 1327, f. 58. His dying words were reported to be: 'I am adiudged to dye for plottinge a plott never acted, and for actinge

an Acte never plotted' (MS. Harleian 1327, f. 55ᵛ) – a neat summary of some of the paradoxes of the whole Essex adventure.

28. *DNB*, vol. 14, p. 144; *APC*, vol. 31 (1600–1), p. 159.

29. W. Camden, *The historie of the most renowned and victorious princesse Elizabeth*, trans. R. Norton (London, 1630) book 4, p. 191 (STC: 4500). See also James, 'At a Crossroads of the Political Culture', p. 436, n. 73.

30. According to Constable's statement: '& after diner Thomas Lee came to the play . . . ' (PRO, SP12/278/72 (dated 16 February 1601), printed in: Chambers, *William Shakespeare*, vol. 2, p. 324).

31. *DNB*, vol. 11, pp. 821–3; *APC*, vol. 31 (1600–1601), p. 159.

32. 'Thenne he was at the same play and Cam in somwhat after yt was begon . . . ' (PRO, SP12/278/78 (dated 17 February 1601), printed in Chambers, *William Shakespeare*, vol. 2, p. 324).

33. *APC*, vol. 31 (1600–1), p. 159; *DNB*, vol. 37, p. 318.

34. See James, 'At a Crossroads of the Political Culture', p. 425, note 34. A. H. Dodd emphasizes the importance of the Earl of Essex's Catholic supporters in those parts: 'In North Wales . . . while few of those who took the earl's part were open recusants, all had either Catholic sympathies or Catholic connexions. . . . Indeed, although Essex was Leicester's stepson, his successor in royal favour and in some sense his political heir, it was from the very quarters where opposition to Leicester had been fiercest that Essex got his strongest support' ('North Wales in the Essex Revolt of 1601', *English Historical Review*, 59 (1944) 369).

35. *DNB*, vol. 15, p. 285.

36. *APC*, vol. 31 (1600–1), pp. 159, 353, 485. *DNB*, vol. 15, pp. 856–8.

37. *DNB*, vol. 15, pp. 854–6.

38. *APC*, vol. 31 (1600–1), p. 284.

39. J. Bruce, ed., *Correspondence of King James VI of Scotland with Sir Robert Cecil and Others in England* (London: Camden Society, 1861), p. 74.

40. See *DNB*, vol. 15, p. 857.

41. See James, 'At a Crossroads of the Political Culture', p. 426, n. 38.

42. Italics mine. PRO SP12/278/78, printed in: Chambers, *William Shakespeare*, vol. 2, p. 324.

43. SP12/278/78.

44. PRO SP12/278/85, printed in Chambers, *William Shakespeare*, vol. 2, p. 325.

45. 'Report of the Trial of Sir Gilly Meyricke and others', in *A Complete Collection of State Trials*, ed. S. Emlyn, 8 vols. (London, 1735) vol. 7, p. 47, cited in Chambers, *William Shakespeare*, vol. 2, pp. 325–6 (the original report was a *Le Neve MS.* according to Chambers).

46. Camden, *The historie of the most renowned and victorious princesse Elizabeth*, book 4, p. 192.

47. F. Bacon, *A declaration of the practices and treasons attempted and committed by Robert late Earle of Essex and his Complices* (London, 1601), sig. K2ᵛ (STC: 1133).

48. Bacon even glossed Augustine Phillips' deposition in a way which was meant to leave no doubt as to Meyrick's determination and political intent: 'And not so onely, but when it was told him by one of the Players, that the Play was olde, and they should haue losse in playing it, because fewe would

come to it: there was fourty shillings extraordinarie giuen to play it, and so thereupon playd it was' (Bacon, *A declaration*, sig. K2^v).

49. PRO, SP12/278/98. This further allusion to the play had not so far been uncovered.

50. 'the play of the deposyng and kyllyng of Kyng Rychard the Second' and 'that play of Kyng Rychard' (SP12/278/85).

51. I am quoting here Jonathan Dollimore's essay, 'Shakespeare, Cultural Materialism and the New Historicism', in *Political Shakespeare*, ed. J. Dollimore and A. Sinfield (Ithaca, NY: Cornell University Press, 1985) p. 88. For a critique of such views, see Barroll, 'A New History for Shakespeare and His Time', pp. 442–4 *et passim*; and P. Yachnin, 'The Powerless Theater', *English Literary Renaissance*, 21.1 (1991) 49–74.

52. This is Richard Simpson's conjecture, cited by Clement Mansfield Ingleby, who also prints a transcript of the letter (C. M. Ingleby, ed., *Shakespeare's Centurie of Prayse* (London: New Shakespeare Society, 1879 [1874]), p. 39). The letter was also mentioned by Evelyn May Albright, who used it in the course of her polemic with the critic Ray Heffner, but failed to explore its full implications (E. M. Albright 'Shakespeare's *Richard II*, Hayward's History of Henry IV, and the Essex Conspiracy', *PMLA*, 46 (1931) 708–9).

53. PRO SP12/275/146. My transcription. Charles Percy gave no indication of the year in which he composed this letter; it has, however, been tentatively assigned to 1600 by the editor of *CSP Dom*. (in which another transcription can be found).

54. W. Shakespeare, *Henry IV, Part 2*, ed. R. Weis, Oxford Shakespeare (Oxford: Clarendon Press, 1998). All further references are to this edition.

55. This scene was absent from the first 1600 quarto of *Henry IV, Part 2*, perhaps because it was deemed too dangerous (see Shakespeare, *Henry IV, Part 2*, p. 80).

56. Strangely, though, *Henry IV, Part 2* contained also an ominous warning to all rebels, showing how dissent could be ruthlessly crushed by royal authority. Prince John is merciless: 'But for you rebels, look to taste the due / Meet for rebellion' (4.1.343–4), or indeed, 'Some guard these traitors to the block of death, / Treason's true bed and yielder up of breath' (4.1.349–50).

57. Richard Simpson surmises also that: Charles Percy 'was evidently one of Shakespeare's admirers, perhaps one of his friends' (cited in Ingleby, ed., *Shakespeare's Centurie of Prayse*, p. 39). This, unfortunately, is unverifiable.

58. The earlier date is argued by René Weis in his edition of the play, the later is proposed by Michael Dobson (*The Oxford Companion to Shakespeare*, ed. M. Dobson and S. Wells (Oxford: Oxford University Press, 2001), p. 193).

59. This has been deduced from a survey of all his available correspondence for these years both in the State Papers and those made available by the Historical Manuscripts Commission (*Calendar of the Manuscripts of the Most Honourable the Marquis of Salisbury, K. G. . . . preserved at Hatfield House, Hertfordshire*, ed. S. R. Scargill-Bird *et al.* (London, 1899), part 7, vol. 7, pp. 464–5 (hereafter *Salisbury MSS.*); *Calendar of the Carew Manuscripts, preserved in the Archiepiscopal Library at Lambeth*, ed. J. S. Brewer and W. Bullen, 6 vols. (London, 1867–73), vol: 1589–1600, p. 280; *Salisbury MSS.*, part 9, vol. 8, p. 416; p. 448; *Salisbury MSS.*, part 9, vol. 9, pp. 93–4; *Calendar of the State Papers, relating to Ireland, of the reign of Elizabeth*, ed. E. G. Atkinson *et al.*,

5 vols. (London, 1893–1905) vol.: March–October 1600, p. 191 (hereafter *CSP Ireland*); *CSP Ireland*, 1601–3, p. 628).

60. In a letter dated 22 November [1600], he writes from Winchester to Mr Carlington, asking him to remind 'my Lord' – Essex perhaps? – to write a letter to Trinity College, Oxford, supporting his grant of a lease of tithes for Dumbleton Hall (the university owned some land in Gloucestershire) (PRO SP46/22/143; the year is not given in the original and is a surmise on the part of the *CSP Dom.* editor).

61. René Weis remarks interestingly that 'Twenty-one copies survive, ten of Q[uarto] A, eleven of Q[uarto] B, which makes it the commonest of extant Shakespeare first quartos' (Shakespeare, *Henry IV, Part 2*, p. 78).

62. Privy Council to the Lord Deputy and Council of Ireland, 17 January 1574, *CSP Ireland*, p. 2. The reference is to 'Mr. Carleton', but, as the editors indicate, Carleton and Carlington were variant spellings.

63. 'He [i.e. Essex] asked liberty to set down in writing his whole project of coming to Court in that sort, which he has done, and this concurs with the confessions of Sir Chas. Danvers, Sir John Davies, Sir Ferd. Gorges, and *Mr. Carleton*' (Italics mine. Robert Cecil to the Lord Deputy in Ireland, 26 February 1601, *CSP Dom.*, p. 597). N.B.: The *CSP* editor indicates that Carleton was a variant of the name Carlington.

64. PRO SP12/278/85, printed in: Chambers, *William Shakespeare*, vol. 2, p. 325.

65. In 1601, the principal players in the company were probably Richard Burbage, William Shakespeare, Augustine Phillips, William Sly, Thomas Pope, John Heminges and Robert Armin (cf. A. Gurr, *The Shakespearean Stage 1574–1642*, 3rd edn. (Cambridge: Cambridge University Press, 1994), p. 44).

66. Among the sharers was also Richard Burbage's elder brother Cuthbert who was not an actor (Gurr, *The Shakespearean Stage*, p. 45).

67. MS. in the Hatfield collection, part 93, f. 74ᵛ, summarized in: *Salisbury MSS.*, part 12, vol. 99, p. 165. See also E. B. De Fonblanque, *Annals of the House of Percy, From the Conquest to the Opening of the Nineteenth Century*, 2 vols. (London, 1887), vol. 2, pp. 252–3.

68. Henry Percy, 9th Earl of Northumberland to Robert Cecil, Lord Salisbury, 20 November 1606 (De Fonblanque, *Annals of the House of Percy*, vol. 2, p. 297). Malicious rumours circulated also about Charles Percy's collusion with Jesuit priests (see Sir Thomas Edmondes to the Earl of Salisbury, 5 December 1605, *Salisbury MSS.*, part 9, vol. 17, p. 546).

69. PRO SP12/278/85, printed in: Chambers, *William Shakespeare*, vol. 2, p. 325.

70. Ian Wilson remarks also that 'the performance was to be at the Globe, clearly then intended not to be for any private purpose, but aimed squarely at the general populace' (*Shakespeare: The Evidence, Unlocking the Mysteries of the Man and His Works*, London: Headline, 1993), p. 275).

71. P. Thomson, *Shakespeare's Professional Career* (Cambridge: Cambridge University Press, 1992), p. 139.

72. Gurr, *The Shakespearean Stage*, p. 45.

73. T. W. Baldwin, *The Organization and Personnel of the Shakespearean Company* (Princeton: Princeton University Press, 1927), p. 136 (note). Baldwin suggests also that Augustine Phillips may have taken the role of Bolingbroke when the play was first performed (p. 407). On Phillips' relation to the other members of his company and on his personal life, see E. A. J. Honigmann, *Playhouse*

Wills, 1558–1642 (Manchester and New York: Manchester University Press, 1993), pp. 72–5; and W. Ingram, 'The Wife of Augustine Phillips', *Notes and Queries* 30.3 (new series), p. 157.

74. Paul Yachnin, in an otherwise sophisticated argument, appears convinced by Augustine Phillips' statement, forgetting that it is a deposition and that it may not necessarily reflect the whole truth. He claims that the players were not hiding behind commercial arguments and that Phillips was even 'dry and almost condescending to the Earl's followers' (Yachnin, 'The Powerless Theater', p. 65). Louis Montrose – who sees Meyrick as the person responsible for hiring the players – seems also to take much of the primary evidence at face value. His analysis of the episode falls short of exploring the possible implications of the players' involvement (*The Purpose of Playing, Shakespeare and the Cultural Politics of the Elizabethan Theatre* (Chicago and London: University of Chicago Press, 1996), p. 75).

75. Schoenbaum, ' "Richard II" and the Realities of Power', p. 6.

76. Robert Sharpe's suggestion that the play in question might have been *Richard II* seems wildly far-fetched (*The Real War of the Theaters* (Boston, MA: Heath, 1945), p. 183.

77. Knight argues that the dramatist and the Master of Chancery William Lambard may have known each other (*Shakespeare's Hidden Life: Shakespeare at the Law, 1585–1595* (New York: Mason & Lipscomb, 1973), p. 227 *et passim*).

78. The title was changed interestingly when the play was printed (see T. Cain, ' "Satyres, That Girde and Fart at the Time": *Poetaster* and the Essex Rebellion', in *Refashioning Ben Jonson, Gender, Politics, and the Jonsonian Canon*, ed. J. Sanders *et al.* (Basingstoke: Macmillan, 1998), p. 54).

79. B. Jonson, *Poetaster, or The Arraignement*, in *Ben Jonson*, ed. C. H. Herford and P. Simpson, 11 vols. (London: Oxford University Press, 1966), vol. 4, respectively: 3.4.201; 5.3.123–5. All references to this edition.

80. See E. K. Chambers, *The Elizabethan Stage*, 4 vol. (Oxford: Clarendon Press, 1923), vol. 1, p. 385. Cf. also R. Dutton, *Mastering the Revels, The Regulation and Censorship of English Renaissance Drama* (Basingstoke: Macmillan, 1991), pp. 138–9.

81. See B. N. de Luna, *Jonson's Romish Plot, A Study of Catiline and its Historical Context* (Oxford: Clarendon Press, 1967). Ian Donaldson explains indeed that: 'Versed initially in the ways of the Roman Church while in prison in 1598, perhaps by the Yorkshire Jesuit, Father Thomas Wright, Jonson was (so to speak) re-versed back into the ways of the established church in 1606 on the instructions of the Consistory Court . . .' (*Jonson's Magic Houses: Essays in Interpretation* (Oxford: Clarendon Press, 1997), p. 52).

82. Respectively, 4.4.6–7; 4.4.11–12; 4.4.15; 4.4.17–20. Tom Cain also emphasizes this intriguing parallel, adding that Lord Monteagle, who accompanied Charles Percy when he hired the players, was a patron of Jonson and, like him, he was a Catholic (see Cain, ' "Satyres, That Girde and Fart at the Time"', pp. 63–4). The only possible allusion to the Essex Rebellion in Shakespeare may be found in *Hamlet*, in a passage where Rosencrantz explains to Hamlet why 'the tragedians of the city' are forced to travel: 'I think their inhibition comes by the means of the late innovation' (2.2.330–1), even if, as Harold Jenkins explains cautiously, the play is notoriously difficult to date precisely

(see W. Shakespeare, *Hamlet*, ed. H. Jenkins, Arden Shakespeare (London and New York: Routledge, 1982), p. 472).

83. *APC*, vol. 31 (1600–1), pp. 147–8.
84. J. Hayward, *The First Part of the Life and raigne of King* Henrie *the IIII.* (London, 1599), sig. I4ʳ. S.T.C.: 12995.
85. F. J. Levy, 'Hayward, Daniel, and the Beginning of Politic History in England', *Huntington Library Quarterly*, 50 (1987) 6.
86. J. Hayward, *The life and raigne of King Edward the Sixt* (London, 1630), p. 2 (To the Reader). S.T.C.: 12998.
87. Cited in R. Dutton, 'Buggeswords: Samuel Harsnett and the Licensing, Suppression and Afterlife of Dr. John Hayward's *The first part of the life and reign of King Henry IV*', *Criticism*, 35.3 (1993) 308.
88. As Richard Dutton points out: 'The rebellion had, in fact, transformed the status of all such *representations* of rebellion' ('Buggeswords', p. 319).
89. Jonson, *Sejanus*, in *Ben Jonson*, vol. 4, p. 405 (Act 3, ll. 383–5).
90. Camden, *The historie of the most renowned and victorious princesse Elizabeth*, book 4, p. 193. Eager to deny that he had not betrayed his former patron, Francis Bacon published in 1604 his *Apologie, in certaine imputations concerning the late Earle of Essex* in which he claims to have played down in the Queen's presence the political importance of Hayward's *History of Henry IV* (*Sir Francis Bacon his apologie, in certaine imputations concerning the late Earle of Essex* (London, 1604), pp. 36–7. S.T.C.: 1111).
91. See in particular Hayward, *The First Part of the Life and raigne of King Henrie the IIII*, p. 86 onwards.
92. Hayward, *The First Part of the Life and raigne of King Henrie the IIII*, p. 105.
93. James, 'At a crossroads of the political culture: the Essex revolt, 1601', pp. 460–1.
94. Essex's title of Earl Marshal figures prominently in the epistle dedicatory of Hayward's book. As Richard McCoy has shown, as soon as Essex was appointed Earl Marshal in 1597, he commissioned extensive research on the status and privileges of the office. This research resulted in the writing of treatises which underlined the ancient rights and prerogatives of the office, one of these being, the right to call a parliament in case of tyranny or crisis in the state (see McCoy, *The Rites of Knighthood*, pp. 90, 93, 95).
95. Camden, *The historie of the most renowned and victorious princesse Elizabeth*, book 4, p. 181. When the Queen called her tenth and last parliament, it was hardly surprising that she seemed intent on defending her prerogative which she felt had been threatened by recent events. This is what she commanded the Speaker to read in parliament: 'She said that her kinglye prerogatyve (ffor soe she termed it) was tender, and therefore desireth us not to speake or dowbte of her carefull reformacion, ffor she said that her commaundemente given a little before the late trobles (meaninge the earle of Essex' matters) by the unfortunate event of them was not soe hindered, but that she had since that tyme . . . thought uppon them . . . ' (T. E. Hartley, ed., *Proceedings in the Parliaments of Elizabeth I*, 3 vols. (Leicester: Leicester University Press, 1981–95), vol. 3, p. 395).
96. PRO SP12/274/133, Earl of Essex to the Queen, 12 May 1600, printed in: *Calendar of State Papers, Domestic series, of the reign of Elizabeth, preserved in the State Paper Department of Her Majesty's Public Record Office*, ed. M. A. E. Green (London, 1869), p. 435.

97. Thomas Sackville (1536?–1608) presided the trial as Lord High Steward. He and Thomas Norton (1532–1584) penned this play about the dangers of a divided kingdom. *Gorboduc* was performed in 1561 in the Inner Temple Hall.

98. Cited in J. Nichols, *Bibliotheca Topographica Britannica*, 10 vols. (New York: AMS Press, 1968 [facsimile reprint of 1780–90 edn.]), vol. 1, appendix 7, p. 525.

99. 'Rebellion is the sinne of witch-craft nam'd', as Richard Vennard proclaimed in a propaganda pamphlet entitled *Englands Joy* ((London, 1601?), sig. A3^v. S.T.C.: 24636.3). Regarding witchcraft trials, Marion Gibson remarked that 'Since it was the representation of events by victim and witch to the justice and then to the judge and jury which mattered in preliminary hearings and in court . . . this circular need for coherence and plausibility is important. . . . The literary, storytelling stereotype is more important in shaping the account and the consequences of its telling than are the inaccessibilities of whatever really happened' (M. Gibson, *Reading Witchcraft, Stories of Early English Witches* (London and New York: Routledge, 1999), pp. 8–9). See also Chapter 1.

100. Analytical abstract, July 1600, PRO SP12/275/33, printed in: Albright, 'Shakespeare's *Richard II*, Hayward's History of Henry IV, and the Essex Conspiracy', p. 697.

101. R. Devereux, *An Apologie of the Earle of Essex, against those which fasly and maliciously taxe him to be the onely hinderer of ther peace, and quiet of his countrey* (London, 1598). S.T.C.: 6788.

102. James, 'At a Crossroads of the Political Culture', p. 445.

103. Cited in James, p. 459.

104. PRO SP12/278/102.

105. Cited in Camden, *The historie of the most renowned and victorious princesse Elizabeth*, book 4, p. 127.

106. G. Chapman, *The Tragedy of Charles Duke of Byron*, ed. J. Margeson (Manchester and New York: Manchester University Press, 1988), p. 210 (4.1.19–20).

107. Camden, *The historie*, book 4, p. 173. Bacon had already denounced what he considered to be Essex's opportunism: 'And knowing there were no such strong and drawing cordes of popularitie, as religion: he had not neglected, both at this time, and long before, in a profane pollicy to serue his turne (for his own greatnesse,) of both sorts & factions, both *Catholicks* and *Puritans*, as they terme them, etc. . . . giuing assurance to *Blunt, Davies*, and diuers others, that (if hee might preuaile in his desired greatnesse,) hee would bring in a toleration of the *Catholike* religion' (F. Bacon, *A Declaration of the Practises & Treasons attempted and committed by* Robert *late Earle of* Essex *and his complices* (London, 1601), sig. D3^r. S.T.C.: 1133).

108. Camden, *The historie*, book 4, p. 173.

109. This was later held as evidence against him as Cuffe summarized the contents of Essex's instructions to the Scottish ambassador at Cecil's demand (Bruce, ed., *Correspondence of King James VI of Scotland with Sir Robert Cecil and Others in England*, pp. 81–4).

110. Paul E. J. Hammer explains this: 'Essex and other privy councillors used agents actually to foment conspiracies against the Queen, a technique

sometimes termed 'projection'. Such plots were exposed when the time seemed right and the participants were tried and executed with maximum publicity. By this means, Catholic exiles could be discredited and Elizabeth could be encouraged to maintain a hard line against Spain, whose support was blamed for each new conspiracy' (*The Polarisation of Elizabethan Politics*, p. 157).

111. Bacon, *A Declaration*, sig. H2^v.
112. Bacon, sig. H3^v.
113. Lucy Aitkin reports indeed that 'The life of the earl of Southampton was spared, at the intercession chiefly of Cecil...' (*Memoirs of the Court of Elizabeth*, 2 vols. (London, 1818), vol. 2, p. 479).
114. Leo Hicks tries to demonstrate that Cecil *did* support at one point the claims of the Infanta. The evidence he brings in is interesting but certainly not conclusive (L. Hicks, S. J., 'Sir Robert Cecil, Father Persons and the Succession', *Archivum Historicum Societatis Iesu*, 24 (1955) 95–139). Joel Hurstfield qualifies Hicks' conclusions and paints a more nuanced picture: 'In practice, the Cecil-Infanta story was more important as a move in the internal struggle between the Jesuits and the Appellants than as a serious proposal to the pope or the king of Spain' (J. Hurstfield, 'The Succession Struggle in Late Elizabethan England', in *Elizabethan Government and Society, Essays Presented to Sir John Neale*, ed. S. T. Bindoff *et al.* (London: Athlone Press, 1961), p. 389).
115. See *DNB*, vol. 1, p. 1152. The anonymous 'A direction for the preachers', dated 14 February 1601 reads indeed very much like Cecil's handiwork directed against a man for whom he had very little sympathy: 'As concerninge matters of religion, his dissimulation and hipocrisye therein is now discovered to haue ben verie admirable' (PRO SP12/278/63). The preachers were thus well briefed.
116. W. Barlowe, *A Sermon preached at Paules Crosse. With a short discourse of the late Earle of Essex* (London, 1601), sig. B5^v. S.T.C.: 1454.
117. Barlowe, sig. C1^v.
118. I am quoting here from the text of one of the many ballads on the earl of Essex, *A lamentable Dittie composed vpon the death of Robert Lord Devereux late Earle of Essex* (London, 1603). S.T.C.: 6791.
119. There were limits as to how far Cecil could 'tune the pulpits'. Barlowe's sermon tried not to overstate its case so as not to alienate the mainstream and dissident Protestants who had supported Essex. The government was never in full control of the pulpits, it was a matter 'not of imposing uniformity, or ensuring that all preachers spoke with one voice, but simply of using sermons as a channel of communication, a 'point of contact' between the state and its subjects' (A. Hunt, 'Tuning the Pulpits: the Religious Context of the Essex Revolt', in *The English Sermon Revised, Religion, Literature and History 1600–1750*, ed. L. A. Ferrell and P. McCullough (Manchester: Manchester University Press, 2000), p. 109).
120. Barlowe, *A Sermon preached at Paules Crosse*, sig. D2^r.
121. PRO SP12/278/127. The massacre of French Protestants began in Paris on 24 August 1572 and subsequently spread to other parts of France.
122. James, 'At a Crossroads of the Political Culture', p. 460, n. 154.

123. Folger Library MS. V.b.214, printed in A. J. Loomie, 'A Catholic Petition to the Earl of Essex', *Recusant History*, 7.1 (1963) 38–41. See also on this same topic J. MacManaway, 'Elizabeth, Essex, and James', in *Elizabethan and Jacobean Studies Presented to Frank Percy Wilson*, ed. H. Davis and H. Gardner (Oxford: Clarendon University 1959), pp. 219–30. On Catholic loyalism and the Essex circle, consult A. Shell, *Catholicism, Controversy and the English Literary Imagination* (Cambridge: Cambridge University Press, 1999), pp. 127–8.

124. See M. Heinemann, 'Rebel Lords, Popular Playwrights, and Political Culture: Notes on the Jacobean Patronage of the Earl of Southampton', *Yearbook of English Studies*, 21 (1991) 83. Sandys' treatise was *A Relation of the State of Religion* (London, 1605). S.T.C.: 21716. Sandys, for example, condemned the lies, on both sides, of religious propaganda: 'And verily in this kinde, both the Protestants and Papistes seeme generally in the greatest part of their stories, to be both to blame, though both not equally, having by their passionate reports much wronged the truth, abused this present age, and preiudiced posteritie: insomuch, that the onely remedie now seeming to remaine, is to read indifferently the stories on both parts, to count them as advocates and to play the Iudge betweene them' (sig. K1^V.)

125. Both Nahum Tate's Drury Lane altered version of the play in 1680 (under the reign of Charles II) and John Rich's Covent Garden production performed in 1738 (as George II was on the throne) amply demonstrate *Richard II*'s potential for topicality (for details of these two productions, see Shakespeare, *King Richard II*, ed. Forker, pp. 50–5).

126. Bacon, *A declaration of the practices and treasons attempted and committed by Robert late Earle of Essex and his Complices*, sig. K3^r.

127. Shakespeare, *King Richard II*, ed. Andrew Gurr, p. 145 (3.4.63–4).

128. R. Verstegan, *Odes in Imitation of the Seaven Penitential Psalmes, With Sundry other Poemes* (n.p., 1601), sig. H^{r-v}. S.T.C.: 21359. See also another collection of poems attributed tentatively to Essex himself: *The Passion of a Discontented Minde* (London, 1601), sig. D2^v, more specifically. S.T.C.: 3679.5.

129. R. Pricket, *Honors Fame in Triumph Riding* (London, 1604), sig. B2^v. S.T.C.: 20339.

130. Pricket, sig. B3^r.

131. Pricket, *Honors Fame in Trivmph Riding*, sig. C3^r. On the same page Pricket also speaks of an 'vp-start groome sprung from the Cart', which again could refer to Cecil.

132. S. Daniel, *The Tragedie of Philotas* (London, 1607), sig. C4^r. S.T.C.: 6263. Hugh Gazzard, in an important article, offers a convincing reading of *Philotas* as a '*drame à clef*' (' "Those graue presentments of antiquitie", Samuel Daniel's *Philotas* and the Earl of Essex', *Review of English Studies*, 51 (2000) 423–50).

133. S. Daniel, *A Panegyrike Congratulatorie, Deliuered to the Kings Most excellent Maiestie* (London, 1607), sig. D4^r. S.T.C.: 6263.

134. Camden, *The historie of the most renowned and victorious princesse Elizabeth*, book 4, p. 178.

6 Revisiting the Reformation: Shakespeare and Fletcher's *King Henry VIII*

1. R. Holinshed, *Chronicles of England, Scotland, and Ireland*, 6 vols. (London, 1808 [1586]), vol. 3, p. 675.
2. All references are taken from the following edition: W. Shakespeare and J. Fletcher, *King Henry VIII*, ed. G. McMullan, Arden Shakespeare (London: Thomson, 2000). As the consensus is growing around the dual authorship of this play, I shall assume – with the Arden 3 editor of *King Henry VIII* – that the play is the work of William Shakespeare and John Fletcher. For textual remarks regarding the collaboration see: Shakespeare and Fletcher, *King Henry VIII*, pp. 180–99 and 445–9.
3. G. McMullan, *The Politics of Unease in the Plays of John Fletcher* (Amherst, MA: University of Massachusetts Press, 1994), p. xi.
4. McMullan, *The Politics of Unease*, p. 25; also p. 29.
5. The present study will not examine the still controversial question of the attribution and composition of the different scenes of *All Is True*. This essay considers the work of Shakespeare and Fletcher as a whole. Readers interested in this question may refer to Gordan McMullan's useful summary of the various hypotheses (Shakespeare, *King Henry VIII*, pp. 448–9 (appendix 3).
6. 'Most scholars whether they agree or not with the link between *Henry VIII* and the wedding celebrations of February 1613, accept the long-held view that the play was written late in 1612 or early in 1613' (W. Shakespeare, *King Henry VIII*, ed. J. Margeson, New Cambridge Shakespeare (Cambridge: Cambridge University Press, 1990), p. 4). McMullan suggests that the play might have been staged at the Blackfriars Theatre before the Globe performances of 1613; if he is right this could not have been before 1610 due to outbreaks of plague (Shakespeare and Fletcher, *King Henry VIII*, p. 9).
7. I. Ribner, *The English History Play in the Age of Shakespeare* (London: Methuen, 1965 [1957]), p. 209. See also G. Taylor, 'The date and auspices of the additions to *Sir Thomas More*', in *Shakespeare and* Sir Thomas More, *Essays on the Play and its Shakespearian Interest*, ed. T. H. Howard-Hill (Cambridge: Cambridge University Press, 1989), p. 125. Lady Jane Grey was a great-granddaughter of Henry VII. She reigned very briefly as Queen of England (9–19 July 1553). The Duke of Northumberland, her father-in-law, persuaded Edward VI to alter the succession in her favour, but after ten days as Queen she was imprisoned and later executed.
8. On Shakespeare and the Essex rebellion, see Chapter 5.
9. Ribner, *The English History Play*, p. 205.
10. R. B. Sharpe, *The Real War of the Theatres, Shakespeare's Fellows in Rivalry with the Admiral's Men, 1594–1603*, Modern Language Association (Boston, MA: Heath; London: Oxford University Press, 1935), p. 194.
11. Anonymous, *The Life and Death of the Lord Cromwell*, in *The Shakespeare Apocrypha*, ed. C. F. Tucker Brooke (Oxford: Clarendon Press, 1908), [4.1.6–7], p. 180.
12. Anonymous, *The Life and Death of the Lord Cromwell*, [5.5.146–7] p. 190.
13. M. Drayton, *The Historie of the Life and Death of the Lord Cromwell, sometimes Earle of Essex, and Lord Chauncellor of England* (London, 1609), sig. A4ᵛ. S.T.C.: 7201.

14. See D. Norbrook, *Poetry and Politics in the English Renaissance* (London: Routledge, 1984), pp. 210–11. Brooke also held the view that if the King could 'impose by his absolute Power, then no Man [would be] certain what he hath: for it shall be subject to the King's Pleasure' (cited in: Norbrook, p. 211). Richard III's ghost addresses a warning to tyrants in no uncertain terms: 'Asswage your Thirst betimes; remit your height, / For if yee fall y'are crush't with your owne weight' (C. Brooke, *The ghost of Richard the third* (London, 1614), sig. L3ʳ. S.T.C.: 3830).

15. Drayton, *The Historie of the Life and Death of the Lord Cromwell*, p. 33.

16. Drayton, *The Historie*, p. 38.

17. Drayton, *The Historie*, p. 39.

18. Drayton, *The Historie*, p. 41.

19. On the 'Bluff-King-Harry' tradition, see Shakespeare and Fletcher, *King Henry VIII*, ed. McMullan, p. 177.

20. See G. Bullough, *Narrative and Dramatic Sources of Shakespeare*, 8 vols. (London: Routledge; New York: Columbia University Press, 1962), vol. 4, p. 494.

21. On Prince Henry and his possible influence on Shakespeare and Fletcher's *Henry VIII* see: F. O. Waage, Jr., '*Henry VIII* and the Crisis of the English History Play', *Shakespeare Studies*, 8 (1975) 297–309.

22. For the dating of the play, see A. Munday and Others, *Sir Thomas More*, ed. V. Gabrieli and G. Melchiori, Revels Plays (Manchester: Manchester University Press, 1990), p. 12. All references to the play are taken from this edition.

23. Munday and Others, *Sir Thomas More*, p. 33.

24. J. W. Veltz, '*Sir Thomas More* and the Shakespeare Canon: Two Approaches', in *Shakespeare and* Sir Thomas More, p. 183.

25. W. Shakespeare, *The Complete Works*, ed. S. Wells and G. Taylor (Oxford: Clarendon Press, 1986), p. 785.

26. Veltz, '*Sir Thomas More* and the Shakespeare Canon', p. 184.

27. 'The author avoids raising the specific question of the conflict between the Roman and the English Church, replacing it with that of the freedom of the individual conscience from worldly authority' (G. Melchiori, '*The Book of Sir Thomas More*: dramatic unity', in *Shakespeare and* Sir Thomas More, p. 77). This was no doubt why such an ambiguous and apparently anti-Catholic figure as Anthony Munday could be among the authors of a play on the life of a Catholic martyr. Yet Munday may not have been so rabidly anti-Catholic after all. See D. B. Hamilton: 'Anthony Munday and *The Merchant of Venice*', *Shakespeare Survey*, 54 (2001) esp. 90–1.

28. G. McMullan, 'The Dialogics of Reformation in *Henry VIII*', in *Shakespeare and Carnival, After Bakhtin*, ed. R. Knowles (Basingstoke and London: Macmillan, 1998), p. 219.

29. Susannah Brietz Monta finds that the play 'is ambivalent about the ability of constant consciences to form a collective witness to historical and religious continuity, a project central to martyrological controversialists' (' "Thou fall'st a blessed martyr": Shakespeare's *Henry VIII* and the Polemics of Conscience', *English Literary Renaissance*, 30.2 (2000) 272).

30. Italics mine.

31. This was probably inspired by Holinshed: 'Thus my conscience being tossed in the waues of a scrupulous mind, and partlie in despaire to haue anie other

issue that I had alredie by this ladie now my wife, it behooued me further to consider the state of this realme, and the danger it stoode in for lacke of a prince to succeed me . . . ' (Holinshed, *Chronicles*, p. 738).

32. McMullan, 'The Dialogics of Reformation', p. 214. See also these other seminal studies: L. Bliss, 'The Wheel of Fortune and the Maiden Phenix of Shakespeare's *King Henry the Eighth*', *English Literary History*, 42 (1975) 1–25; J. H. Anderson, *Biographical Truth: The Representation of Historical Persons in Tudor-Stuart Writing* (New Haven, CT and London: Yale University Press, 1984), p. 126 *et passim*; P. Rudnytsky, 'Shakespeare and the Deconstruction of History', *Shakespeare Survey*, 43 (1991) 43–58. G. McMullan, 'Shakespeare and the End of History', *Essays and Studies*, 48 (1995) 16–37.

33. On rumour, see Pierre Sahel, 'The Strangeness of a Dramatic Style: Rumour in *Henry VIII*', *Shakespeare Survey*, 38 (1985) 145–51.

34. G. Wickham, 'The Dramatic Structure of Shakespeare's *King Henry the Eighth*: An Essay in Rehabilitation', in *British Academy Shakespeare Lectures 1980–89*, ed. E. A. J. Honigmann (Oxford: Oxford University Press, 1993), p. 132.

35. See Shakespeare and Fletcher, *King Henry VIII*, p. 9.

36. Wickham, 'The Dramatic Structure', p. 133.

37. In Holinshed, Katherine's obstinacy is interpreted by Henry as a sign of her allegiance to the Pope: 'With this answer the lords departed to the king, which was sorie to heare of hir wilfull opinion, and in especiall that she more trusted in the popes law, than in keeping the precepts of God' (Holinshed, *Chronicles*, p. 772). In Shakespeare and Fletcher she finds her estrangement from the English nation painful.

38. For V. B. Richmond, 'Katherine is thus a Catholic with a conscience, not a superstitious follower of the Church'. She adds: 'one of the most compelling scenes stages a "vision" that resonates with medieval stories of saints and heroes of romance to whom God gives a foretelling of eternal life and their own nearing life' (*Shakespeare, Catholicism and Romance* (New York and London: Continuum, 2000), pp. 203, 204).

39. R. Vanita, 'Mariological Memory in *The Winter's Tale* and *Henry VIII*', *Studies in English Literature 1500–1900*, 40.2 (2000) 329.

40. Wolsey asks Katherine to 'Be patient yet' in 2.4.71, and later in the same scene she admits that 'They vex me past my patience' (l. 127). In another scene with Wolsey she confronts him with 'Yet will I add an honour: a great patience' (3.1.137).

41. Shakespeare and Fletcher, *King Henry VIII*, ed. McMullan, p. 133.

42. See Shakespeare and Fletcher, *King Henry VIII*, p. 134.

43. Shakespeare and Fletcher, *King Henry VIII*, p. 134–5.

44. McMullan, 'The Dialogics of Reformation', p. 222.

45. K. H. Noling, 'Grubbing Up the Stock: Dramatizing Queens in *Henry VIII*', p. 299. Linda McJ. Micheli writes on the same lines: 'However much weight is given to the at least superficially positive portrait of Anne, mother of the Protestant Elizabeth, Katherine earns a larger share of respect and sympathy' ('Visual Imagery and the Two Queens in Henry VIII', *Shakespeare Quarterly*, 38.4 (1987) 465).

46. See Shakespeare and Fletcher, *King Henry VIII*, ed. McMullan, p. 295 (note to l. 72).
47. Paradoxical because of her mercantilist attitude to the birth of Elizabeth in 5.1.171–6.
48. Holinshed, *Chronicles*, p. 745.
49. Holinshed, *Chronicles*, p. 675.
50. McMullan, 'The Dialogics of Reformation', pp. 219–20.
51. In the play the Chancellor is Thomas More, even though the post was held by Thomas Wriothesley at the time. See: Shakespeare and Fletcher, *King Henry VIII*, p. 406, n.
52. Interestingly, in Pedro Calderón de la Barca's *La cisma de Inglaterra* (1627) the Henrician Reformation is depicted not as the result of the King's whims, but as a tragic moral error. Indeed, the sovereign is forced to admit that he has burnt his bridges: 'Lend me your aid. Give help, since I desire / To repent. But it's too late, and I cannot. / What evil have I done, what evil done!' (*The Schism in England (La cisma de Inglaterra)* [1627], trans. K. Muir and A. L. Mackenzie, ed. A. L. Mackenzie, Hispanic Classics (Warminster: Aris and Phillips, 1990), p. 183).
53. Shakespeare and Fletcher, *King Henry VIII*, p. 135.
54. Holinshed, *Chronicles*, p. 745.
55. 'if I had serued God as diligentlie as I haue doone the king, he would not haue giuen me ouer in my greie haires: but it is the iust reward that I must receiue for the diligent paines and studie that I haue had to doo him service, not regarding my seruice to God, but onelie to satisfie his pleasure' (Holinshed, *Chronicles*, p. 755).
56. Holinshed, *Chronicles*, p. 766.
57. Shakespeare and Fletcher, *King Henry VIII*, pp. 87–8.
58. A. Fox, 'Prophecies and politics in the reign of Henry VIII', in *Reassessing the Henrician Age: Humanism, Politics and Reform, 1500–1550*, ed. A. Fox and J. Guy (Oxford, 1986) pp. 77–94.
59. Holinshed, *Chronicles*, p. 790.
60. Gordon MacMullan interprets the fact that Shakespeare probably let Fletcher write the ending of the play as 'a significant gesture' of a playwright ensuring his own artistic succession: 'Shakespeare's *not* writing the scene of Cranmer's prophecy can in itself be regarded as a testamentary act, disabling all readings of the play which view the scene as a culmination, a conclusion. It is no more final than any of the other episodes that have made up the play. To project a future, it returns to the past, a progression at once linear and cyclical, sustaining the hegemony both of Shakespeare and of the King's company, succession assured. As a memorial to the ending of epochs, *Henry VIII* can thus be seen as both a testamentary act and a self-consuming artifact' ('Shakespeare and the End of History', *Essays and Studies*, 48 (1995) 35).
61. In this way, their work was the product 'of an era of doubt, conflict and dilemma' (J. Gasper, 'The Reformation Plays on the Public Stage', *Theatre and Government under the Early Stuarts*, ed. J. R. Mulryne and M. Shewring (Cambridge: Cambridge University Press, 1993), p. 213).
62. J. Harington, *A Tract on the Succession to the Crown, A. D. 1602*, ed. C. R. Markham (London: Roxburghe Club, 1880), p. 99.

Conclusion

1. W. Prynne, *Histrio-mastix. The Players Scourge, or, Actors Tragœdie* (London, 1633), f. 1ᵛ ('To the Christian Reader') S.T.C.: 20464.
2. W. Allen, *An Admonition to the Nobility and People of England and Ireland concerninge the present warre* (n.p., 1588), sigs. A2ʳ⁻ᵛ; A6ʳ; B2ʳ. S.T.C.: 368.
3. Cited in A. Walsham, *Church Papists: Catholicism, Conformity, and Confessional Polemic in Early Modern England* (Woodbridge: Boydell Press, 1993), pp. 118–19.
4. P. Lake, 'Religious Identities in Shakespeare's England', in *A Companion to Shakespeare*, ed. D. S. Kastan (Oxford: Blackwell, 1999), pp. 70–1. Lake's point is about the radical Protestant (Puritan) agenda.
5. J. Harington, *A Tract on the Succession to the Crown, A.D. 1602*, ed. C. R. Markham (London: Roxburghe Club, 1880), p. 114.
6. E. Sandys, *A Relation of the State of Religion* (London, 1605), sig. K1ᵛ. S.T.C.: 21716.
7. Maurice Hunt also finds that 'Shakespeare's religious allusiveness precludes a naiveté about the prospect of achieving consensus or unity in matters of religion' (*Shakespeare's Religious Allusiveness: Its Play and Tolerance* (Aldershot: Ashgate, 2004), p. 130).
8. R. Holinshed,*Chronicles*, ed. H. Ellis, 6 vols. (London, 1807–8, repr. with an intro. by V. Snow, New York: AMS Press, 1965), vol. 4, p. 264, cited in A. Patterson, *Reading Holinshed's Chronicles* (Chicago and London: University of Chicago Press, 1994), p. 130.
9. T. Watt, *Cheap Print and Popular Piety 1550–1640* (Cambridge: Cambridge University Press, 1991), p. 126.
10. C. Marsh, *Popular Religion in Sixteenth-Century England, Holding their Peace* (Basingstoke: Macmillan, 1998), p. 11.
11. Marsh, *Popular Religion in Sixteenth-Century England*, p. 145.
12. Cited in Marsh, *Popular Religion in Sixteenth-Century England*, p. 213; and Walsham, *Church Papists*, p. 41.
13. Indeed, the point has been, as Peter Lake writes, 'to recapture the unstable, labile nature of religious identity during this period, to unearth some of the myriad available answers to the ubiquitously problematic question of what it meant to be a Christian in post-reformation England' (P. Lake, with M. Questier, *The Antichrist's Lewd Hat: Protestants, Papists and Players in Post-Reformation England* (New Haven, CT and London: Yale University Press, 2002), p. 714).

Bibliography

Manuscript sources

British Library, London

Harleian 1327, ff. 58–60 ('Aphorismes Political, gathered out of the Life & End of that most noble Robert Devereux Earl of Essex, not long before his death; by Mr. Henry Cuffe his Secretary', 1601?).

Public Record Office, London

SP12/274/133 (Earl of Essex to the Queen, 12 May 1600).

SP12/275/146 (Charles Percy to Mr Carlington, 27 December [1600]).

SP 12/278/23 ('A Skeltonian satirical ballad on some principal personages of Elizabeths Court', 1601).

SP12/278/63 ('A direction for the preachers', February 1601).

SP12/278/85 ('The examination of Augustyn Phillypps servant unto the Lord Chamberlyne and one of hys players taken the xviii[th] of Februarii 1600 upon hys oth').

SP12/278/98 (Attorney-general Coke's notes on the Essex trial, 1601).

SP12/278/102 (Account of the arraignement of the Earls of Essex and Southampton, 1601).

SP12/278/127 ('Memorial about the insurrection of the Earl of Essex' in Robert Cecil's hand, 1601).

SP46/22/143 (Charles Percy to Mr Carlington, 22 November [1600]).

Jesuit Provincial Archives, London

ARSJ Fondo Gesuitico 651, ff. 143–6 (Henry Garnet to the General, 16 April 1596 [reproduction of the Vatican Archive original]).

Early texts and editions

A lamentable Dittie composed vpon the death of Robert Lord Devereux late Earle of Essex (London, 1603). S.T.C.: 6791.

Allen, W. *An Admonition to the Nobility and People of England and Ireland concerninge the present warre* (n.p., 1588). S.T.C.: 368.

Allen, W. *A Defense and Declaration of the Catholike Churchies Doctrine, touching Purgatory, and Prayers for the Soules Departed* (Antwerp, 1565). S.T.C.: 371.

Anno xxiii. Reginæ Elizabethæ. At this present session of Parliament by prorogation holden at Westminster the xvi day of Januarie (London, 1581). S.T.C.: 9484.

Articles agreed on by the Bishoppes, and other learned menne in the Synode at London, in the yere of our Lorde Godde, M.D.LII. for the avoiding of controversie in opinions, and the establishment of a godlie concorde, in certeine matters of Religion (London, 1553). S.T.C.: 10034.

Articles ecclesiastical (London, 1571). S.T.C.: 10036ᵃ.

Atkinson, E. G. et al. *Calendar of the State Papers, relating to Ireland, of the reign of Elizabeth*, 5 vols. (London, 1893–1905).

Bacon, F. *A Declaration of the Practises & Treasons attempted and committed by Robert late Earle of Essex and his complices* (London, 1601). S.T.C.: 1133.

Bacon, F. *Sir Francis Bacon his apologie, in certaine imputations concerning the late Earle of Essex* (London, 1604). S.T.C.: 1111.

Barlowe, W. *A Sermon preached at Paules Crosse. With a short discourse of the late Earle of Essex* (London, 1601). S.T.C.: 1454.

Brewer, J. S. and W. Bullen, eds. *Calendar of the Carew Manuscripts, preserved in the Archiepiscopal Library at Lambeth*, 6 vols. (London, 1867–73).

Brooke, C. *The ghost of Richard the third* (London, 1614). S.T.C.: 3830.

Bruce, J., ed. *Correspondence of King James VI of Scotland with Sir Robert Cecil and Others in England* (London: Camden Society, 1861).

Bullough, G., ed. *Narrative and Dramatic Sources of Shakespeare*, 8 vols. (London: Routledge; New York: Columbia University Press, 1960).

Calderón de la Barca, P. *The Schism in England (La cisma de Inglaterra)* [1627], trans. K. Muir and A. L. Mackenzie, ed. A. L. Mackenzie, Hispanic Classics (Warminster: Aris and Phillips, 1990).

Camden, W. *The historie of the most renowned and victorious princesse Elizabeth* (London, 1630). S.T.C.: 4500.5.

Cecil, W. *The Execution of Justice in England* (London, 1583). S.T.C.: 4902.

Chapman, G. *The Tragedy of Charles Duke of Byron*, ed. J. Margeson (Manchester and New York: Manchester University Press, 1988).

Cotton, R. *An Armor of Proofe, brought from the Tower of David, to fight against Spannyardes, and all enimies of the trueth* (London, 1596). S.T.C.: 5865.

Creigh, G. and J. Belfield, eds. *The Cobler of Caunterburie and Tarlton's Newes out of Purgatorie* (Leiden: Brill, 1987).

Daniel, S. *The first fovvre bookes of the ciuile wars between the two houses of Lancaster and Yorke* (London, 1595). S.T.C.: 6244.

Daniel, S. *A Panegyrike Congratulatorie, Deliuered to the Kings Most excellent Maiestie* (London, 1607). S.T.C.: 6263.

Daniel, S. *The Tragedie of Philotas* (London, 1607). S.T.C.: 6263.

Dasent, J. R., ed. *Acts of the Privy Council of England* (London, His Majesty's Stationery Office, 1905), vol. 30 (1599–1600).

Davenport, R. *The Works of Robert Davenport*, ed. A. H. Bullen, Old English Plays New Series, vol. 3 (New York and London: Blom, 1964 [1882–89]).

Devereux, R. *An Apologie of the Earle of Essex* . . . (London, 1598). S.T.C.: 6788.

Doleman, R. (*vere* R. Parsons). *A Conference About the Next Succession to the Crowne of Ingland* ([Antwerp], 1594). S.T.C.: 19398.

Drayton, M. *The Historie of the Life and Death of the Lord Cromvvell, sometimes Earle of Essex, and Lord Chauncellor of England* (London, 1609). S.T.C.: 7201.

Dyce, A., ed. *The Dramatic and Poetical Works of Robert Greene and George Peele* (London: Routledge, 1861).

Froissart, J. *Of the Chronicles of Englande, fraunce, Spayne, etc.* (1525). S.T.C: 11397.

G. B., *A most wicked worke of a wretched witch* . . . (London, 1592). S.T.C.: 1030.5.

Gibbon, C. *A Watch-worde for Warre* . . . (London, 1596). S.T.C.: 11492.

Gifford, G. *A Dialogue Concerning Witches and Witchcraftes* (1593), intro. B. White (London: Shakespeare Association, 1931).

Gifford, G. *A Discourse of the subtill Practises of Devilles by Witches and Sorcerers. By which men are and have bin greatly deluded* . . . (London, 1587). S.T.C. 11852.

Green, M. A. E., ed. *Calendar of State Papers, Domestic series, of the reign of Elizabeth, preserved in the State Paper Department of Her Majesty's Public Record Office* (London, 1869).

Halle, E. *The Vnion of the two noble and illustrate famelies of Lancastre & Yorke* (1548). S.T.C.: 12721.

Harington, J. *A Tract on the Succession to the Crown, A.D. 1602*, ed. C. R. Markham (London: Roxburghe Club, 1880).

Hartley, T. E., ed. *Proceedings in the Parliaments of Elizabeth I*, 3 vols. (Leicester: Leicester University Press, 1981–95).

Hayward, J. *The First Part of the Life and raigne of King* Henrie *the IIII*. (London, 1599). S.T.C.: 12995.

Hayward, J. *The First and Second Parts of the Life and Raigne of King Henrie IIII*, ed. J. J. Manning, Camden Society 4th series, vol. 42 (London: Royal Historical Society, 1991).

Higgons, T. *The First Motive of T. H. Maister of Arts, and Lately Minister, To Suspect the Integrity of his Religion*, 2 parts (London, 1609). S.T.C.: 13454.

Holinshed, R. *Chronicles of England, Scotland and Ireland*, 6 vols. (London, 1807 [1586]).

Holinshed, R. *Chronicles*, ed. H. Ellis, 6 vols. (London, 1807–8, repr. with an intro. by V. Snow, New York: AMS Press, 1965).

Holland, H. *A Treatise Against Witchcraft* (Cambridge, 1590). S.T.C.: 13590.

Ingleby, C. M., ed. *Shakespeare's Centurie of Prayse* (London: New Shakespeare Society, 1879 [1874]).

James VI, *Daemonologie, in Forme of a Dialogue, Divided into three Bookes* (Edinburgh, 1597). S.T.C.: 14364.

Jewel, J. *An Apologie, or aunswer in defence of the Church of England, concerninge the state of Religion used in the same* (London, 1562). S.T.C.: 14590.

Jonson, B. *Ben Jonson*, eds. C. H. Herford and P. Simpson, 11 vols. (London: Oxford University Press, 1966).

Kyd, T. *The Works of Thomas Kyd*, ed. F. S. Boas (Oxford: Clarendon Press, 1955 [1901]).

Lyly, J. *Endymion*, ed. D. Bevington, Revels Plays (Manchester and New York: Manchester University Press, 1996).

Marlowe, C. *The Complete Works of Christopher Marlowe*, ed. F. Bowers, 2 vols. (Cambridge: Cambridge University Press, 1981).

Milward, P. *Religious Controversies of the Elizabethan Age: a Survey of Printed Sources* (Lincoln and London: University of Nebraska Press, 1977).

Milward, P. *Religious Controversies of the Jacobean Age: a Survey of Printed Sources* (London: Scolar Press, 1978).

More, T. *The Complete Works of Thomas More*, eds. G. L. Carroll, J. B. Murray, et al., 21 vols. (New Haven, CT and London: Yale University Press, 1963–97).

Munday A. and Others *Sir Thomas More*, eds. V. Gabrieli and G. Melchiori, Revels Plays (Manchester: Manchester University Press, 1990).

Munday, A. *A Watch-woord to Englande To beware of traytours and tretcherous practises* . . . (London, 1584). S.T.C.: 18282.

Nashe, T. *The Terrors of the night, Or, A Discourse of Apparitions* (London, 1594). S.T.C.: 18379.

Newes from Scotland. Declaring the damnable life of Doctor Fian a notable Sorcerer, who was burned at Edenbrough in Ianuarie last. 1591... [London]: Printed [by T. Scarlet] for William Wright, [1592?]. S.T.C. 10841.

Nichols, J. *Bibliotheca Topographica Britannica*, 10 vols. (New York: AMS Press, 1968 [facsimile reprint of 1780–1790 edn.]).

Nun, T. *A Comfort against the Spaniard* (London, 1596). S.T.C.: 18748.

Peele, G. *The Battle of Alcazar* (pr. 1594), ed. W. W. Greg (Oxford: Oxford University Press, 1963 [1907]).

Perkins, W. *A golden chaine, or the description of theologie, containing the order of the causes of salvation and damnation according to Gods woord* (London, 1591). S.T.C.: 19657.

Pricket, R. *Honors Fame in Triumph Riding* (London, 1604). S.T.C.: 20339.

Prynne, W. *Histrio-mastix. The Players Scourge, or, Actors Tragœdie* (London, 1633). S.T.C.: 20464.

Rainolds, W. *Calvino-Turcismus. Id est Calvinisticæ perfidiae, cum Mahumetana Collatio... Quatuor libris explicata... Authore G. Reginaldo* (Antwerp, 1597).

Sandys, E. *A Relation of the State of Religion* (London, 1605). S.T.C.: 21716.

Scargill-Bird, S. R. et al., eds. *Calendar of the Manuscripts of the Most Honourable the Marquis of Salisbury, K.G.... preserved at Hatfield House, Hertfordshire* (London, 1899).

Scot, R. *The Discoverie of Witchcraft* [1584], intro. H. R. Williamson (Arundel: Centaur Press, 1964).

Shakespeare, W. *The Comedy of Errors*, ed. C. Whitworth (Oxford: Oxford University Press, 2002).

Shakespeare, W. *The Complete Works*, eds. S. Wells and G. Taylor (Oxford: Clarendon Press, 1986).

Shakespeare, W. *Hamlet*, ed. H. Jenkins, Arden Shakespeare (London and New York: Routledge, 1982).

Shakespeare, W. *Henry IV, Part 2*, ed. R. Weis, Oxford Shakespeare (Oxford: Clarendon Press, 1998).

Shakespeare, W. *King Henry VI, Part 1*, ed. E. Burns, Arden 3 (London: Thomson Learning, 2000).

Shakespeare, W. *King Henry VI, Part 2*, ed. R. Knowles, Arden 3 (London: Thomson Learning, 2001 [1999]).

Shakespeare, W. *King Henry VIII*, ed. J. Margeson, New Cambridge Shakespeare (Cambridge: Cambridge University Press, 1990).

Shakespeare, W. and J. Fletcher, *King Henry VIII*, ed. G. McMullan, Arden Shakespeare (London: Thomson, 2000).

Shakespeare, W. *King John*, ed. E. A. J. Honigmann, Arden Shakespeare (London and New York: Routledge, 1954 (repr. 1991)).

Shakespeare, W. *The Life and Death of King John*, ed. A. R. Braunmuller (Oxford and New York: Oxford University Press, 1989).

Shakespeare, W. *The Life and Death of King John*, ed. C. McEachern (Harmondsworth: Penguin, 2000).

Shakespeare, W. *Richard II*, ed. P. Ure, Arden Shakespeare (London and New York: Routledge, 1961).

Shakespeare, W. *King Richard II*, ed. A. Gurr, New Cambridge Shakespeare (Cambridge: Cambridge University Press, 2003 [1984]).

Shakespeare, W. *King Richard II*, ed. C. R. Forker, Arden 3 (London: Thomson Learning, 2002).

Shakespeare, W. *King Richard III*, ed. A. Hammond, Arden 2 (London: Methuen, 1981).

Shakespeare, W. *The Tragedy of King Richard III*, ed. J. Jowett, Oxford World Classics (Oxford and New York: Oxford University Press, 2000).

Sidney, P. *The Defence of Poesie, Political Discourses, Correspondence, Translations*, ed. A. Feuillerat (Cambridge: Cambridge University Press, 1923).

Speed, J. *The Theatre of the Empire of Great Britain* (n.p., 1611). S.T.C.: 23041.

Stow, J. *The Annales of England, faithfully collected out of the most autenticall Authors, Records, and other Monuments of Antiquitie* (London, 1592). S.T.C.: 23334.

Tarltons newes out of Purgatorie (London, 1590) S.T.C.: 23685.

The Passion of a Discontented Minde (London, 1601). S.T.C.: 3679.5.

The seconde Tome of Homelyes (London, 1563). S.T.C.: 13663.

The Troublesome Raigne of John, King of England, ed. J. W. Sider (New York and London: Garland, 1979).

The True Tragedie of Richard The Third (1594), ed. W. W. Greg, Malone Society (Oxford: Oxford University Press, 1929).

Thomas of Woodstock, or Richard the Second, Part One, eds. P. Corbin and D. Sedge (Manchester: Manchester University Press, 2002).

Tucker Brooke, C. F., ed. *The Shakespeare Apocrypha* (Oxford: Clarendon Press, 1908).

Tyndale, W. *An Answer to Sir Thomas More's Dialogue* (Cambridge: Parker Society, 1850).

Tyndale, W. *The obedience of a Christen man . . .* (London, 1528). S.T.C.: 2446.

Vennard, R. *Englands Joy* (London, 1601?). S.T.C.: 24636.3.

Verstegan, R. *Odes in Imitation of the Seaven Penitential Psalmes, With Sundry other Poemes* (n.p., 1601). S.T.C.: 21359.

Wentworth, P. *A Pithie Exhortation to her Maiestie for Establishing her Svccessor to the Crowne, Wherevnto is added a Discovrse containing the Authors opinion of the true and lawful svccessor to her Maiestie* ([Edinburgh], 1598). S.T.C.: 25245.

Critical and historical scholarship

Aitkin, L. *Memoirs of the Court of Elizabeth*, 2 vols. (London, 1818).

Albright, E. M. 'Shakespeare's *Richard II*, Hayward's History of Henry IV, and the Essex Conspiracy', *PMLA*, 46 (1931) 694–719.

Alexander, M. 'Shakespeare's Catholicism? or "You would pluck out the heart of my mystery" ', *Quadrant*, 42.12 (1998) 46–51.

Anderson, J. H. *Biographical Truth: The Representation of Historical Persons in Tudor-Stuart Writing* (New Haven, CT and London: Yale University Press, 1984).

Anglo, S. *Images of Tudor Kingship* (London: Seaby, 1992).

Ash, D. F. 'Anglo-French Relations in *King John*', *Études Anglaises*, 3 (1939) 349–58.

Asquith, C. *Shadowplay: The Hidden Beliefs and Coded Politics of William Shakespeare* (New York: Public Affairs, 2005).

Baldwin, T. W. *The Organization and Personnel of the Shakespearean Company* (Princeton, NJ: Princeton University Press, 1927).

Barish, J. *The Antitheatrical Prejudice* (Berkeley: University of California Press, 1981).

Barroll, L. 'A New History for Shakespeare and His Time', *Shakespeare Quarterly*, 39.4 (1988) 441–64.

Batson, E. B., ed. *Selected Comedies and Late Romances of Shakespeare from a Christian Perspective* (Lewiston, Queenston, Lampeter: Edwin Mellen Press, 2002).

Battenhouse, R. 'On *King John*: An Answer to Billington and Hobson', *Connotations*, 2.2 (1992) 172–81.

Battenhouse, R. 'Religion in *King John*: Shakespeare's View', *Connotations*, 1.2 (1991) 140–9.

Bearman, R. ' "John Shakespeare's Spiritual Testament": A Reappraisal', *Shakespeare Survey*, 56 (2003) 184–203.

Bearman, R. ' "Was William Shakespeare William Shakeshafte?" Revisited', *Shakespeare Quarterly*, 53.1 (2002) 83–94.

Beauregard, D. N. 'New Light on Shakespeare's Catholicism: Prospero's Epilogue in *The Tempest*', *Renascence*, 49.3 (1997) 159–74.

Bliss, L. 'The Wheel of Fortune and the Maiden Phenix of Shakespeare's *King Henry the Eighth*', *English Literary History*, 42 (1975) 1–25.

Bowden, H. S. *The Religion of Shakespeare, Chiefly from the Writings of the Late Mr. Richard Simpson* (London: Burns & Oats, 1899).

Boyd, B. '*King John* and *The Troublesome Raigne*: Sources, Structure, Sequence', *Philological Quarterly*, 74.1 (1995) 37–56.

Briggs, K. M. *Pale Hecate's Team, An Examination of the Beliefs on Witchcraft and Magic among Shakespeare's Contemporaries and His Immediate Successors* (London: Routledge, 1962).

Brooks, H. F. '*Richard III*: Antecedents of Clarence's Dream', *Shakespeare Survey*, 32 (1979) 145–50.

Brownlow, F. W. 'John Shakespeare's Recusancy: New Light on an Old Document', *Shakespeare Quarterly*, 40.2 (1989) 186–91.

Brownlow, F. W. *Shakespeare, Harsnett, and the Devils of Denham* (Newark, London and Toronto: University of Delaware Press; Associated Ups, 1993).

Buckhardt, S. *Shakespearean Meanings* (Princeton: Princeton University Press, 1968).

Cain, T. ' "Satyres, That Girde and Fart at the Time": *Poetaster* and the Essex Rebellion', in *Refashioning Ben Jonson, Gender, Politics, and the Jonsonian Canon*, eds. J. Sanders et al. (Basingstoke: Macmillan, 1998), pp. 48–70.

Campbell, L. B. *Shakespeare's Histories, Mirrors of Elizabethan Policy* (London: Methuen, 1964).

Candido, J., ed. *King John, Shakespeare: The Critical Tradition* (London and Atlantic Highlands, NJ: Athlone, 1996).

Chambers, E. K. *The Elizabethan Stage*, 4 vols. (Oxford: Clarendon Press, 1923).

Chambers, E. K. *William Shakespeare, A Study of Facts and Problems*, 2 vols. (Oxford: Clarendon Press, 1930).

Clare, J. 'The Censorship of the Deposition Scene in *Richard II*', *The Review of English Studies*, 41 (1990) 89–94.

Clark, S. *Thinking with Demons, The Idea of Witchcraft in Early Modern Europe* (Oxford: Oxford University Press, 1997).

Clegg, C. S. ' "By the choise and inuitation of al the realme": *Richard II* and Elizabethan Press Censorship', *Shakespeare Quarterly*, 48.4 (1997) 432–48.

Collinson, P. 'John Stow and Nostalgic Antiquarianism', in *Imagining Early Modern London, Perceptions and Portrayals of the City from Stow to Strype, 1598–1720*, ed. J. F. Merritt (Cambridge: Cambridge University Press, 2001), pp. 27–51.

Collinson, P. 'The Monarchical Republic of Queen Elizabeth I', *Bulletin of the John Rylands University Library of Manchester*, 69.2 (1987) 394–424.

Collinson, P. *The Birthpangs of Protestant England* (Basingstoke: Macmillan, 1988).

Collinson, P. *Elizabethan Essays* (London and Rio Grande: Hambledon Press, 1994).

Collinson, P. 'The Mongrel Religion of Elizabethan England', in *Elizabeth, The Exhibition at the National Maritime Museum*, ed. S. Doran (London: Chatto & Windus, 2003), pp. 27–32.

Cox, J. D. *The Devil and the Sacred in English Drama, 1350–1642* (Cambridge: Cambridge University Press, 2000).

Cressy, D. *Birth, Marriage and Death: Ritual, Religion, and the Life-Cycle in Tudor and Stuart England* (Oxford: Oxford University Press, 1997).

Crockett, B. *The Play of Paradox, Stage and Sermon in Renaissance England* (Philadelphia: University of Pennsylvania Press, 1995).

Curren-Aquino, D. T., ed. *King John, New Perspectives* (Newark: University of Delaware Press, 1989).

Davies, M. 'On this Side Bardolatry: the Canonisation of the Catholic Shakespeare', *Cahiers Élisabéthains*, 58 (2000) 31–47.

De Fonblanque, E. B. *Annals of the House of Percy, From the Conquest to the Opening of the Nineteenth Century*, 2 vols. (London, 1887).

De Groot, J. H. *The Shakespeares and 'The Old Faith'* (Fraser: Real-View-Books, 1995 [1946]).

De Luna, B. N. *Jonson's Romish Plot, A Study of Catiline and its Historical Context* (Oxford: Clarendon Press, 1967).

Devlin, C. *Hamlet's Divinity* (London: Rupert Hart-Davis, 1963).

Diehl, H. *Staging Reform, Reforming the Stage: Protestantism and Popular Theater in Early Modern England* (Ithaca, NY: Cornell University Press, 1997).

Dillon, A. *The Construction of Martyrdom in the English Catholic Community* (Aldershot: Ashgate, 2002).

Dobson M. and S. Wells, eds. *The Oxford Companion to Shakespeare's Works* (Oxford: Oxford University Press, 2001).

Dockray, K. *Henry VI, Margaret of Anjou and the War of the Roses: A Sourcebook* (Stroud: Sutton, 2000).

Dodd, A. H. 'North Wales in the Essex Revolt of 1601', *English Historical Review*, 59 (1944) 348–70.

Dollimore, J. 'Shakespeare, Cultural Materialism and the New Historicism', in *Political Shakespeare*, eds. J. Dollimore and A. Sinfield (Ithaca, NY: Cornell University Press, 1985), pp. 2–17.

Donaldson, I. *Jonson's Magic Houses: Essays in Interpretation* (Oxford: Clarendon Press, 1997).

Doran, S. *Elizabeth I and Foreign Policy 1558–1603* (London and New York: Routledge, 2000).

Duffy, E. *The Stripping of the Altars, Traditional Religion in England c. 1400–c. 1580* (New Haven, CT and London: Yale University Press, 1992).

Duffy, E. 'Was Shakespeare a Catholic?', *The Tablet*, 27 April 1996, pp. 536–8.

Dutton, R. 'Buggeswords: Samuel Harsnett and the Licensing, Suppression and Afterlife of Dr. John Hayward's *The first part of the life and reign of King Henry IV*', *Criticism*, 35.3 (1993) 305–40.

Dutton, R. *Mastering the Revels, The Regulation and Censorship of English Renaissance Drama* (Basingstoke: Macmillan, 1991).

Dutton, R. 'Shakespeare and Lancaster', *Shakespeare Quarterly*, 49 (1998) 1–21.

Dutton, R., A. Findlay and R. Wilson, eds. *Theatre and Religion, Lancastrian Shakespeare* (Manchester and New York: Manchester University Press, 2003).

Elton, W. R. *King Lear and the Gods* (San Marino: Huntington Library, 1966).

Fernie, E., ed. *Spiritual Shakespeares* (Abingdon and New York: Routledge, 2005).

Flynn, D. *John Donne and the Ancient Catholic Nobility* (Bloomington and Indianapolis: Indiana University Press, 1995).

Fox, A. 'Prophecies and Politics in the Reign of Henry VIII', in *Reassessing the Henrician Age: Humanism, Politics and Reform, 1500–1550*, eds. A. Fox and J. Guy (Oxford, 1986), pp. 77–94.

Fox, A. 'Richard III's Pauline Oath: Shakespeare's Response to Thomas More', *Moreana* 15 (1978) 13–23.

Freeman, T. 'Demons, Deviance and Defiance: John Darrell and the Politics of Exorcism in Late Elizabethan England', in *Conformity and Orthodoxy in the English Church, c. 1560–1660*, eds. P. Lake and M. Questier (Woodbridge: Boydell Press, 2000), pp. 34–63.

Frye, R. M. *Shakespeare and Christian Doctrine* (Princeton, NJ: Princeton University Press, 1963).

Garber, M. *Dream in Shakespeare: From Metaphor to Metamorphosis* (New Haven, CT: Yale University Press, 1974).

Gasper, J. 'The Reformation Plays on the Public Stage', *Theatre and Government under the Early Stuarts*, eds. J. R. Mulryne and M. Shewring (Cambridge: Cambridge University Press, 1993), pp. 190–216.

Gazzard, H. ' "Those graue presentments of antiquitie", Samuel Daniel's *Philotas* and the Earl of Essex', *Review of English Studies*, 51 (2000) 423–50.

Gibson, M. *Reading Witchcraft, Stories of Early English Witches* (London and New York: Routledge, 1999).

Greenblatt, S. *Hamlet in Purgatory* (Princeton, NJ and Oxford: Princeton University Press, 2001).

Greenblatt, S. *Shakespearean Negotiations, The Circulation of Social Energy in Renaissance England* (Oxford: Clarendon Press, 1988).

Greenblatt, S. *Will in the World: How Shakespeare became Shakespeare* (London: Cape, 2004).

Griffiths, R. A. 'The Trial of Eleanor Cobham: An Episode in the Fall of Duke Humphrey of Gloucester', *Bulletin of the John Rylands Library Manchester*, 51.2 (1969) 381–99.

Gurr, A. *The Shakespearean Stage 1574–1642*, 3rd edn. (Cambridge: Cambridge University Press, 1994).

Guy, J., ed. *The Reign of Elizabeth I, Court and Culture in the Last Decade* (Cambridge: Cambridge University Press, 1995).

Guy, J. *Tudor England* (Oxford: Oxford University Press, 1988).

Hadfield, A. *Shakespeare, Spenser and the Matter of Britain* (Basingstoke: Palgrave, 2003).

Haigh, C. 'The Continuity of Catholicism in the English Reformation', *Past and Present*, 93 (1981) 37–69.

Haigh, C. *English Reformations, Religion, Politics, and Society under the Tudors* (Oxford: Clarendon Press, 1993).

Haigh, C. 'From monopoly to minority: Catholicism in early modern England', *Transactions of the Royal Historical Society*, 5th series, 31 (1981) 129–47.

Haigh, C. 'Puritan Evangelism in the Reign of Elizabeth I', *The English Historical Review*, 72 (1977) 30–58.

Haigh, C. 'Success and Failure in the English Reformation', *Past and Present*, 173 (2001) 28–49.

Halliday, F. E. *A Shakespeare Companion* (Harmondsworth: Penguin, 1964).

Halliwell-Phillips, J. O. *Outlines of the Life of Shakespeare*, 2 vols. (London, 1898).

Hamilton, D. B. *Anthony Munday and the Catholics, 1560–1633* (Aldershot: Ashgate, 2005).

Hamilton, D. B. 'Anthony Munday and *The Merchant of Venice*', *Shakespeare Survey*, 54 (2001) 89–99.

Hamilton, D. B. *Shakespeare and the Politics of Protestant England* (Lexington: University of Kentucky Press, 1992).

Hamilton, D. B. and R. Strier, eds. *Religion, Literature, and Politics in Post-Reformation England, 1540–1688* (Cambridge: Cambridge University Press, 1996).

Hammer, P. E. J. *The Polarisation of Elizabethan Politics, The Political Career of Robert Devereux, 2nd Earl of Essex, 1585–1597* (Cambridge: Cambridge University Press, 1999).

Hammerschmidt-Hummel, H. *Die verborgene Existenz des William Shakespeare: Dichter und Rebell im katholischen Untergrund* (Freiburg: Herder, 2001).

Harcourt, J. B. ' "Odde Old Ends, Stolne . . . ": King Richard and Saint Paul', *Shakespeare Studies*, 7 (1974) 87–100.

Hardin, R. F. 'Chronicles and Mythmaking in Shakespeare's Joan of Arc', *Shakespeare Survey*, 42 (1990) 25–34.

Heinemann, M. 'Rebel Lords, Popular Playwrights, and Political Culture: Notes on the Jacobean Patronage of the Earl of Southampton', *Yearbook of English Studies*, 21 (1991) 63–86.

Hicks, L. 'Sir Robert Cecil, Father Persons and the Succession', *Archivum Historicum Societatis Iesu*, 24 (1955) 95–139.

Hillman, R. *Shakespeare, Marlowe and the Politics of France* (Basingstoke: Palgrave, 2002).

Hobson, C. Z. 'A Comment on Roy Battenhouse, "Religion in *King John*: Shakespeare's view" ', *Connotations*, 2.1 (1992) 69–75.

Holmes, P. 'The Authorship and Early Reception of *A Conference about the Next Succession to the Crown of England*', *Historical Journal*, 23.2 (1980) 415–29.

Holmes, P. *Resistance and Compromise, The Political Thought of the Elizabethan Catholics* (Cambridge: Cambridge University Press, 1982).

Honan, P. *Shakespeare, A Life* (Oxford: Oxford University Press, 1998).

Honigmann, E. A. J. 'Catholic Shakespeare? A Response to Hildegard Hammerschmidt-Hummel', *Connotations*, 12.1 (2002/3) 52–60.

Honigmann, E. A. J. *Playhouse Wills, 1558–1642* (Manchester and New York: Manchester University Press, 1993).

Honigmann, E. A. J. *Shakespeare: the 'Lost Years'* (Manchester and New York: Manchester University Press, 1998 [1985]).

Honigmann, E. A. J. 'The Shakespeare/Shakeshafte Question, Continued', *Shakespeare Quarterly*, 54.1 (2003) 83–6.

Howard, J. E. and P. Rackin *Engendering a Nation: A Feminist Account of Shakespeare's English Histories* (London and New York: Routledge, 1997).

Howard-Hill, T. H. *Shakespeare and* Sir Thomas More, *Essays on the Play and its Shakespearian Interest* (Cambridge: Cambridge University Press, 1989).

Hunt, A. 'Tuning the Pulpits: The Religious Context of the Essex Revolt', in *The English sermon Revised, Religion, Literature and History 1600–1750*, eds. L. A.Ferrell and P. McCullough (Manchester: Manchester University Press, 2000), pp. 86–114.

Hunt, M. *Shakespeare's Religious Allusiveness: Its Play and Tolerance* (Aldershot: Ashgate, 2004).

Hurstfield, J. 'The Succession Struggle in Late Elizabethan England', in *Elizabethan Government and Society, Essays Presented to Sir John Neale*, eds. S. T. Bindoff, et al. (London: Athlone Press, 1961), pp. 369–96.

Ingram, M. 'From Reformation to Toleration: Popular Religious Cultures in England, 1540–1690', in *Popular Culture in England, c. 1500–1850*, ed. T. Harris (Basingstoke: Macmillan, 1995), pp. 95–123.

Ingram, W. 'The Wife of Augustine Phillips', *Notes and Queries*, 30.3 (new series) 157.

Jackson, K. and A. F. Marotti 'The Turn to Religion in Early Modern English Studies', *Criticism*, 46 (2004) 167–90.

James, M. 'At a Crossroads of the Political Culture: the Essex Revolt, 1601', in *Society, Politics and Culture: Studies in Early Modern England* (Cambridge: Cambridge University Press, 1986), pp. 416–66.

Jones, E. *The Origins of Shakespeare* (Oxford: Clarendon Press, 1977).

Kastan, D. S. *Shakespeare after Theory* (London and New York: Routledge, 1999).

Kastan, D. S. ' "To Set a Form upon that Indigest": Shakespeare's Fictions of History', *Comparative Drama*, 17.1 (1983) 1–16.

Knapp, J. 'Jonson, Shakespeare, and the Religion of Players', *Shakespeare Survey*, 52 (2000) 57–70.

Knapp, J. *Shakespeare's Tribe: Church, Nation, and Theater in Renaissance England* (Chicago and London: University of Chicago Press, 2002).

Knight, W. N. *Shakespeare's Hidden Life: Shakespeare at the Law, 1585–1595* (New York: Mason & Lipscomb, 1973).

Knowles, R. 'The Farce of History: Miracle, Combat, and Rebellion in *2 Henry VI*', *Yearbook of English Studies*, 21 (1991) 168–86.

Kozuka, T. 'Shakespeare in Purgatory: a Study of the Catholicising Movement in Shakespeare Biography' (unpublished PhD thesis, University of Warwick, 2003).

Lake, P. 'Religious Identities in Shakespeare's England', in *A Companion to Shakespeare*, ed. D. S. Kastan (Oxford: Blackwell, 1999), pp. 57–84.

Lake, P. with M. Questier, *The Antichrist's Lewd Hat: Protestants, Papists and Players in Post-Reformation England* (New Haven, CT and London: Yale University Press, 2002).

Lake, P. and M. Questier, eds. *Conformity and Orthodoxy in the English Church, c. 1560–1660* (Woodbridge: Boydell Press, 2000).

Larner, C. *Enemies of God, The Witch-hunt in Scotland* (Edinburgh: John Donald, 2000 [1983]).

Le Goff, J. *The Birth of Purgatory*, trans. A. Goldhammer (Chicago: University of Chicago Press, 1984).

Levin, C. ' "I Trust I May Not Trust Thee": Women's Visions of the World in Shakespeare's *King John*', in *Ambiguous Realities Women in the Middle Ages and Renaissance*, eds. C. Levin and J. Watson (Detroit: Wayne State University Press, 1987), pp. 219–34.

Levine, N. S. 'The Case of Eleanor Cobham: Authorizing History in *2 Henry VI*', *Shakespeare Studies*, 22 (1994) 104–21.

Levy, F. J. 'Hayward, Daniel, and the Beginning of Politic History in England', *Huntington Library Quarterly*, 50 (1987) 1–34.

Lilly, W. S. *Studies in Religion and Literature* (London: Chapman and Hall, 1904).

Loomie, A. J. 'A Catholic Petition to the Earl of Essex', *Recusant History*, 7.1 (1963) 33–43.

MacCulloch, D. *The Later Reformation in England, 1547–1603*, 2nd edn. (Basingstoke: Palgrave, 2001 [1990]).

MacManaway, J. 'Elizabeth, Essex, and James', in *Elizabethan and Jacobean Studies Presented to Frank Percy Wilson*, eds. H. Davis and H. Gardner (Oxford: Clarendon Press, 1959), pp. 219–30.

Marotti, A. F. *Catholicism and Anti-Catholicism in Early Modern English Texts* (Basingstoke: Macmillan, 1999).

Marsh, C. *Popular Religion in Sixteenth-Century England, Holding their Peace* (Basingstoke: Macmillan, 1998).

Marshall, P. *Beliefs and the Dead in Reformation England* (Oxford and New York: Oxford University Press, 2002).

Marshall, P. *Reformation England 1480–1642* (London: Arnold, 2003).

Mason Carr, V. *The Drama as Propaganda: a Study of* The troublesome raigne of King John (Salzburg: Institut für Englische Sprache, 1974).

Mason Vaughan, V. 'Between Tetralogies: *King John* as transition', *Shakespeare Quarterly*, 35.4 (1984) 407–20.

Mayer, J.-C., ed. *Breaking the Silence on the Succession, A Sourcebook of Manuscripts and Rare Elizabethan Texts* (c. *1587–1603*) (Montpellier: Université Paul Valéry, 2003).

Mayer, J.-C. 'Late Elizabethan Theatre and the Succession', in *The Struggle for the Succession in Late Elizabethan England, Politics, Polemics and Cultural Representations*, ed. J.-C. Mayer (Montpellier: Université Paul Valéry, 2004), pp. 371–93.

Mayer, J.-C., 'Power of Myths and Myths of Power: Shakespeare's History Plays and Modern Historiography', in *Shakespeare and History*, eds. H. Klein and R. Wymer, Shakespeare Yearbook 6 (Lewiston, Queenston, Lampeter: Edwin Mellen Press, 1996), pp. 37–51.

Mazzola, E. *The Pathology of the English Renaissance, Sacred Remains and Holy Ghosts* (Leiden, Boston, Köln: Brill, 1998).

McCoy, R. C. *Alterations of State: Sacred Kingship in the English Reformation* (New York: Columbia University Press, 2002).

McCoy, R. C. *The Rites of Knighthood, The Literature and Politics of Elizabethan Chivalry* (Berkeley, Los Angeles, London: University of California Press, 1989).

McEachern, C. and D. Shuger, eds. *Religion and Culture in Renaissance England* (Cambridge: Cambridge University Press, 1997).

McKisack, M. *The Fourteenth Century 1307–1399* (Oxford: Clarendon Press, 1959).

McManaway, J. G. 'John Shakespeare's "Spiritual Testament"', *Shakespeare Quarterly*, 18.3 (1967) 197–205.

McMullan, G. *The Politics of Unease in the Plays of John Fletcher* (Amherst, MA: University of Massachusetts Press, 1994).

McMullan, G. 'Shakespeare and the End of History', *Essays and Studies*, 48 (1995) 16–37.

McMullan, G. 'Swimming on Bladders: The Dialogics of Reformation in *Henry VIII*', in *Shakespeare and Carnival, After Bakhtin*, ed. R. Knowles (Basingstoke and London: Macmillan, 1998), pp. 211–27.

Micheli, L. M. 'Visual Imagery and the Two Queens in Henry VIII', *Shakespeare Quarterly*, 38.4 (1987) 452–66.

Milward, P. *The Catholicism of Shakespeare's Plays* (Southampton: Saint Austin Press, 1997).

Milward, P. *Shakespeare the Papist* (Ann Arbor: Sapientia Press, 2005).

Monta, S. B. ' "Thou fall'st a blessed martyr": Shakespeare's *Henry VIII* and the Polemics of Conscience', *English Literary Renaissance*, 30.2 (2000) 262–83.

Montrose, L. *The Purpose of Playing, Shakespeare and the Cultural Politics of the Elizabethan Theatre* (Chicago and London: University of Chicago Press, 1996).

Moorman, F. W. 'The Pre-Shakespearean Ghost', *Modern Language Review*, 1 (1906) 85–95.

Mullaney, S. 'After the New Historicism', in *Alternative Shakespeares vol. 2*, ed. T. Hawkes (London and New York: Routledge, 1996), pp. 17–37.

Mutschmann, H. and K. Wentersdorf, *Shakespeare and Catholicism* (New York: Sheed and Ward, 1952).

Neill, M. ' "*Exeunt with a Dead March*": Funeral Pageantry on the Shakespearean Stage', in *Pageantry in the Shakespearean Theater*, ed. D. M. Bergeron (Athens, GA: University of Georgia Press, 1985), pp. 153–93.

Neill, M. *Issues of Death, Mortality and Identity in English Renaissance Tragedy* (Oxford: Clarendon Press, 1997).

Norbrook, D. *Poetry and Politics in the English Renaissance* (London: Routledge, 1984).

O'Connell, M. *The Idolatrous Eye, Iconoclasm and Theater in Early-Modern England* (Oxford: Oxford University Press, 2000).

Patterson, A. *Reading Holinshed's Chronicles* (Chicago and London: University of Chicago Press, 1994).

Piesse, A. J. 'King John: Changing Perspectives', in *The Cambridge Companion to Shakespeare's History Plays*, ed. M. Hattaway (Cambridge: Cambridge University Press, 2002), pp. 126–40.

Poole, K. *Radical Religion from Shakespeare to Milton, Figures of Nonconformity in Early Modern England* (Cambridge: Cambridge University Press, 2000).

Poole, K. 'Saints Alive! Falstaff, Martin Marprelate, and the Staging of Puritanism', *Shakespeare Quarterly*, 46 (1995) 47–75.

Pugliatti, P. *Shakespeare the Historian* (Basingstoke and London: Macmillan, 1996).

Questier, M. C. *Conversion, Politics and Religion in England, 1580–1625* (Cambridge: Cambridge University Press, 1996).

Raffel, B. 'Shakespeare and the Catholic Question', *Religion and Literature*, 30.1 (1998) 35–51.

Ribner, I. *The English History Play in the Age of Shakespeare* (London: Methuen, 1965 [1957]).

Richmond, H. M. '*Richard III* and the Reformation', *Journal of English and Germanic Philology*, 83 (1984) 509–21.

Richmond, V. B. *Shakespeare, Catholicism, and Romance* (New York: Continuum, 2000).

Rio, A.-F. *Shakespeare catholique* (Paris: Bray et Retaux, 1864).

Rist, T. *Shakespeare's Romances and the Politics of Counter-Reformation* (Lewiston: Edwin Mellen Press, 1999).

Rudnytsky, P. 'Shakespeare and the Deconstruction of History', *Shakespeare Survey*, 43 (1991) 43–58.

Sahel, P. 'The Strangeness of a Dramatic Style: Rumour in *Henry VIII*', *Shakespeare Survey*, 38 (1985) 145–51.

Sams, E. *The Real Shakespeare, Retrieving the Early Years, 1564–1594* (New Haven, CT and London: Yale University Press, 1995).

Santayana, G. *Interpretations of Poetry and Religion* (1900), ed. W. G. Holzberger and H. J. Saatkamp (Cambridge, MA: MIT Press, 1989).

Saul, N. *Richard II* (New Haven and London: Yale University Press, 1997).

Scarisbrick, J. J. *The Reformation and the English People* (Oxford: Oxford University Press, 1984).

Schoenbaum, S. '"Richard II" and the Realities of Power', *Shakespeare Survey*, 28 (1975) 1–13.

Sharpe, J. *Instruments of Darkness, Witchcraft in Early Modern England* (Philadelphia: University of Pennsylvania Press, 1996).

Sharpe, R. B. *The Real War of the Theatres, Shakespeare's Fellows in Rivalry with the Admiral's Men, 1594–1603*, Modern Language Association (Boston, MA: Heath; London: Oxford University Press, 1935).

Shell, A. *Catholicism, Controversy and the English Literary Imagination, 1558–1660* (Cambridge: Cambridge University Press, 1999).

Shirley, F. A., ed. *King John and Henry VIII: Critical Essays* (New York and London: Garland, 1988).

Shuger, D. K. *Habits of Thought in the English Renaissance* (Berkeley, Los Angeles and Oxford: University of California Press, 1990).

Shuger, D. K. *Political Theologies in Shakespeare's England, The Sacred and the State in* Measure for Measure (Basingstoke: Palgrave, 2001).

Simpson, R. 'Was Shakespeare a Catholic?', *The Rambler, A Catholic Journal and Review*, New Series, vol. 2, part 7 (1854) 19–36.

Simpson, R. 'What was the religion of Shakespeare?' [parts 1–3], *The Rambler, A Catholic Journal and Review*, new series, vol. 9 (1858) 168–87, 232–319, 302–87.

Spevack, M. *Harvard Concordance to Shakespeare* (Cambridge, MA: Harvard University Press, 1973).

Steible, M. 'Jane Shore and the Politics of Cursing', *Studies in English Literature*, 43.1 (2003) 1–17.

Strohm, P. *England's Empty Throne, Usurpation and the Language of Legitimation, 1399–1422* (New Haven, CT and London: Yale University Press, 1998).

Targoff, R. ' "Dirty" Amens: Devotion, Applause, and Consent in *Richard III*', *Renaissance Drama*, 31 (2002) 61–84.

Targoff, R. 'The Performance of Prayer: Sincerity and Theatricality in Early Modern England', *Representations*, 60 (1997) 49–69.

Taylor, D. and D. N. Beauregard, eds. *Shakespeare and the Culture of Christianity in Early Modern England* (New York: Fordham University Press, 2003).

Taylor, G. 'Divine [Sences]', *Shakespeare Survey*, 52 (2000) 13–30.

Taylor, G. 'Forms of Opposition: Shakespeare and Middleton', *English Literary Renaissance*, 24.2 (1994) 283–314.

Tetzeli von Rosador, K. 'The Power of Magic: From *Endimion* to *The Tempest*', *Shakespeare Survey*, 43 (1991) 1–13.

Thomas, D. L. and N. E. Evans, 'John Shakespeare in The Exchequer', *Shakespeare Quarterly*, 35.3 (1984) 315–18.

Thomas, K. *Religion and the Decline of Magic, Studies in Popular Beliefs in Sixteenth- and Seventeenth-Century England* (Harmondsworth: Penguin, 1971).

Thomson, P. *Shakespeare's Professional Career* (Cambridge: Cambridge University Press, 1992).

Thurston, H. 'A Controverted Shakespeare Document', *The Dublin Review*, 173 (1923) 161–76.

Traister, B. H. *Heavenly Necromancers, The Magician in English Renaissance Drama* (Columbia: University of Missouri Press, 1984).

Tyacke, N. *England's Long Reformation 1500–1800* (London: University College London Press, 1998).

Vanita, R. 'Mariological Memory in *The Winter's Tale* and *Henry VIII*', *Studies in English Literature 1500–1900*, 40.2 (2000) 311–37.

Vickers, B. '*The Troublesome Raigne*, George Peele, and the Date of *King John*', in *Words that Count*, ed. B. Boyd (Newark: University of Delaware Press, 2004), pp. 78–116.

Waage, F. O., Jr. '*Henry VIII* and the Crisis of the English History Play', *Shakespeare Studies*, 8 (1975) 297–309.

Waith, E. M. 'King John and the Drama of History', *Shakespeare Quarterly*, 29.2 (1978) 192–211.

Walker, D. P. *Unclean Spirits, Possession and Exorcism in France and England in the Late Sixteenth and Early Seventeenth Centuries* (London: Scolar Press, 1981).

Walsham, A. *Church Papists: Catholicism, Conformity and Confessional Polemic in Early Modern England* (Woodbridge: Boydell and Brewer, 1993).

Walsham, A. *Providence in Early Modern England* (Oxford and New York: Oxford University Press, 1999).

Watson, C. K. 'Was Shakespeare a Roman Catholic?', *The Edinburgh Review*, 123 (1866) 146–85.

Watt, T. *Cheap Print and Popular Piety 1550–1640* (Cambridge: Cambridge University Press, 1991).

Wells, S. 'Staging Shakespeare's Ghosts', in *The Arts of Performance in Elizabethan and Early Stuart Drama, Essays for G. K. Hunter*, eds. M. Biggs, P. Edwards, I. -S. Ewbank and E. M. Waith (Edinburgh: Edinburgh University Press, 1991), pp. 50–69.

Wells, S. and G. Taylor *A Textual Companion* (Oxford: Clarendon Press, 1987).

Wheeler, R. P. 'History, Character and Conscience in *Richard III*', *Comparative Drama*, 5 (1971) 301–21.

White, P. W. *Theatre and Reformation, Protestantism, Patronage and Playing in Tudor England* (Cambridge: Cambridge University Press, 1993).

White, P. W. 'Theater and Religious Culture', in *A New History of Early English Drama*, eds J. D. Cox and D. S. Kastan (New York: Columbia University Press, 1997), pp. 133–53.

Wickham, G. 'The Dramatic Structure of Shakespeare's *King Henry the Eighth*: An Essay in Rehabilitation', in *British Academy Shakespeare Lectures 1980–89*, ed. E. A. J. Honigmann (Oxford: Oxford University Press, 1993), pp. 149–66.

Willis, D. 'Shakespeare and the English Witch-Hunts: Enclosing the Maternal Body', in *Enclosure Acts, Sexuality, Property, and Culture in Early Modern England*, eds. R. Burt and J. M. Archer (Ithaca, NY and London: Cornell University Press, 1994), pp. 96–120.

Wills, G. *Witches and Jesuits: Shakespeare's Macbeth* (New York: Oxford University Press, 1995).

Wilson, I. *Shakespeare: The Evidence, Unlocking the Mysteries of the Man and His Works* (London: Headline, 1993).

Wilson, R. *Secret Shakespeare, Studies in Theatre, Religion and Resistance* (Manchester and New York: Manchester University Press, 2004).

Womack, P. 'Imagining Communities: Theatres and the English Nation in the Sixteenth Century', in *Culture and History 1350–1600* (Detroit: Wayne State University Press, 1992), pp. 91–145.

Worden, B. 'Which Play was Performed at the Globe Theatre on 7 February 1601?', *London Review of Books*, 10 July 2003, pp. 22–3.

Yachnin, P. 'The Powerless Theater', *English Literary Renaissance*, 21.1 (1991) 49–74.

Index

Globe theatre, 66, 105, 106, 107, 108,
110, 117, 122, 196 n 70, 202 n 6
Goodland, Katherine, 177 n 55
Greenblatt, Stephen, 9–10, 50, 51,
92, 157 n 14, 162 n 44, 164 n 51,
171 n 64, 177 n 53, 178 n 72
Greene, Robert, 15, 24
*The Honourable History of Friar
Bacon and Friar Bungay*, 15, 86,
169 n 32
Grey, Jane, 131, 202 n 7
Griffiths, Ralph A., 170 n 46
Grindal, Matthew (Archbishop of
Canterbury), 6
Gunpowder Plot, 108, 116
Gurr, Andrew, 66, 75, 182 n 21, 185 n
51, 193 n 15
Guy, John, 160 n 28

Hades, 47, 48
Hadfield, Andrew, 182 n 13
Haigh, Christopher, 6–7, 160 n 27 n
30 n 33, 162 n 40
Hall, Edward, 30, 32, 56
*The Union of the Two Noble and
Illustre Famelies of Lancastre and
Yorke*, 171 n 50, 178 n 69,
183 n 27
Halliwell-Phillips, J. O., 159 n 22
Hamel, Guy, 80
Hamilton, Donna B., 94, 162 n 44,
166 n 66, 187 n 32, 190 n 65,
203 n 27
Hammer, Paul E. J., 199 n 110
Hammerschmidt-Hummel, Hildegard,
157 n 14
Hammond, Anthony, 173 n 2
Harcourt, John B., 174 n 14
Hardin, Richard F., 171 n 53
Harington, John, 150, 154
*A Tract on the Succession to the
Crown*, 205 n 62, 206 n 5
Harsnett, Samuel, 34, 37, 170 n 47
*Declaration of Egregious Popish
Impostures, A*, 29–30, 34, 170 n
47, 171 n 64
*Discovery of the Fraudulent Practices
of John Darrell, A*, 34
Hatton, Christopher, 109

Hayward, John,
*First and Second Parts of the Life and
Raigne of King Henrie IIII, The*,
104, 112, 119, 120, 121, 192 n
9, 198 n 84 n 90 n 91 n 92 n 94
*Life and raigne of King Edward VI,
The*, 120, 198 n 86
Heffner, Ray, 195 n 52
Heinemann, Margot, 201 n 124
Heminges, John, 116, 196 n 65
Henri IV (King of France), 85
Henry VI (King of England), 168 n 15,
173 n 7
Henry VII (King of England), 17, 168
n 15, 202 n 7
Henry VIII (King of England), 9, 25,
79, 84, 130, 132, 134, 142, 144–5,
146, 148, 150, 203 n 31, 204 n 37
as 'Defender of the Faith', 142
Henrician Schism (the) 61, 130–51
passim, 205 n 52
Henslowe, Philip, 131, 167 n 9,
168 n 14
heresy, 75, 143, 147, 168 n 20,
181 n 11
Heywood, Thomas,
*If You Know Not Me, You Know
Nobody*, 139
Hicks, Leo, 200 n 114
Higgons, Theophilus, 58
*The First Motive of T. H. Maister of
Arts, and Lately Minister, To
Suspect the Integrity of his
Religion*, 179 n 81
Hillman, Richard, 171 n 53
historiography, 70, 160 n 33, 184 n 38
Catholic, 70, 78, 79, 80
Protestant, 70, 78, 79
Hobson, Christopher Z., 189 n 52
Hoghton Tower (Lancashire), 3
Holinshed, Raphael, 32, 68, 71, 80,
82, 121, 139, 142, 145, 146, 148,
154, 183 n 30, 184 n 40, 203 n 31
*Chronicles of England, Scotland, and
Ireland*, 69, 96, 148, 178 n 68,
183 n 28, 186 n 13, 187 n 14
n 15, 202 n 1, 204 n 37,
205 n 48 n 49 n 54 n 55
n 56 n 59, 206 n 8